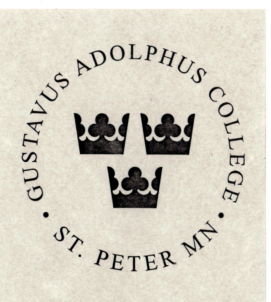

OXFORD TELEVISION STUDIES

General Editors **Charlotte Brunsdon**
John Caughie

Television Drama

Television Drama: Realism, Modernism, and British Culture

John Caughie

OXFORD
UNIVERSITY PRESS

OXFORD

UNIVERSITY PRESS

Great Clarendon Street, Oxford OX2 6DP

Oxford University Press is a department of the University of Oxford.
It furthers the University's objective of excellence in research, scholarship,
and education by publishing worldwide in

Oxford New York

Athens Auckland Bangkok Bogotá Buenos Aires Calcutta
Cape Town Chennai Dar es Salaam Delhi Florence Hong Kong Istanbul
Karachi Kuala Lumpur Madrid Melbourne Mexico City Mumbai
Nairobi Paris São Paulo Singapore Taipei Tokyo Toronto Warsaw

and associated companies in Berlin Ibadan

Oxford is a registered trade mark of Oxford University Press
in the UK and certain other countries

Published in the United States
by Oxford University Press Inc., New York

British Library Cataloguing in Publication Data

Data available

Library of Congress Cataloging in Publication Data

Data available

ISBN 0–19–874219–3
ISBN 0–19–874218–5 (Pbk.)

1 3 5 7 9 10 8 6 4 2

Typeset by Graphicraft Limited, Hong Kong
Printed in Great Britain
on acid-free paper by
Biddles Ltd, Guildford and King's Lynn

Oxford Television Studies

General Editors
Charlotte Brunsdon and **John Caughie**

OXFORD TELEVISION STUDIES offers international authors—both established and emerging—an opportunity to reflect on particular problems of history, theory, and criticism which are specific to television and which are central to its critical understanding. The perspective of the series will be international, while respecting the peculiarities of the national; it will be historical, without proposing simple histories; and it will be grounded in the analysis of programmes and genres. The series is intended to be foundational without being introductory or routine, facilitating clearly focused critical reflection and engaging a range of debates, topics, and approaches which will offer a basis for the development of television studies.

Acknowledgements

THIS book has been a long time coming, and has therefore acquired more debts of gratitude than I can properly acknowledge here. Many students, friends, and colleagues may recognize echoes of conversations or fragments of arguments for which I can only make a general acknowledgement. The book, though my responsibility, is not all my own work.

I owe a lot to students and colleagues in the Department of Theatre, Film and Television Studies at Glasgow University and in the John Logie Baird Centre. Parts of the book have been test-driven with students in my Television Drama courses. The postgraduate course for the Baird Centre in the spring term of 1998 sharpened up my ideas before I started writing, and many of the changes between first draft and second took their inspiration from some quite passionate arguments in my undergraduate course in the autumn term of the following session. Among my colleagues, I am particularly grateful to Tony Pearson for keeping the faith with television, to Karen Lury for her refusal to allow film and television theory to be the property of my generation, and, more generally, to Jan McDonald for a little more than two decades of academic competition and collaboration and for making it good fun along the way. The experience of co-teaching and co-directing with Simon Frith in the Baird Centre has been a process of challenge and exchange and a model of what academic collegiality might be.

I am happy to acknowledge a general indebtedness to *Screen* as a formative influence and now as a kind of intellectual home (though a home in which the furniture keeps shifting), and I value the commitment and collectivity of my colleagues on the present editorial board.

The book benefited from two experiences of teaching British television outside Britain. A semester as a Visiting Professor in the Centre for Twentieth Century Studies at the University of Wisconsin-Milwaukee in 1988 gave me a sense of the peculiarity of British television and injected a necessary estrangement effect to some of the things which I had taken for granted. It also brought me into contact with people for whom I have an enduring admiration. Patrice Petro's classes on the Frankfurt School shifted my critical perspective in ways which I value, and I owe a continuing debt to the intellectual excitement, commitment and toughness which Pat Mellencamp brought to everything in general and television in particular.

Much of the book was written during a three-month Visiting Professorship in the English Department at the Federal University of Santa Catarina in Florianopolis, Brazil. The graduate students on my Television Drama course there were willing and generous collaborators, responding to ideas critically and enthusiastically while they were still wet on the page. It was they who made clear to me how restrictive some of the British debates about realism were. I am grateful to Anelise Corseuil for arranging my visit and for her participation in my course; and I am grateful to the staff and students of the Department for the quite overwhelming generosity of their hospitality. I am also grateful to the British Council and to CAPES, the Brazilian academic funding body, for making my visit possible.

Though the book was a long time germinating, the delivery was quite quick: the first draft was written between May and September, 1998. This was largely because it was written in places remote from Glasgow: Brazil, Knoydart in the Scottish West Highlands, and Shetland. I am grateful to the University of Glasgow for allowing me the study leave which permitted this. The fact that I could not put off the writing until I had checked just one more book in the library played a large part in getting the book finished by the deadline I had set myself: it allowed me the space to think without the seductive displacement activity of endless reading. The process of writing the draft was one of the most enjoyable I have had, and this owed a lot to a wonderful routine in which periods of undistracted writing were punctuated by periods of relaxed conviviality in some of my favourite places. For the conviviality, I am grateful in particular to Anelise and Henry in Brazil, to Ann and Peter in Shetland (and to Jenny and Joe), and to Ian and Jackie in Knoydart (not forgetting The Old Forge—the most remote pub on mainland Britain). Ouainé Bain was with me for some of the time in all of these places and added to the pleasure. She also read bits of the book and discussed many of the ideas, and I have valued her friendship and her engagement in all kinds of ways.

Andrew Lockett commissioned this book and the series, Oxford Television Studies, of which it is a part before he moved to the British Film Institute. I am grateful for his early commitment when we didn't have much to show for it, and I am grateful to the editors at Oxford University Press, and to Katie Ryde, my copy editor, who saw it through the final stages.

Finally, the book has benefited from two of the best (and sharpest) readers a writer could ask for. Charlotte Brunsdon has been a collaborator in thinking about ways of teaching and writing about television for many years, and is my co-editor in the Oxford Television Studies series. She not only made a detailed reading of the manuscript full of necessary corrections and suggestive possibilities, but also, crucially, clarified for me what the book was actually about. Even if I could not follow all of the possibilities she suggested, I hope that a better sense of what the book is actually about has informed the final version. Simon Frith did what I knew, and feared, he would do: he spotted the bits I thought I might just get away with, and nailed me for them. I am grateful for his belief that the book could be better than it was, and hope that, even if I haven't done everything, I have done enough to justify his faith.

Some of the material in this book is revised from articles written over almost twenty years. Chapter 2 marries two earlier articles: the beginning of 'Broadcasting and cinema (1): converging histories', in Charles Barr (ed.), *All Our Yesterdays: Ninety Years of British Cinema* (London: BFI Publishing, 1986) with a slightly revised form of 'Before the Golden Age: early television drama', in J. Corner (ed.), *Popular Television in Britain: Studies in Cultural History* (London: BFI Publishing, 1991), 22–41. Chapter 3 draws in part on material and arguments which I first proposed in 'Progressive television and documentary drama', *Screen*, 21:3 (1980), 9–35, but which I have substantially developed here. Chapter 5 similarly develops arguments which I made in 'Rhetoric, pleasure and art television', *Screen*, 22:4 (1981), 9–31 and in 'Adorno's reproach: repetition, difference and television genre', *Screen*, 32:2 (1991), 127–53. Chapter 7 uses some material from 'The logic of convergence', in J. Hill and M. McLoone (eds.), *Big Picture, Small Screen: The Relations between Film and Television*, Academia Research Monograph 16 (Luton: John Libbey Media/University of Luton, 1996), 215–23. Chapter 8 is based on an article, 'Small pleasures: adaptation and the past in British film and television', first commissioned for a special issue on Film, Literature and History of *Ilha do Desterro: A Journal of English Language, Literatures in English and Cultural Studies* (Editora da Universidade Federal de Santa Catarina, 1997). The work on acting in this chapter was developed for the conference on television drama organized by the Wednesday Play project at Reading University, and will appear in a collection of the papers from that conference to be published by Macmillan. The epilogue in Chapter 9 reproduces the introduction to 'Adorno's reproach'. I am grateful to many editors for refining the initial ideas to the point at which I could develop them here.

Contents

1

Introduction: 'Serious Drama'

I T is worth saying briefly what this book is not. Though the arguments follow a chronological line of development since the beginnings of television in the 1930s, it is not intended to be a history of British television drama. It does not claim to chronicle with historical detail the achievements and transformations of television drama through the period, nor does it explain with scholarly objectivity the evolutions and revolutions. Nor is the book a survey, covering the territory and identifying the major players, plays, and playwrights. Both of these are necessary and long overdue, but this book does not fill that gap, and any reading which starts out expecting the comprehensiveness which either implies is likely to be frustrated by a quite apparent selectivity.

If this book is a history of anything it is a history of the arguments and debates which seem to me to have been formative for British television drama, at least since 1946. These arguments were sometimes initiated by the practitioners of television drama, sometimes by its critics, and sometimes were conducted between the two. They were arguments about liveness; about the gap between fact and fiction; about realism, naturalism, and, implicitly, about modernism; and above all they were debates about the place and the politics of drama in public service broadcasting, and in public—and sometimes popular—culture. They were arguments which reached out to something wider in the culture and allow us to trace the shifting place of television drama in recent British cultural history. If, as the book progresses towards the present, a sense of the elegiac creeps in, it is not an elegy for a lost Golden Age of Television Drama, but for the loss of that sense of engagement—the sense that television drama really mattered within the culture—of which the arguments and debates were part symptom and part cause.

In tracing the history of these debates I have tried to tie them back into the cultural and institutional histories which gave them their wider significance. I have also tried to relate them to the aesthetic adventures, formal arguments and political interventions in the plays and films and series which make up the kind of television drama with which I am concerned. It is these adventures and interventions which not only focus the debates but complicate them, and I have tried to materialize the arguments wherever I can by analysis of the texts which inform them. The result, I hope, is a breaking down of apparently fixed aesthetic categories—realism, naturalism, modernism—into the fluidity and complexity of aesthetic forms when they meet practical determinations or political contexts or popular audiences.

Underpinning all this is a wider argument which is central to the purpose and the economy of the book. Put simply, the central argument of the book is that television drama is a central component of postwar British culture, and that its arguments and debates are both an extension and a complication of social, political, aesthetic, and cultural debates which have been going on at least since the second world war in cinema, theatre, literature, the fine arts and culture in general. Put this simply, and in its generality, the argument may seem unexceptionable, and there is always the possibility that the wider culture, having already capitulated to the popular, may welcome television drama into the fold without feeling any need to redefine itself. Television drama is, after all, the respectable end of television. Fair enough. At this level, I simply want to put the emphasis on the extent to which television drama complicates many of the terms of aesthetic debate and gives a new and very important significance to the notion of public culture.

At another level, however, in arguing that television drama is central to the culture, there is a desire to drag discussion of television drama out of the isolation ward in which it demanded special treatment and a protected vocabulary, and to reconnect it with a wider critical vocabulary which is adequate to this centrality. This is to say, at its most obvious, that I do not believe that discussion of television drama can any longer hide behind non-terms like 'non-naturalism', and refuse to recognize the complex and shifting relationship between television drama and late British modernism. Nor can we accept the easy contempt for naturalism and the consequent automatic approval of whatever its opposite is taken to be. What I have tried to do is to situate television drama in the context of historical debates and cultural shifts which have been going on in the arts and culture since the end of the nineteenth century—and to add some which are specific to television drama. I have tried to complicate our understanding of television drama by exposing it to historical debates, and, in reverse, to complicate the debates by exposing them to television drama. The underlying argument of the book, therefore, is not simply the familiar demand that television drama be taken seriously by 'official culture', but that the criticism of television drama take itself seriously, and that it accept the responsibility which that seriousness implies to engage with modern cultural debate on its own terms.

The 'serious drama' of this chapter heading, replete with scare quotes, designates in shorthand the tradition in British television drama which stretches from the single play to the television-commissioned art film, including on the way certain 'authored' series and serials and 'quality' and 'classic' adaptations. When I have said, over the past few years, that I was working on television drama, colleagues who inhabit the same area of film and television studies as I do, and share the same history of studying popular culture, have quite naturally assumed that my category would or should include soap opera, crime series and hospital melodrama. Or when I offered a course called 'Television Drama', students have complained that we did not talk about *NYPD Blue* or *ER*. 'Well, no,' I have said, a little defensively, 'what I'm interested in is "serious drama"', hoping that my scare quotes would be audible, and that my shorthand would not be taken seriously to imply that some areas of television or popular culture are not serious.

Short-hand explanations, with or without scare quotes, have a way of causing trouble. The term 'serious drama' brings with it a long history in formal and informal criticism and in everyday conversation, referring to forms of drama which are approved by 'serious' critics or 'serious' people. In most of these contexts, 'seriousness' comes bearing the weight of casual cultural elitism. 'Serious drama' lacks the institutional and legal history which gave meaning to the term 'legitimate theatre' of the nineteenth century (referring to the officially approved theatre which operated under state licence), but it inherits some of its implicit significance. Just as the notion of the 'legitimate' came to serve as a way of distinguishing a culturally approved theatre from the popular theatre of melodrama and music hall, so 'serious drama' operates to mark off a 'legitimate' cultural territory within television from other areas which are not legitimated by the official discourses of cultural approval. Used in this way, the territory of 'serious drama' is undefined because it does not need to be defined: it is the shared currency of those who own the cultural capital. Stripped of its scare quotes, it is not a term which anyone would own up to or defend seriously in the circles in which I move—and yet the idea still seems to creep in like a code understood by like-minded people, signalling a sense of worth which is assumed to be shared but which there never seems to be enough time or need to elaborate.

Despite the risks, I find myself persisting with the term and giving it prominence at the beginning of this book. Partly, this is provocation. I have found in recent teaching that the term 'serious drama' provokes quite fruitful discussion about where the boundaries of cultural value lie. In what sense is *ER* not 'serious'? How can you talk about television drama in Britain and not talk about *EastEnders*? A recent introductory class for a postgraduate course on television drama began with scorn and contempt for the term and shock/horror that I could propose it, and ended with an extremely interesting empirical research project based on interviews with television producers and newspaper critics to find out what the term 'quality' meant in professional and critical discourse, and what were the professional values implicit in taking television drama seriously.[1] However much the critical orthodoxy of popular cultural studies may insist that culture is not arranged in hierarchies of value, people (a category which includes television producers, intellectuals and critics of popular culture as well as the woman viewer much noted by researchers who self-deprecatingly jokes about her own taste for soap operas) do seem to approach their culture with systems of inherited, reasoned, or intuitive boundaries in which some things appear more valuable, or more serious, or seem to matter more than other things; and if these systems are not interrogated they easily slip into the mythology of a natural order—whether that order is founded on 'the people's culture' or on an 'elite culture'. The mildly scandalous provocation of 'serious drama' is intended to throw these boundaries into question.

At another level, within the politics of criticism, what the term 'serious drama' identifies is an area of television drama which is already taken seriously within public culture. This seems important. The development of cultural studies as an area of scholarship and criticism within the humanities, the kind of academic study which has formed my intellectual history, seems often to have been marked by the felt need to insist, in the face of those who saw only specious entertainment, that popular culture could and should be taken seriously. Culture, the refrain went, was to be considered not as the property of a cultivated elite, but as part of what Raymond Williams in *The Long Revolution* famously called a 'way of life', 'a structure of feeling' which defined and determined identities and subjectivities, setting limits and exerting pressures on ways of being. A 'structure of feeling', he said,

> is as firm and definite as 'structure' suggests, yet it operates in the most delicate and least tangible parts of our activity. In one sense, this structure of feeling is the culture of a period: it is the particular living result of all the elements in the general organization.[2]

Such an extension of the field of culture led enquiry and engagement out of the established paths of humanities scholarship sign-posted

1 I am indebted to Inge Sorenson, Lone Sorensen, and Marie Olesen, the 'three Danes' on our 1997/8 Media and Culture course, for their work on this applied research project.

2 Raymond Williams, *The Long Revolution* (Harmondsworth: Penguin, 1965), 64 ff.

by its canonical texts, and into foreign territory in which intellectuals *as intellectuals* appeared as strangers with no privileged knowledge and no native language. The foreignness was particularly marked in television, where the territory seemed, from the perspective of traditional academic enquiry, peculiarly exotic and eccentric—soap opera, sport, chat shows, the ontology of *Star Trek*. Such voyages into strange environments did not proceed without resistance back home: the popular press scoffed at 'Professors of Soap'; the academy dismissed this 'Mickey Mouse' subject, good for attracting students but not part of the serious academic agenda; and television professionals watched with bemusement as academics took seriously programme material which they themselves dismissed as 'bread and butter work' or 'ratings fodder'. The early explorations of popular forms, however, were of immense value within the discipline, opening up new modes of enquiry and engagement, staking out key critical debates, forging new vocabularies of criticism and theory, and redefining what it meant to be a discipline. The hostility and suspicion with which they were greeted merely increased the sense of excitement in the intellectual adventure, drawing the participants into a supportive, self-sustaining and sometimes, it should be said, self-confirming community. This is the common history of most new academic disciplines: English Literature and Sociology, now thoroughly domesticated within the academy, have their own relatively recent histories and memories of the wilderness.

These histories are, in many ways, defining for the discipline. Explicitly they set the critical agenda and establish priorities; at a rather more implicit level, they carry traces of the struggles of inception in interiorized prejudices and predilections and unacknowledged canon formations, setting the limits between home ground and territory which still belongs to the enemy. In early film studies in Britain, formed in reaction to Cambridge English and the elitist tradition associated, rightly or wrongly, with Leavis, European art cinema—the cinema which appealed to 'serious' critics in Britain—was not high on the agenda of the emerging discipline. For television studies, 'serious drama' was, similarly, uncertain territory, caught between the validation of 'low' culture and an edginess around television's particular forms of participation in 'high' culture. There was a flurry of interest in the late 1970s and early 1980s in *Days of Hope* and the possibility or impossibility of a politically progressive form of realism, and there has been the growth, particularly since his death, of a small branch industry in Dennis Potter Studies. If, however, one reads symptomatically the various readers and textbooks in television or media studies which have appeared recently, it becomes clear that debates about 'serious drama' are not taken to be definitive for the discipline.[3] The reference points for a theoretically informed study of television were popular forms and actuality. In this context, television drama came to mean popular drama: soap opera in particular offered the possibility of a critical feminism more rooted in the social than the psychoanalytical feminism which had come to dominate film studies. As well as opening up vistas, the histories of development (and memories of underdevelopment) created blind-spots. There does not seem to have been a sustained and coherent attention to the form of television which the surrounding culture took seriously. For a television studies informed by critical theory and cultural studies, 'serious drama' belonged to the bourgeoisie, placing it in a territory which was just below the horizon, only visible in certain lights.

Despite a renewed scholarly interest in the history of the single play in recent years,[4] there still remains a significant critical backlog around television drama: a historical reticence which, in the late 1990s, becomes more and more surprising. Pragmatically, in terms of the cultural politics and political economy of British television, it neglects an area which is absolutely central to both the ideals and the official discourse of public service broadcasting in all its complex forms within Britain. Culturally, in terms of the local and the global, it gives us little to say about a tradition of television drama which has become a central component among the marketable images of Britishness in the national and international imaginary. Theoretically, a study of television drama offers the opportunity to complicate some of the orthodoxies which have accumulated around television and cultural studies: the intellectual's relationship to the popular, the nature of authorship and creativity, the place of the text, and the possibility of a viewer who is neither distracted nor indifferent nor even resistant, but is engaged in both active and affective ways. And from the perspective of cultural history, I want to argue that television drama is central to an understanding of what happened to British modernism in the second half of the twentieth century.

In the end, then, I suppose I do believe that the television drama which I want to write about is serious in particular and specific ways: not exclusively serious, or more serious, but serious in a slightly different way. The fact that it is already taken seriously within the culture (often under the heading of 'quality television') may be symptomatic

3 I am thinking in particular of the very useful reader edited by Christine Geraghty and David Lusted, *The Television Studies Book* (London: Arnold, 1998), or the textbook, *Studying the Media* written by Tim O'Sullivan, Brian Dutton, and Philip Rayner (2nd edn., London: Arnold, 1998).

4 Here, I am thinking of Jason Jacobs's forthcoming book on early television drama in this series, *British Television Drama: The Intimate Screen* (Oxford: Oxford University Press, forthcoming 2000); and the work of the Reading University/British Academy Wednesday Play Research Project.

of systems of values of which television studies has traditionally, and correctly, been suspicious, but it also presents an opportunity to engage with wider debates about modernity, modernism, and modern culture, and about the place of television within what Simon Frith has called 'capitalist culture',[5] a term which seeks to escape the boundaries set by the division into 'high' and 'low' cultures or by the self-confirming prejudices of 'the popular' and 'the elite'.

So let me go a little beyond the ironic short-hand of 'serious drama', and offer a working definition which is brief, schematic and preliminary. The television drama in which I am interested involves three formal, institutional and cultural categories:

1. A category which derives from the theatre, and finds its classical form in the single play;
2. A category which is associated with cinema, and finds its most recognizable form in a number of the films commissioned by Channel 4;
3. A category which is more or less specific to television, and finds its forms in certain authored or adapted series and serials.

What I want to trace—formally, institutionally, and culturally—is the historical movement from the first category to the second, and the ways in which this movement is crossed at various points—the authored serial or series, the adaptation of classic literature—by its intersection with the third.

In their pioneering article, 'Television: a world in action', Stephen Heath and Gillian Skirrow refer to the problem of 'television itself'.

> When Raymond Williams writes . . . that 'one of the innovating forms of television is television itself', this cannot be allowed to confine 'television itself' to a technology or a single isolable element of the viewing experience: 'television itself' is everywhere in television, everywhere in the operation of 'form' and 'content' that a communication based analysis takes for granted.[6]

Clearly, television as a medium presents its own problems of critical method and theoretical approach, and the question of 'television itself', its languages and routines, constraints and determinations, needs to be acknowledged. It sometimes seems, however, that writing about television (despite the exemplary instance of Heath and Skirrow's very detailed analysis of a single programme) is so caught by

---

5 Simon Frith, 'Hearing secret harmonies', in Colin MacCabe (ed.), *High Theory, Low Culture: Analysing Popular Television and Film* (Manchester: Manchester University Press, 1986), 53–70.

6 Stephen Heath and Gillian Skirrow, 'Television: a world in action', *Screen*, vol. 18, no. 2 (1977), 8. The quotation from Raymond Williams is from *Television: Technology and Cultural Form* (London: Fontana Collins, 1974), 77.

the fascination of the problem of 'television itself' that it cannot see beyond it, cannot say anything about television in particular until it has said everything about television in general. The result is a phenomenology of television which is endlessly described and redescribed, 'television itself' functioning as an alibi for avoiding the hard business of critical analysis in favour of the more relative and negotiable pleasures of description.

This book does not propose a theory of everything or a new general theory of television, but proposes instead a historical and critical analysis of one bit of television, a particular corner of the field of dramatic narrative which has a particular political, cultural, and aesthetic efficacy of its own, at the same time, of course, as it shares in the efficacy of 'television itself'. If I seem to take some things as read— the determinations of audience, the nature of flow—it is not because I regard them as unimportant, but simply because I want to move on. I no longer believe that because flow is the characteristic experience of television it is pointless to isolate individual programmes for analysis without constant qualification to accommodate their place in the flow; nor do I believe that because viewers make their own differential readings and creative resistances and inhabit a condition of semiotic democracy (or not), it is no longer our business to try to define meanings and values. Texts provide the conditions of possibility of meaning and value, and they make some meanings more possible than others—and analysis can show how this works.

But having said that the generality of 'television itself' is not my primary focus, I want to begin by identifying some problems of critical method in 'television studies itself' which seem to me to provide the conditions of possibility for writing about television drama. These are not intended to add up to a general theory, but to provide a context of determinations which have an effect on the ways in which I want to write about television drama, and the ways in which television criticism and theory has been written. I have arranged these problems somewhat schematically under six headings.

The Problem of Specificity

Like many academics of my generation, I come to television studies by way of film studies. Also like many academics of my generation, I have no formal training in either film or television studies, but come to both as a refugee, escaping more established academic disciplines —in my case, English Literature and Theatre Studies—which seemed in the mid-1970s to be a little removed from the cutting edge of post-1968 academic and intellectual dissidence. In Britain, what drew many of us to film studies was theory: the magical object which opened up new ways of thinking not simply about film but about culture, language, ideology and, above all, about subjectivity. When departments began to form in the mid- to late-1970s and the discipline began to take shape, many of us felt that, politically, if we had any pretensions to be a radical discipline as well as a theoretically sophisticated one, television could not be ignored. After all, the canon which was forming in film studies—John Ford, Douglas Sirk, *film noir*, Godard—was not constituted by the films which people would recognize as forming *their* popular culture, or which packed real audiences into the high street cinemas. Television seemed to be the place in which you could engage with actual audiences as opposed to textual subjects, and in which you could give sharper definition to the political materiality of culture. And so, television was brought into the fold, an extension of film studies which made the discipline honest.

This potted biography may be more particular, and perhaps more confessional, than I imagine. It is certainly generationally particular, and many younger academics may not recognize it as their history. But what I am trying to identify are the origins of an uncertainty in television studies: an uncertainty about the specificity of television theory and analysis. Drawn to film studies by the glamour of theory and the excitement of textual analysis and symptomatic reading— *Young Mr Lincoln*, *Touch of Evil*—many of us (not all of us) seem to have assumed that we could import into the study of television the same theoretical matrix and analytical procedures. Much of the writing about television from my generation seemed to be haunted by the desire for film.[7]

The forms of analysis appropriated from film—semiotics, structuralism, psychoanalysis—seemed to stumble over the diversity of the television text, the programme in all its variety, which turned out to be less like a film than we had thought. Analysis seemed to go beyond or to fall short of its object, caught out by banality and unaccustomed to television's ways of being popular. In our disappointment, we turned away from the text to a more general cultural and institutional analysis or to the new object of fascination: the audience. However personal this account may be, it does seem to be the case that the development of television studies is not anchored, in the way that film studies is, by the analytical reading of texts; or, more exactly, it is hard to find textual analyses of television as a signifying practice which move with explanatory power from the specifics of the text to the generality of signification and the signifying system. We seem to have no precise understanding of how identification or point of view

7 A symptomatic reference point for this may be Robert C. Allen's influential textbook, *Channels of Discourse, Reassembled: Television and Contemporary Criticism* (2nd edn., London: Routledge, 1992), in which the familiar critical categories of film studies—semiotics, structuralism, psychoanalysis, genre, feminism—are 'adapted' for television.

works in television, other than to assume that it must be broadly the same as film—always with a qualifying nod to the domestic context of viewing.

There is, of course, a much longer tradition of the academic study of television in sociology and social sciences stretching back to the work of the emigrés of the Frankfurt School in the New School for Social Research in New York in the 1940s. Imported into the television studies which developed in the 1970s and 1980s, or into the more hybrid 'media studies', the vocabulary and disciplined empirical methodologies of the social sciences seemed to promise a way of disciplining the new fascination with the social audience, in the same way that structural linguistics had disciplined the fascination with the text in film studies. Some of the key texts of television studies—David Morley's *Family Television*[8] or Ann Gray on domestic technologies[9]— come from this tradition, and give real insight into the ways in which television operates within gendered relations to technology and within the distribution of domestic power. Coupled with this, work such as Stuart Hall's 'Encoding/decoding'[10] gave a theoretical framework for understanding differential readings. The very success of this work offered temptations to the unwary, and ambition often seemed to outstrip methodological competence, resulting in an appeal to a somewhat uncertain 'ethnography' as the guarantee for claims about an audience which seemed to be more and more a projection of the writer's intellectual wishes and ideological needs. Such work on the social, as David Morley pointed out[11], lacked an adequate sociology. The object of these criticisms was John Fiske, whose *Television Culture*[12] threatened to become the textbook for the discipline; but in many ways, Fiske was a scapegoat for our uncertainties, a kind of court jester playing out in grotesque form the logic of a much wider insecurity about the position of intellectuals in popular television, pushing to the point of absurdity the drama of a more general desperation to identify, and identify with, 'ordinary viewers'.

This appropriation of ethnography was characteristic of a wider system of appropriations, and it seemed that if you wanted to understand television, you had to read about something else: not only film and literary theory, but geography, economic theory, tourism studies,

8 David Morley, *Family Television* (London: Comedia, 1986).

9 Ann Gray, *Video Playtime: The Gendering of a Leisure Technology* (London: Routledge, 1992).

10 Stuart Hall, 'Encoding/decoding', in Stuart Hall *et al.* (eds.), *Culture, Media, Language: Working Papers in Cultural Studies, 1972–79* (London: Hutchinson/Centre for Contemporary Cultural Studies, 1990), 128–38.

11 David Morley, 'Where the global meets the local: notes from the sitting room', *Screen*, vol. 32, no. 1 (1991), 3.

12 John Fiske, *Television Culture* (London: Methuen, 1987).

cybernetics. Now, it seems to me that one of the glories of television studies is its insistence on an interdisciplinarity which breaks with formalist or sociological reductionisms in which television's meanings are the product *either* of formal procedures *or* of social forces. There are even real strengths in radical eclecticism, and it may be in the nature of the study of a television which inhabits so many spheres of experience that, in the absence of a secure theoretical foundation of its own, it will turn to analogical rather than deductive reasoning: it is genuinely illuminating, as Margaret Morse has shown, to compare the experience of watching television to the experience of being in a shopping mall. [13] But the risks of an undisciplined eclecticism which appropriates a language and procedures selectively and instrumentally are considerable. What it often seems to produce in television studies is a kind of 'wild theory', a theory which can never be held to account because it prides itself on its lack of discipline, a 'disobedience' which allows it the continual freedom to slip off the hook of difficult engagement because it is politically subversive, academically undomesticated or charmingly playful.

The more fundamental uncertainty around theory of which 'wild theory' is a symptom seems to be one of the conditions of writing about the specificity of television. Many of the tensions which it creates are productive, and some are simply frustrating. I do not expect to place myself outside them, and I am conscious that much of the intellectual luggage which I carry to a study of television drama is formed in film studies or in the wider fields of cultural theory and cultural history. My focus, however, is on the historical and material conditions of the production of meanings and values in television drama: conditions of language, technology, institution, and culture; the conditions, that is, which frame meaning and make some meanings probable and others unexpected, and which create specific forms of subjectivity. What I hope is that this may say something more widely about the possibilities of meaning and subjectivity on television, and ways of thinking about them. While the convergence of film and television is a consistent thread of the analysis, I am concerned with the difference of television, and its specificity.

The Problem of History

One of the characteristics which defines the specificity of television is a very problematic relationship to its own past. In the retrospective glance of academic, professional, and public discourses, 'old

---

13 Margaret Morse, 'The ontology of everyday distraction: the freeway, the mall and television', in Patricia Mellencamp (ed.), *Logics of Television: Essays in Cultural Criticism* (Bloomington/London: Indiana University Press/BFI Publishing, 1990), 193–221.

television' seems to begin around 1980 and to recede into antiquity some time around 1955 when programmes become irrecoverable. There is still a catch of surprise for many people, even those who have an academic or professional interest in television, when they are reminded that there were three years of public broadcasting of television in Britain in the 1930s before the service was suspended at the outbreak of the war in Europe. While cinema historians have a continuous, though incomplete, history of films from the 1890s, a significant part of television's past inhabits a dim pre-history in which programmes themselves do not exist in recorded form.

This, as we shall see, begins from the nature of the early technology. Transcription, the ability to record an electronic television signal on 35mm. celluloid, was not developed till 1948 by the engineers of the BBC, and recording on tape was developed first in the United States in 1953. Neither was in routine use till the late 1950s or early 1960s, and even when recording was possible there is a long chain of missing links which have been wiped from the record either to reuse the tapes or to save storage space. For television drama, as for other forms, the early history of form and style is an archaeological, rather than a strictly historical procedure, piecing together the fragments from the potsherds of the paper record.[14]

A number of things follow from this which are significant for our understanding of television, and for our relationship to television's history. The routine wiping of early television recordings seems symptomatic of a professional view of the essential nature of early television which leaves traces in later attitudes, both professional and academic. Television was ephemeral. Even after technology had solved the problem of recording and had given selected programmes a potentially permanent form, there seems to have persisted a fairly casual attitude to the establishment of the record. This lack of self-regard seems characteristic of television, marking out a symptomatic difference from cinema both in terms of its early circulation as a commodity form (it is only recently that new technologies of dissemination have made apparent the value of the programme archive), and in terms of its eye on posterity. Where this attitude to the record persists, in British television at least, is in the way it now begins to present its past in retrospectives—at least of popular programming—which seem always to be introduced by an embarrassed—and embarrassing—cuteness. Television's past is generally not regarded as 'serious'. Programmes in Britain like *Television Hell* or *Television Heaven* which reclaim programmes from the 1960s and 1970s for our amused attention, linking them with joky graphics and funny voices which disavow

14 For an excellent use of the written record in reconstructing early British television drama, see Jacobs, *British Television Drama*.

any suspicion of being serious about the past, may irritate historians but may, at the same time, indicate a correct perception of how television fits into our lives and our memories. Television seldom claims any of the historical dignity of 'classic cinema'; rather, 'old television' presents itself like the family album, inviting us to gather round and be amused by the way we once were—'I remember that' shading into 'Did we really dress like that?' and implying 'Were we really like that then?' However damaging to the dignity of history, this may tell us a great deal about the ways in which television establishes commonalities of shared experience and communities of memory. Our glimpses of old television, in a way which is curiously and interestingly different from our fascination with films of the same period, seem to function—like old photographs—as a kind of *musée imaginaire*, a museum which, as Andreas Huyssen suggests,[15] may remind us of the non-synchronicity of the past, of our difference from ourselves. This would clearly be an important component of a social theory of television, and would compensate for the lack of monuments which seems for Jameson to be purely a negative, consigning television to indifference.[16]

I stress the generality of this disregard for the past, because there are a few particular exceptions. It is symptomatic of its cultural and professional prestige that these exceptions seem to occur most frequently in 'serious' television drama. Armchair Theatre, The Wednesday Play, single plays like *Cathy Come Home*, serials like *The Singing Detective*, and the tentative emergence of a canon around a few writers, producers, and directors (Dennis Potter, Ken Loach, Tony Garnett; even, from early history, Rudolph Cartier) begin to constitute a crest-line history of television marked out by monuments. This usefully calls into question the universalizing reach of Jameson's theory of the non-monumentality of television. It is also part of what makes the study of television drama important, offering a record of the difference of the past which reminds us, naggingly, of what the present might be—or might have been.

This notwithstanding, for an understanding of the history of television programmes and the development of television language the weakness of the record constitutes a problem. The sheer volume of output seems to create an amnesia-producing pandemonium, leaving little space for a critical and contemplative history or for a

15 Andreas Huyssen, *Twilight Memories: Marking Time in a Culture of Amnesia* (New York/London: Routledge, 1995).

16 Fredric Jameson, 'Reading without interpretation: postmodernism and the video-text', in N. Fabb *et al.* (eds.), *The Linguistics of Writing: Arguments between Language and Literature* (Manchester: Manchester University Press, 1987), 199–223. Another version of this essay appears in F. Jameson, *Postmodernism, or, The Cultural Logic of Late Capitalism* (London: Verso, 1990).

careful recovery of programmes and language. Television studies as a discipline seems to fasten onto the contemporary and the current in a way which risks essentializing television into a perpetual present: a present which distracts attention from the process of change and transformation in which the grammar of meanings and representations is formed, by which the routines of language and 'specific signifying practices' came to be institutionalized, or the ways in which 'good television' learned to be good.

Much of the most productive recent work in film theory has been informed by cinema history, tracing the paths by which cinema moved through the 'primitive' towards what Noël Burch calls the 'Institutional Mode of Production', or what Bordwell, Staiger, and Thompson call the 'Classical Hollywood Cinema'.[17] While television belongs to a very different set of histories and practices (which calls into question, for instance, whether something like a 'classical' television is a meaningful concept), nevertheless, the historical method which seeks to piece together the steps by which practices become routines seems to offer a way of understanding some of the working assumptions which persist long after the conditions which legitimated them have withered away. As Geoffrey Nowell-Smith has argued, all histories of representations are histories of subjectivities,[18] and without a history of the production of meaning it is not only television which is essentialized into the present, but subjectivity.

For television studies, it is worth pointing to another absence in the record. Just as we are distracted from programmes of the past which might establish the difference of the present, so also there seems to be an absence of 'monumental' figures from the past with whom contemporary theory and criticism might argue. The standard introductory readers and textbooks in television and media studies all tend to gather together critical articles from the 1980s and 1990s, with the 1970s as some all-but-forgotten pre-history; and the rest is silence. There are no figures who stand in the same relationship to television theory as Eisenstein and Bazin have done for film, staking out the territory of the defining debates. It is not that figures do not exist with a different framework—McLuhan and Adorno might have provided some theoretical starting points—but they seem to have been covered with amnesia or obliquy, forgotten as the gurus of a more innocent age or derided as cultural pessimists, with no purchase on the immediacy of the present.

---

17 See Noël Burch, *Correction Please; or, How We Got Into Pictures* (London: Arts Council, undated), and 'Porter, or, ambivalence', *Screen*, vol. 19, no. 4 (1978/9), 91–105; David Bordwell, Janet Staiger, and Kristin Thompson, *The Classical Hollywood Cinema: Film Style and Mode of Production to 1960* (London: Routledge & Kegan Paul, 1985).

18 Geoffrey Nowell-Smith, 'On history and the cinema', *Screen*, vol. 31, no. 2 (1990), 160–71.

The monumental figure of British television, and, by extension, of much world television derived from the model of the BBC, is, of course, John Reith, the patriarch of a system and ideology now known as 'Reithian'. Undoubtedly, any account of what television is and what its place in the culture might be has to engage with the Reithian model, and in the late 1990s, at the point of its dissolution, that model may offer more interesting challenges to the present than we may have imagined in the 1970s when it was in its dominance. Reith's importance, however, is as a cultural and institutional model—often posed for the sake of argument in extremely general and attenuated forms. The 'Reithian' stands as an almost abstract discursive formation rather than as a material practice, or as a body of reflective writing or critical thinking with which we might engage.

Richard Dienst, in *Still Life in Real Time*, a very exciting engagement with theory after television,[19] reminds us that Rudolph Arnheim had registered the significance of television, and that Dziga Vertov anticipated it intriguingly with his writing on 'radio eye'. But, for Dienst, the history of television theory proper begins with Raymond Williams, and the theoretical understanding which he initiated in 1974 with *Television: Technology and Cultural Form*[20] —most particularly in its identification of 'flow' as the defining characteristic—stands as the first point of orientation. For the rest, Dienst's complex engagements are with theory which could not, did not, or would not engage with television: Marx, Derrida, Deleuze, and Heidegger. It seems at least worth noting that—'flow' apart— Dienst's engagement with television theory is written quite explicitly as theory *after* television, its debates conducted with an elsewhere. The narrow aperture of the historical framework of television theory seems to define the window out of which that theory is written, and the kind of television which is taken as its material reference point.

This may seem an odd and somewhat dubious complaint, this yearning for a parentage. My point, however, is that it is one of the specificities of television theory that its founding moment is written in the context of a television which has already achieved a mature form, a context which precedes the present by only two decades, four decades after the first public transmission, and two decades after television had become a mass popular form. Theory is, in some sense, retrospective, catching up with what already exists, concerned with the condition of having become. While there are symptomatic speculations, descriptions, and polemics written largely by practitioners, there seems, almost uniquely, to be no formative and elaborated

19 Richard Dienst, *Still Life in Real Time: Theory after Television* (Durham/London: Duke University Press, 1994).

20 Williams, *Television: Technology and Cultural Form*.

theoretical intervention in thinking about television which is written in the process of becoming, in the context of the theoretical uncertainties and the practical possibilities of what it was that was going to be formed.

Though they are organized chronologically, the chapters in this book do not claim to be a history of television drama. With any luck, they may point to the need for many more detailed, scholarly, and particular histories. The book is, however, written from a historical perspective. As a general project, I hope to establish the debates and transformations and material histories which seem to me to have been definitive for British television drama and its place within the culture of the last fifty years or so.

The Problem of the National

When Fredric Jameson writes about the lack of monumental texts in television, he is writing about both video and broadcast television. When he applies his argument to television, he seems to me to be writing from the North American experience of television. When I question the universality of his argument, I am arguing from my rather different experience of British television. This points to another problem of writing about television which can be noted quite briefly. Rightly or wrongly, film studies has grown up with some kind of shared language, a system of references which provides the points of consensus or argument: monuments, precisely as Jameson says, which seem to unify the field. Love it or loathe it, the classic Hollywood cinema provides an international standard which allows us to agree or disagree, whether at the academic or the popular level, whether in São Paulo or San Francisco. While postcolonial theory would challenge Hollywood's rights of definition, it would not contest its global power. Hollywood seems to be the common sense of cinema.

Television, on the other hand, is local, defined by quite different systems of national regulation, different historical relations with the state and with capital—even with different points of entry. Brazil, now an important television country in the international market, did not begin its television service till the early 1950s; Mozambique did not begin its service till 1977 (in consultation, famously if somewhat eccentrically, with Jean-Luc Godard[21]); and even within Britain, the nation which began the first public transmission in 1936, television did not reach Scotland till 1952. These different histories add up to different national experiences, and different understandings of what television is. The experience of using *The Singing Detective* in

---

21 See special issue of *Cahiers du cinéma*, 300 (May 1979).

an undergraduate course on television in Milwaukee in 1988, or showing *Cathy Come Home* and David Mercer's *The Parachute* in a graduate course in Brazil in 1998, is to challenge, and to throw into question the common sense of what television is.

The specificity of the local has an 'up side' and a 'down side'. The 'up side' lies in the resistance which television poses to universal theories and the confusion it brings to hegemonic common sense and international standards of what television is. Clearly, in the face of global systems of diffusion this becomes more of an uphill struggle, but the global media always come into being in specific relations to the local, and these little contests of the local and the global are what make the difference.

Where this resistance to universalization becomes particularly important is in critical writing which seeks to celebrate television as the child of postmodernity, the place where postmodernism finds its logic and its quintessential cultural form. Against this, it seems important to insist that postmodernity is not an achieved condition, but a process of becoming, and it is a process which is marked by uneven development. For the record, British terrestrial television, with its regulated duopoly operating in the public interest derived from the Victorian regulation of public utilities, seems to me still rooted in modernity. While that 'still' comes to seem increasingly conditional, and while the mix of competition and regulation, national and international, terrestrial broadcasting and new technologies of distribution, is constantly shifting and converging, the end result will be a specific local formation of the residual and the emergent which will mark out a particular (and probably peculiar) relationship to the global and the postmodern. Critical writing which assumes that American television always already forms the same kind of international standard as the classical Hollywood cinema seems to founder on quite sharp local differences. For television at least, celebrations of the end of history and the birth of 'in-difference' seem premature.

The 'down side' of the local specificity of national systems is that it is more difficult to form an international community of interest and a common language of reference. The discipline seems threatened on the one side by 'universalism' and on the other by 'parochialism'. The ways in which the economics of publishing crosses with the politics of the academy plays some part in this: publishers need large markets, and academics need to publish. The seduction of universal theory, despite the evidence of history, may be that 'the universe' is a very attractive publishing market.

What is clear is that questions of the local and the global, the national and the international come to form a central problematic for the study of television. It is precisely the interest of television drama in Britain that it allows us to trace a particular historical path from the local to the global, from the television play as an ephemeral event which had no existence outside the moment of transmission, through the television play as an event in the national polity, to the art film or the classic serial which circulate as commodities in the international market in images. In its national peculiarities, British television also allows us to imagine different boundaries of definition and common sense.

The Problem of the Text

I have already referred to the problem which the television text presents to the development of theory. I want to develop the point here, pursuing an argument which I have introduced elsewhere.[22]

Cinema and broadcasting have neatly contrasting histories of development. Cinema spends the first thirty years of its existence with the image and no speech; broadcasting spends its first thirty years with speech and no image. As a result, cinema develops a narrative based on a highly elaborated visual rhetoric and spectacle which continues even after sound is added; broadcasting is a medium of speech, carrying a respect for the written word forward into its dramas after the development of television. Cinema narrative deploys its visual rhetoric to seduce us into a fantasmatic relationship to its narrative space; television drama uses the word to tell us about the world. Film allows us to dream; television drama invites us to be responsible.

The comparison is clearly too pat: too neat and too general to be sustained for very long or very seriously. And yet I think it points to a certain fascination, a system of seduction which informs film criticism and which is much less marked in writing about television. The *mise en scène* of cinema holds secrets—even from its creators—which criticism can uncover. More than that, it creates desire: it is, as Laura Mulvey says, 'an illusion cut to the measure of desire'.[23] Cinema writing seems often to be marked by the tones of intellectuals trying to come to terms with their own 'incorrect' pleasures. Mulvey sets out to destroy the pleasure of a Hollywood cinema which has stolen women's image (a cinema on whose decline women can only look back with 'sentimental regret' from the shores of a feminist politics),[24] but there is no doubt that the writing with which she seeks to destroy that cinema also feels the power of its seduction. This is what gives her

22 See John Caughie, 'Rhetoric, pleasure and "art television"—*Dreams of Leaving*', *Screen*, vol. 22, no. 4 (1981), 14.

23 Laura Mulvey, 'Visual pleasure and narrative cinema', *Screen*, vol. 16, no. 1 (1975), 17.

24 Ibid. 18.

essay its authority. It seems characteristic of much television writing that the critic can see the seduction but is not seduced. The fascination is transferred from the text to the audience—the housewife, the teenage girl (it is so often a woman)—and her seduction. The terms of creativity, negation, and difference are reassigned from the modernist producer of meaning to the postmodern consumer, and the critic engages with an object which is external to herself or himself and to which she or he is external.

Simon Frith writes of the criticism of popular culture as a 'fantasy land', but the fantasies, he says, 'are those projected onto it by (male) intellectuals themselves: intellectuals, longing, daring, fearing to transgress; intellectuals wondering what it would be *not to be an intellectual*.'[25] In the romance of criticism, the text of popular culture often seems resistant to the blandishments of the intellectual, who responds by taking it away from all that, removing it from the conditions of its popularity. This is not an argument that the intellectual should get down and dirty with the television text, but is only to try to explain (if only to myself) some of the reticences and silences of television theory and criticism, and the effects of what Bourdieu calls our 'distinction'[26] on and in our writing.

The Problem of the Everyday

The problem of the text is further complicated for criticism by the conditions in which it is received. So much has been said about this, and it has become so much part of the orthodoxy of the study of 'television itself', that little needs to be added here. It is clearly crucial to the way in which 'television itself' functions within the culture that, as a domestic technology, it does not inhabit a 'specialized time'[27] or a specialized place, but takes its place, in the midst of distraction, as part of everyday life, a way of passing or spending or wasting time. This is one of the determining conditions of television, and it undoubtedly complicates the extent to which a criticism based on

25 Simon Frith, review article in *Screen*, vol. 31, no. 2 (1990), 235.

26 See Pierre Bourdieu, *Distinction: A Social Critique of the Judgement of Taste* (Cambridge, Mass.: Harvard University Press, 1984).

27 'Everyday life, defined elliptically as "whatever remains after one has eliminated all specialized activities", is, Lefebvre argues, a limited historical phenomenon. It is inextricably tied to two parallel developments: first, to the rise of a middle class and the demise of the great "styles" formerly imposed on western societies by Church and Monarch; second, to the vast migration of those middle classes to urban centres, spaces where their everyday activities would become increasingly organized—hence perceptible.' Alice Kaplan and Kristin Ross, Introduction to a Special Issue on 'Everyday Life', *Yale French Studies*, no. 73 (1987), 2. For the development of Lefebvre's argument, see Henri Lefebvre, *Critique of Everyday Life*, vol. 1, trans. John Moore (London: Verso, 1991; first published: Paris, 1947).

respect for the integrity of the text can make sense of a text which is continually subject to everyday distraction. The complication has sometimes produced a paralysis in which criticism can say nothing at all about the text without dissolving it into the endless relativities of the distracted audience.

So be it. But against this, it is worth recalling that Dennis Potter's *The Singing Detective* (1986), a six-part serial which is one of the significant works of postwar British modernism, had an audience of around eight million people in Britain for its first episode (around one in seven of the total population), and six million people were still watching the last episode six weeks later. Within all the qualifications and variables of ratings, and after subtracting a million distracted viewers and unwatched televisions switched on in empty rooms, it seems reasonable to guess that perhaps a little more than one in ten of the adult population of Britain had created a little piece of specialized time during which they were prepared to give a particular form of attention to something which bore all the marks—and all the marketing—of a very 'serious' television drama. Other particular forms of attention with varying degrees of concentration and telephones taken off the hook are commanded night after night by *EastEnders*, or week after week by *The X-Files*. My point is that the fact that television as a technology takes its place alongside the telephone or the washing machine in everyday domestic life does not mean that we do not make quite specialized uses of it, sometimes using it distractedly to pass time, sometimes arresting everyday time with quite demanding engagement. There is no single form of attention appropriate to television; the viewer who is distracted at eight o'clock may be absorbed and engaged at ten o'clock; flow is not undifferentiated, but moves in currents of distraction and eddies of engagement.

Forms of attention produce forms of subjectivity, and are the products of forms of address. I am interested in the particular forms of subjectivity which television drama seems to address, and in the historically variable forms of attention which it seems to expect of its audience. Gus Macdonald, then Managing Director of Scottish Television, one of the regional commercial franchises dependent for its funding on advertising, insisted once, in a discussion programme on one of the many Government policy papers of the late 1980s and early 1990s, that he wanted to see a strong BBC, with a commitment to culture and quality, maintained as the cornerstone of public service broadcasting: 'I want the BBC to address the public as citizens', he said, 'so that I can be free to address them as consumers.'

What seems interesting about this is the frank recognition that viewers do not always already exist as consumers or citizens but are invited to occupy these roles by forms of address. Television drama seems to bring these terms into particularly complex forms of relationship. I am interested in the ways in which, at various points in its history, it has negotiated the terms, sometimes refusing to compromise with 'television itself' and the everyday space which it inhabits, sometimes struggling to subvert it, sometimes using the everyday conventions of television ironically against themselves, sometimes playing the market and sometimes constructing a niche. In the terms which Raymond Williams used, the everyday is a central determination of television, but only in the sense of 'setting limits, exerting pressures', never absolutely determining its possibilities of meaning.[28] The point of analysis is to understand the specific forms—of address, attention, and subjectivity—which that condition calls into being.

The Problem of Value

The question of value has become pervasive in contemporary criticism and cultural studies—almost to the point of becoming fashionable. I will return to it briefly in the conclusion to this book, but I want to insert it at the outset as a filter through which many of the arguments of the book can be read. In particular, I want to identify two aspects to the question.

The first part of the problem is historical. The particular current of film, and subsequently television studies which seemed to establish the hesitant academic recognition of the discipline (or the community of interest) staked its claim to that recognition with a form of criticism which was more concerned with the ways in which meaning was produced than with the ranking of works on a scale of value. There were various sleights of hand in this, and canons and pantheons emerged in practice. The project was very far from being value free, a pure space created between the reader and the text, but nevertheless, in a quite formative way, film and television studies developed in reaction to the school of criticism associated with English literary criticism (the 'lit crit' which was sometimes more imagined than real) which saw its purpose as being to assign, agree, and protect the values of the culture.

For television studies, this was, at least in part, a necessary strategic move. If we were to concede a single scale of values which contained both *King Lear* and *Coronation Street*, it would be difficult to argue for the seriousness of soap opera. Rather than get into the absurdities of a later debate about whether or not Keats was better than Bob Dylan, it was better to disengage than to fight on that terrain. The political project of this current of film and television studies was more concerned with what made the text seductive than with what made it valuable. Value, in that sense, was, like the texts themselves, ideological,

---

28 See Raymond Williams, 'Base and superstructure in Marxist cultural theory', in *Problems in Materialism and Culture* (London: Verso, 1980), 32.

and the business of critical theory and analysis was to demystify ideology, understanding the discourses of value without itself assigning
value. It was not what made the text good that was important
but what made it pleasurable: what produced pleasure and what
pleasure produced.

And so the question of the value of the text was suspended. The
item which had become definitive for the academic study of literature
was taken off the agenda of the academic study of film and television
in order to allow it to concentrate on something else, on the workings
of language and ideology. This was, in many ways and for many critics,
definitive for the discipline, and, inevitably, while it was liberating in
some respects it was constraining in others. In particular, it separated
film and television studies even further from the realms of public
discourse in which the terms of judgement are taken to be important,
and are seen to be part of the business of people who are professional
and specialized intellectuals. Students must sometimes have been
puzzled by the fact that we were allowed to say that a film was 'very,
very interesting', but not that it was 'very, very good', and the judgements which underpinned our passionate enthusiasms never seemed
to be what our teaching was about. As Charlotte Brunsdon has
pointed out, the evacuation of the field of value removed film and
television studies from important public debates, depriving us of
a vocabulary with which to intervene confidently in debates about,
for example, 'quality television' or the various moral panics around
video violence, or taste and decency on television.[29] Some people did
intervene in these debates, of course, but it seemed to be in spite of
the discipline rather than because of it, their interventions posing a
challenge to the orthodoxy rather than speaking for it.

These reticences are important for an understanding of the political history of the discipline (the reverse sides of which are, of course,
its intellectual strengths). But value and judgement pose an even
more fundamental set of difficulties. The tradition of romantic and
modernist criticism has been to ascribe value to difference. In its
more conservative versions this difference goes under the name of
creativity and originality, and it is assigned to the individual talent
speaking with a unique voice from within a tradition.[30] In the Marxist
variant associated with Adorno and Horkheimer in their essay on
the culture industry (to which I will return),[31] it has its roots in the

29 Charlotte Brunsdon, 'Problems with quality', *Screen*, vol. 31, no. 1 (1990),
   67–90.

30 I am thinking of the *locus classicus*, T. S. Eliot, 'Tradition and the individual
   talent' (1920), in *The Sacred Wood: Essays in Poetry and Criticism* (London:
   Methuen, 1960), 47–59.

31 Theodor Adorno and Max Horkheimer, 'The Culture Industry: enlightenment
   as mass deception', in *Dialectic of Enlightenment* (London: Verso, 1979),
   120–67.

negation of capitalist administrative rationality, the difference and difficulty of 'authentic art' providing the talisman which protects it from commodification. Either variant is hostile to industrial, commodified culture. For television, however, where a significant part of the pleasure seems to lie in repetition, recognition, and familiarity, the assignment of value to difference presents particular problems. The result has been that television studies has simply side-stepped the issue, denouncing Adorno and Horkheimer as cultural pessimists, and preferring to leap beyond the challenge which they pose rather than to think through it.

For film studies, the response was *overtly* to resist judgement, but *covertly* to erect a canon based on systems of difference found in authorship and genre. For television, where repetition seems more foundational, and where authorship seems more invisible, the terms of critical judgement become more uncertain. While there have been attempts at canonization—particularly of genres (soap opera, prime time melodrama, cop shows), and occasionally of authorship (Steve Bochco, Potter)—it has been difficult to generalize difference as a term of value without removing popular television from the pleasures which make it popular. As Tania Modleski has shown,[32] the problem of valuing the repetition and familiarity of popular forms is not confined to a modernist criticism which has assigned them to the 'specious good' (Trilling's phrase), but extends into post-structuralism, and even, despite its claims, into postmodernism: Barthes erects an obvious scale of values when he discriminates for the 'readerly' against the 'writerly', for '*jouissance*' against 'pleasure';[33] and the scales of postmodern judgement are weighted firmly by Lyotard against 'the solace of good forms'.[34]

The question of value, judgement, and evaluation runs through this book, emerging in various ways. It brings me back to the beginning of this introduction, because it is this question which places the protective scare quotes around 'serious drama'. It would seem to be part of the business of the book to whittle away at the scare quotes, to unhedge the bets, and to justify the claim that the tradition of television drama I am concerned with is serious in particular ways. Again, it is not that it is serious on a scale on which other forms are unserious, but that, within the various problematics and conditions I have outlined in this chapter, television drama gives us a purchase on certain questions of theory and criticism, meaning, and value

32 Tania Modleski, 'The terror of pleasure: the contemporary horror film and postmodern theory', in Modleski (ed.), *Studies in Entertainment: Critical Approaches to Mass Culture* (Bloomington: Indiana University Press, 1986), 155–66.

33 Roland Barthes, *The Pleasure of the Text* (New York: Hill & Wang, 1975).

34 Jean-François Lyotard, *The Postmodern Condition* (Manchester: Manchester University Press, 1986), 81.

which are less sharply marked elsewhere in television, and are important for an understanding both of the recent history of British culture and of the possibilities of the future. These questions extend the boundaries of what we mean when we talk about 'television itself', and may allow us still to imagine a television which might be otherwise.

2
Early Television and Television Drama

1927   On 1 January 1927, the British Broadcasting Company, formed as a private monopoly in 1922 to protect the interests of Marconi and the other radio manufacturers, became the British Broadcasting Corporation. The change in title signified a shift from private to public, from protection in the interests of business and private commerce to protection in the public interest. This followed the recommendation of the Crawford Committee of 1926, and significantly reflected the fact that the British Broadcasting Company had demonstrated its trustworthiness during the General Strike of 1926 when the BBC, while retaining its formal independence from government, had managed to reconcile the national interest with the interest of the national government. The aim of the BBC's reporting during the Strike, say Paddy Scannell and David Cardiff,

> was conciliatory, to reconcile opposing factions to each other, to maintain the morale of the population and to restore national unity. The position was, of course, far less innocent and disinterested than it professed to be, for what it systematically filtered out was any account or explanation of the causes that had put a large section of the population in conflict with central government.[1]

Or as John Reith notoriously put it at the time, 'Since the BBC was a national institution, and since the Government in this crisis were acting for the people ... the BBC was for the Government in this crisis too.'[2]

So began a relationship of independence from and common interest with the State, which was to characterize British broadcasting for a long time, punctuating its history sometimes with servile complicity and sometimes with remarkable contradictions.

---

1 Paddy Scannell and David Cardiff, *A Social History of British Broadcasting: Volume 1, 1922–1939* (Oxford: Basil Blackwell, 1991), 33.

2 Quoted ibid.

The new Corporation received its Royal Charter, its funding (a licence fee on receiving sets determined by Government and administered by the Post Office), and its somewhat provisional independence from direct state control on the condition that it used the public airwaves as a national utility through which to provide a public service. In this respect, the regulation of broadcasting followed the pattern established by the late Victorians and the Edwardians for the administration of other national utilities like water, gas, and electricity.

John Reith, subsequently (and consequently) Sir John and ultimately Lord Reith, had been General Manager of the Company since 1922. Having manoeuvred effectively against the commercial interests of his private paymasters, he became in 1927 the first Director General of the new Corporation, stamping on it a character which was to be identified as 'Reithian' long after he had departed. Monopoly, for Reith, was not simply an administrative convenience but was a moral imperative. Without monopoly, he later wrote in his autobiography,

> many things might not have been done so easily that were done. The Christian religion and the Sabbath might not have had the place and the protection which it was right to give them. . . . The Christian religion, not just as a sectional activity but as a fundamental. And as to the Sabbath, one day in the week clear of jazz and variety and such like. . . . Almost everything might have been different. The BBC might have had to play for safety, prosecute the obviously popular lines, count its clients, study and meet their reactions, curry favour, subordinate itself to the vote.[3]

Public monopoly could only be justified by public service; but in order to serve the public, broadcasting had to be free both from the commercial pressures of mass entertainment and from the political pressures of mass persuasion and propaganda. The name which was given to the various forms of negotiated relationships between the State, the public interest, and the market was public service broadcasting.

1927 On 31 January 1927, John Grierson returned to Britain from the United States, where he had spent two years on a scholarship studying mass communications and writing about cinema. In 1927, for a student just out of a Scottish university where he had studied philosophy, the choice of subject seems remarkable, though it may be significant for Grierson's subsequent relationship with the State that he had studied in the Philosophy Department at Glasgow University, then dominated by Hegelians.

---

3 J. C. W. Reith, *Into the Wind* (London: Hodder & Stoughton, 1949), 90–1.

On his return to Britain, he went to see Stephen Tallents (later Sir Stephen Tallents), the civil servant in charge of the recently established Empire Marketing Board (EMB), a government agency charged with the promotion of Britain and British trade in the Empire and at home. The story is well known: Grierson persuaded Tallents, and Tallents persuaded the Treasury, that cinema, and specifically documentary should receive Government funding to 'bring the Empire alive'. On the basis of Government funding and sponsorship, Grierson recruited the filmmakers of the EMB Film Unit, later to become the GPO Film Unit when Tallents moved to the General Post Office, and later still to become the Crown Film Unit to meet the more specific demands of wartime propaganda. This is the familiar narrative of the British Documentary Movement. In its various institutional homes during the 1930s and 1940s, the Movement was supported by a system of state sponsorship, creating a protected cinema outside the commercial sphere, operating within the public sphere as a service to a citizenry whose interests were identified with the interests of the imperial State. For Grierson,

> Cinema is neither an art nor an entertainment: it is a form of publication, and may publish in a hundred different ways for a hundred different audiences. . . . The facts are simple enough. In a world too complex for the educational methods of public speech and public writing, there is a growing need for more imaginative and widespread media of public address. Cinema has begun to serve propaganda and will increasingly do so. It will be in demand. It will be asked to create appreciation of public services and public purposes. It will be asked from a hundred quarters to create a more imaginative and considered citizenship. It will be asked too, inevitably, to serve the narrower viewpoints of political or other party propaganda . . .[4]

And so began another negotiated relationship with the State and the public interest, reminding us in its quite unashamed advocacy of state propaganda that in the early Roman church the *propaganda* were agents in the department of the Vatican responsible for the propagation of the faith.

This, for Grierson, is the future of the '*art* of the cinema', whatever frivolities its business might lead it into. It was a future, he believed, which may not lie in cinemas, but in YMCAs, church halls, 'and other citadels of suburban improvement'; it may even, he suggested in

4 John Grierson, in Forsyth Hardy (ed.), *Grierson on Documentary* (London: Faber, 1966), 118–19.

5 Ibid. 69.

6 Ibid.

1935, lie in television.[5] What is certain is that 'in the commercial cinema there is no future worth serving'.[6]

As for Reith in broadcasting, so for Grierson in the cinema, commerce is the enemy of any serious social or moral purpose. For both, the necessary refuge is provided by the State and by the service of the public interest which can give broadcasting and cinema their necessary independence from the market in commodified public taste. This can make them 'serious', and lift them out of the realm of mere entertainment. The serious job of broadcasting and cinema is to create an audience rather than simply pander to it; the public interest which is defined by Reith in terms of religion and morality is defined by Grierson in terms of civic education and an informed citizenry.

> Many of us after the war [WW1] (and particularly in the United States) were impressed by the pessimism that had settled on Liberal Theory. We noted the conclusions of such men as Walter Lippmann that because the citizen under modern conditions could not know everything about everything all the time, democratic citizenship was therefore impossible. We set to thinking how a dramatic apprehension of the modern scene might solve the problem, and we turned to the new wide-reaching instruments of radio and cinema as necessary instruments both in the practice of government and the enjoyment of citizenship.[7]

To remain for a moment longer with the knots of history which bind British film and television together, the fit between Reith and Grierson does not end with the coincidence of 1927, but extends to a patrimony which may explain something about the history of the attitudes and social formations which are embedded in the institutions associated with them, and their strange accommodations with state and public interests. The fact that both men were Scottish may be seen as more than an interesting biographical curiosity. Reith was the son of a Church of Scotland minister, a son of the manse; Grierson was a dominie's son, brought up in a rural Scottish schoolhouse, his father the local headmaster, his mother the daughter of a family of Ayrshire radicals. Within Scotland, this background, to which both men refer with enormous respect, is more than a question of parentage. Rather, it places them in their formation within the institutions, church and school, which form the backbone of a very particular form of popular democracy: the Scottish presbyterian community. The Church of Scotland, often repressive and authoritarian in its moral and spiritual precepts, was democratic in its forms, operating for most of the nineteenth century, through General Assembly, Presbytery, and local Kirk Session, a system of local government,

---

7   Grierson, in Hardy, *Grierson on Documentary*, 207.

free from aristocratic patronage or state establishment, which under-took not only the moral but also the physical and social welfare of its parishioners. Education, poverty, disability, as well as correction, were under the supervision of Church government. The school was the secular arm of the Church welfare system. Within the community, the dominie was second in authority only to the minister and the elders of the Kirk: education was a thing to be treated with ponderous respect as the agency at the service of a social and geographical mobility which transformed the 'local lad' into a 'lad o' pairts': a lad who, in the words of Arthur Anderson, the Shetland-born founder of P. & O. Steamers, could 'go forth and fare weel'.

It is not necessary, then, to go to the mystical excesses of one of Reith's biographers ('the dark and simple superstitions of Calvinism had been bred in his bones like a hereditary disease'[8]) to see that there might have been something in Reith's experience of institutions which would make it easy for him to find nothing particularly strange or contradictory in an institutional arrangement which attempted to hold together authoritarianism, paternalism, moral guidance, public service, and improvement. Nor is it difficult to find in Grierson's writing—'I look on cinema as a pulpit and use it as a propagandist'[9] —the often biblical tones of a Scottish secular radicalism informed by a passionate respect for universal education and community service. Reith and Grierson, quite different in many respects, and the institutions and attitudes which they shaped, can be seen more clearly if they are placed in the shared tradition of a patrimony which saw no contradiction between serving the people and serving the state.

1927, then, marks the formal opening for both cinema and broad-casting of a relationship with the State and the public which has as its common terms public service, independence from the demands of the market, and conditional independence from state control. For the culture in which it developed, this relationship is the institutional form of an ideological hostility to commerce and a cultural hostility to the frivolities of 'mere' entertainment and the fantasies of the 'dream factory'. The coincidence of 1927 is, of course, fortuitous. What I want to suggest, however, is that in 1927 a certain attitude to entertainment became institutionalized within British broadcasting and cinema, and that the solidity which the attitude gained from its institutionalization has been a defining factor in the development of British film and television. Specifically, it institutionalizes an idea of 'serious' film and television which critics still promulgate and

8 Andrew Boyle, *Only the Wind Will Listen: Reith of the BBC* (London: Hutchinson, 1972), 34.

9 Grierson, in Hardy, *Grierson on Documentary*, 12.

audiences and producers still carry in their heads. Reith left the BBC in 1938 (a strangely disappointed man, according to his best biographer, Ian McIntyre, because he had not achieved any great work[10]), and Grierson left the GPO Film Unit in 1937; but their influence would endure both within and beyond those particular institutions. Public service occupies a position of such conscious and unconscious centrality in thinking about British culture, that it is only now, when it is under various forms of threat, that we begin to discover, with a touch of panic, that it is not the natural condition. The centrality of public service goes a long way towards explaining the quite unusual centrality which television occupies in British culture. It is sometimes difficult to see from the inside how unusual this centrality is; but it evokes at various times a level of public concern which marks British culture as being different from most other national cultures. It is this which gives a particular significance to television drama within the national culture.

1936 On 2 November 1936, the BBC transmitted the first regularly scheduled television programme service in the world from its London Television Station. To viewers within an approximate radius of twenty-five miles from its production centre in Alexandra Palace, it offered broadcasts six days a week (excluding Sundays, of course) for one hour in the afternoon (3–4p.m.) and one hour in the evening (9–10p.m.). Many of the items in the evening schedule were live repeats of the same item in the afternoon: thus, in the *Radio Times* (the weekly British television programme guide) for that first week of television, we find that *The Golden Hind*, transmitted 3.25–3.40p.m. on 3 November—'A model of Drake's famous ship made by L. A. Stock, a bus driver, who will describe its construction'—was repeated live at 9.25–9.40p.m. the same evening, when L. A. Stock returned to the studio and described its construction again. On 5 November, a twenty-five-minute afternoon performance by Marie Rambert's Mercury Ballet was performed again in the evening. But on 6 November, *From the London Theatre*, a twenty-five-minute item in the afternoon schedule featuring Sophie Stewart performing scenes in the studio from the Royalty Theatre production of *Marigold*, 'A Scottish comedy by Allen Harker and F. R. Pryor', was not repeated in the evening, presumably because Sophie Stewart was performing at the time in the Royalty Theatre.

It is worth beginning from these beginnings, partly to establish the pattern of live performances and live repeats which was to be central to the early formation of television drama, partly to anticipate the

10 Ian McIntyre, *The Expense of Glory: A Life of John Reith* (London: Harper Collins, 1994).

surprising popularity of live extracts from West End plays, but partly also to compensate for the very short recall of television in which history begins only with recorded programmes.

For the week beginning 23 October 1936, the *Radio Times* published a 'Special Television Issue', featuring an article by Gerald Cock, the first Director of Television, with the title, 'Looking Forward: A Personal Forecast of the Future of Television'. In this article, Cock ruminates on the questions which he had asked himself when offered the job, and admits to doubts about 'the chances of "selling" the idea of television to a public already satiated with entertainment'. In projecting the future (it is not clear by how far), he suggests: 'We are entitled to imagine that programme hours would still be few—perhaps four a day—and that they would be confined to events of outstanding interest and entertainment value, for television will, I think, mean the end to "background listening"' (p. 6).

For television drama, Cock foresees extracts rather than whole single plays, not as a temporary technological constraint, but as the essential and logical form for a medium which was more concerned with relaying the world and disseminating information than with the production of entertainment or the creation of art:

> for in my view, television is *from its very nature*, more suitable for the dissemination of all kinds of information than for entertainment as such, since it can scarcely be expected to compete successfully with films in that respect. Nevertheless, the lighter forms of entertainment will certainly have their place. (p. 7, my emphasis)

And he takes this view to its logical conclusion:

> I believe viewers would rather see an actual scene of a rush hour at Oxford Circus directly transmitted to them than the latest in film musicals costing £100,000—though I do not expect to escape unscathed with such an opinion. (p. 7)

The view of television which emerges from Cock's predictions can be approached, not as a naively primitive misunderstanding of the medium, but as exemplary of a number of assumptions and uncertainties about the function of television which were formative in the early decades. Part of my argument is that these uncertainties cast residual shadows, stretching into the present, within the discourses which still surround television drama.

Most apparent, right from the moment at which television first appears, is the assertion of immediacy, liveness and the direct transmission of live action as both an opportunity and an aesthetic virtue of the medium rather than as a mere technological constraint. The concept of immediacy is central to an understanding of television, and the 'immediacy effect' which persists as an aesthetic long after the technological necessity had been removed, retains its importance for notions of the 'authenticity' of television drama and is a continuing term in both professional and critical vocabularies. The effect of immediacy, of a directness and spontaneity which comes to signify authenticity, is one of the characteristics of the specific forms of realism in television drama.

Also significant within Cock's prognostication is an uncertainty around the competing claims of the 'dissemination of all kinds of information', 'entertainment as such', and 'the lighter forms of entertainment'. For the postwar period in which the BBC promoted itself as an instrument (if not *the* instrument) of national cultural reconstruction, and in which television was beginning to threaten the primacy of radio, the competing claims of 'information, education and entertainment' within public service broadcasting may account for some of the suspicion with which television was regarded by BBC management. Television, it seems to have been felt, might be a little *too* entertaining, threatening to upset the delicate balance which radio had achieved. Notably and, with hindsight, ironically, information is privileged not simply out of a Reithian reverence but out of a belief that television cannot win in competition with cinema.

Cock recognizes, too, forms of attention specific to television, distinct from both television and radio, which, for him, will impose limits on the number of hours that properly should be available for scheduling in a system which does not yet depend on maximizing its audience. The nature of the audience and the conditions of viewing also determine the kinds of event appropriate to the schedule. While it is hard to square his insistence on programmes 'of outstanding interest and entertainment value' with the early love of demonstration programmes—*The Handy Man*, for instance, in which 'J. T. Baily will demonstrate how to repair a broken window'—such items, though they may have been programme fillers, give a sense of the homeliness of television's early notion of the domestic and the delicacy with which the BBC intruded into the home.

Strikingly, many of the early uncertainties about the function of television echo uncertainties which had been experienced forty years earlier by cinema. The pioneers of cinema, too, had had doubts about a gap in the entertainment market for a public which was already satiated with entertainment in the popular theatres of music hall and vaudeville, and while there was little danger of television being relegated to the fairground, it could have become a mere technological novelty. Was the new medium to be for the dissemination of information or for entertainment as such? Was it to record scenes and events from the real world or to tell stories? Intriguingly, in Cock's preference for the live transmission of the rush hour in Oxford Circus over the latest in screen entertainment, we can begin to imagine an early 'television of attractions' comparable to the early 'cinema of attractions' which Tom Gunning describes.[11] While the 'cinema of attractions', however, was to be based on spectacle, the 'television of attractions' would be firmly founded on the immediacy and liveness of the everyday.

Though they are clearly labelled as 'personal', then, Cock's assumptions and uncertainties point to questions not simply about the history of early television, but about the way the history of television is to be written. The danger of starting the history too late, with, say, the beginnings of the regular recording of programmes in the 1960s, is that we miss the formative stages in which the practices of language and form are still unstable, in which institutional practices are experimental rather than routine, in which 'good television' still has to learn to be 'good', and in which that particular 'goodness' is only one of a number of possibilities.

The television service only ran for a little under three years in the prewar period before it was suspended on 3 September 1939 on the outbreak of war. It was resumed in June 1946. In both the prewar and the immediate postwar period, drama formed a central component of the schedules. In the week beginning 25 December 1938, for instance, of the twenty-two hours and thirty minutes transmitted, fourteen hours and ten minutes were given over to drama (including some repeats). It was, of course, Christmas week, and the productions reflected this, including adaptations of leading West End successes: *Hay Fever, Richard of Bordeaux, The Moon in the Yellow River, Charley's Aunt,* and *The Knight of the Burning Pestle.* In a routine week in the late 1940s, drama usually occupied eight to ten hours of a very slightly expanded schedule.

It is worth recording that in the 1930s, and later in the 1940s and 1950s, the single play seems to have had the status of special attraction which the 'big picture' did not achieve till the 1970s: one of the appetites which television seemed to serve from the beginning was the appetite for dramatic narrative. Until relatively recently when it could be served by the screening of recent Hollywood releases or, more recently still, by rented videos, the appetite for dramatic narrative was served in domestic entertainment by the single play or the dramatic serial.

Perhaps even more significant than the total weekly time allotted to drama was the place it occupied in the evening schedule. By late 1937 week-day schedules ran, roughly, 3–5p.m. and 8–10p.m., with a Sunday schedule, 9–10.30p.m., added in 1938 (interestingly the year

11 Tom Gunning, 'The cinema of attractions: early film, its spectators and the avant garde', *Wide Angle*, vol. 8, no. 3/4 (1986); reprinted in Thomas Elsaesser (ed.), *Early Cinema: Space, Frame, Narrative* (London: BFI Publishing, 1990), 56–62.

Reith left the BBC). In the postwar years the schedule was expanded slightly to include a Children's Hour, but a so-called 'toddlers' truce' between 6 and 8p.m., when parents could dutifully tuck their toddlers into bed without the fear of rival attractions, was not breached until 1954, and then only partially, when a half-hour news programme was added at 7.30p.m. Scheduling, therefore, mainly consisted of two- to three-hour blocks.

On perhaps four out of seven evenings in a routine week the programme mix would be arranged in the magazine format which has become familiar in broadcast television. On any evening, however, when a full-length drama was shown, it dominated the evening schedule, relegating any other programme to the kind of supporting shorts familiar from the cinema. It is important to recall this when thinking about the place of drama within the economy of viewing of early television. The single play was not simply a part of the flow of programming, but constituted a kind of anchor-point within the evening (and perhaps within the week), which structured viewing in a different way and invited a particular kind of attention.

Largely thanks to Reith's contempt for counting clients and currying their favour, BBC audience research did not begin as a formal and routine activity until the 1940s, but targeted research had been started in radio in the late 1930s. A popularity poll conducted in 1939 among the 20,000 London subscribers with joint radio/television licences placed drama in front of sport and only slightly behind variety. This, of course, may say more about the nature of these subscribers than about drama, and the poll covered both television and radio, but it is an indication of the place which drama occupied in domestic culture. Even by 1959, in a year in which the Queen's Christmas message (as much a part of Christmas Day for many families as turkey) had an audience of twenty million viewers from BBC and ITV combined, a BBC World Theatre production of Gogol's nineteenth-century Russian theatre classic, *The Government Inspector*, could get an audience of 9.5 million (beating the nine million of the very popular celebrity quiz show, *What's My Line?*).

Of course, in a Reithian or post-Reithian system, ratings were not everything. Director-General William Haley had re-committed the BBC to its sense of mission in 1949:

> The aim of the BBC must be to conserve and strengthen serious listening. . . . While satisfying the legitimate public demand for recreation and entertainment, the BBC must never lose sight of its cultural mission. . . . The BBC is a single instrument and must see that the nation derives the best advantage from that.[12]

---

12 Quoted in Asa Briggs, *Sound and Vision: History of Broadcasting in the United Kingdom, Vol. 4* (Oxford: Oxford University Press, 1979), 80–1.

This mission was not simply pious rhetoric, but was the expression of quite explicit policy. In 1943, as the end of war began to seem possible and policy-formers in a number of areas were beginning to think of a postwar society, William Haley had already stated very clearly what was to be the role of the BBC in cultural reconstruction: 'The BBC must provide for all classes of listeners equally. This does not mean it shall remain passive regarding the distribution of these classes. It cannot abandon the educative task it has carried on for twenty-one years to improve cultural and ethical standards.'[13] As a part of the fabric of national life, broadcasting was charged by Royal Charter with the duty to inform, educate, and entertain, but in a period of postwar reconstruction its interpretation of the Charter obligation, its self-adopted 'educative task', was a redistribution of classes by raising cultural standards towards an approved level. The very organization of radio broadcasting in the postwar years was designed to facilitate this task: the Light Programme for light entertainment, the Home Service for informative talks, and the Third Programme for serious music and experimental drama. The task was to lead the audience up the ladder of taste, from Mantovani to Mahler, from light entertainment to 'serious listening'. This was policy rather than piety, referred to by Haley unashamedly as 'the slow but rewarding process of raising public taste'[14], and endorsed by the Labour Education Minister of the day as the laudable project of turning Britain into a 'Third Programme' nation.

It is, of course, highly significant that Haley's terms of reference are listening and radio rather than viewing and television. The cultural mission in the postwar years had a slightly edgy relationship to television, preferring the known territory of radio and its place within a homely domesticity to the *terra incognita* of television with its slightly heady potential for entertainment. Asa Briggs points out that 'key figures in the BBC were more interested in 1946 in the starting of the Third Programme than in the resumption of television'[15], and it was not until 1950 that television was promoted to the status of a Department as opposed to that of a Service: the same status, that is, that the Third Programme had enjoyed since it was opened.

This unease about television was not simply to do with the 'educative task' which formed the explicit aim of the cultural mission, but to do with a much more pervasive sense of responsibility towards the home and the preservation of family life. Television, with its demand for concentrated attention, seemed to threaten the stabilities of family

13 Ibid. 28.

14 Ibid. 76. Figures suggest that the national listening figures for the Third Programme in 1950 represented 0.14% of the population.

15 Ibid. 208.

life which had learned to absorb and even ritualize the less compulsive distractions of radio. Whereas radio seemed compatible with the rhythms of domestic life, television threatened to cut time out of the everyday. In an article in the *Radio Times* for the week beginning 7 March 1952, celebrating the opening of the television service in Scotland, Melville Dinwiddie, the Controller of Scottish Broadcasting, is ambivalent about the pleasures of television in relation to the pleasures of the hearth:

> The advent of television is like the opening of a great window in the home. Those who have sets can 'view' in comfort events as they take place near and far, see news items from all over the world, and, in addition, find home entertainment of a most varied kind. This invasion of our homes must cause something of an upset in family life. Sound broadcasting as such is upsetting enough when reading and school lessons and other home tasks have to be done, but here is a more intensely absorbing demand on our leisure hours, and families in mid-Scotland will have to make a decision both about getting a receiver and about using it. At the start, viewing will take up much time because of its novelty, but discrimination is essential so that not every evening is spent in a darkened room, the chores of the house and other occupations neglected. We can get too much even of a good thing. (p. 5)

Where else but in the BBC, before the days of competition, would one find a broadcaster warning the viewer against too much viewing? Dinwiddie's caution, replete with the authentic tones of a public service protected by monopoly, points to a wonderfully BBC-ish, unselfconsciously paternalistic anxiety about the sanctities of home and family.

It is worth pausing here to note another characteristic of television and the public sphere in the years after the war. It is important to recall that with only 4.5 million holders of the combined radio and television licence in 1955 (even after the surge in television ownership around the Coronation of 1953), it was probably more common for most people in the first decades to have their first experience of television in someone else's house. Up until the sharp increase in the late 1950s and early 1960s when television truly became a mass entertainment, people went out to see television instead of staying in. It was common to be invited to 'come over and watch television'. The technology was not yet fully a part of the everyday, and, consequently, the characteristic experience was not yet entirely private or exclusive. Ivor Brown, in the *BBC Yearbook* of 1951, claims, 'In the suburbs, television is plainly acting as a cohesive force';[16] and there is a particu-

---

16 Ivor Brown, 'Television in the Englishman's castle', *BBC Yearbook 1951*, p. 17.

larly quaint viewer's letter in a 1953 *Radio Times* (24 July 1953) which evokes a more innocent age: the viewer had been troubled by inter-ference in his picture caused by hair-dryers in a neighbouring girls' college until he invited the girls over to view with him: 'So now', he says, 'I call my television set my "friend collector"'.

It is a useful historical antidote to the universalisms and essen-tialisms which often mark writing about television to recall that for many of us who had our first experience of television in the early 1950s there was no *essential* connection between television and the family domestic sphere. Quite commonly, the early experience of television, even when it was quite extensive, did not coincide with ownership; it was not, as radio was, a ritual of home and family—and it was not continuous. It was acquired in glimpses as a special occasion—as specialized rather than everyday time—and as a social, even communal, activity.

These, then, are some of the conditions of existence of early tele-vision, the context in which television drama developed: the cultural mission, the educative task, the protection of the home, and the cohesion of the new suburban society. To which might be added, picking up a detail from Dinwiddie, that people often watched in darkened rooms, curtains drawn and lights switched off to enhance the clarity of the 405-line, low resolution, black and white image. Not only was viewing not necessarily privatized, it was almost certainly not distracted.

All of these conditions have some bearing on the status of tele-vision drama within the schedules, on the forms of attention of the viewer, and, consequently, on the history of subjectivities associated with television. Within the sense of special occasion, drama figured strongly, a distinct event cut out of everyday flow. The Sunday night play and the serial offered the possibility of a collective viewing as part of a social gathering, and the letters pages of the *Radio Times* in the 1960s carry a number of complaints when the plays of the new social realism are no longer considered fit and proper for decent communal viewing. Within the BBC's mission of cultural improvement drama lent prestige. In the prewar years, its limited audience gave television drama the freedom to experiment with some of the cutting-edge modernist dramas of the interwar years. In the postwar years, on the evidence of the schedules, the general horizons of television seemed set a little lower, somewhere below those of the Third Programme, targeted at middle-brow rather than high-brow taste, its imaginary viewer distinctly suburban. Quite regularly, however, even television could seek to bring alive in a very exciting way the very best 'that has been thought and written in the world' (Matthew Arnold's resonant phrase): the classics of the world stage secured a place in the schedules in the World Theatre series, as did adaptations from the Great Tradition of English literature. And even when its ambitions were less lofty, television could bring, in the shape of drama, a culture which bore the imprimatur of middle-class taste, carrying a form which had a particular significance in approved British culture into the very heart of everyday entertainment.

The vast majority of the single plays and serials produced by the BBC until the 1960s were adaptations, coming to the viewer with a prior seal of approval from the West End theatre, the classics, or the best-seller list. Plays written specifically for television were the exception rather than the rule, and, interestingly, it was much more common to find distinctive original writing in popular forms like the thriller, or, famously, science fiction. The Quatermass series (*The Quatermass Experiment* [1953], *Quatermass II* [1955]) written by Nigel Kneale and directed by Rudolph Cartier in the mid-1950s was in every sense a sensational success. In the more elevated forms of drama, however, adaptation was the norm. Most of the theatrical classics had been adapted, frequently in very abbreviated form, together with some of the modernist plays of the contemporary stage: Fry and Eliot were regulars, but in the prewar years there had been productions of Capek's *R.U.R.* and a very ambitious production of Auden and Isherwood's *The Ascent of F6*, both in 1938.[17] The institution of the classic serial began in 1956 with *Jane Eyre* and by 1959 the list included *Villette, Nicholas Nickleby, Pride and Prejudice, David Copperfield, Vanity Fair, Kenilworth,* and *Precious Bane*. Best-seller adaptations, such as Mazo de la Roche's *The Whiteoak Chronicles*, serialized in 1954, answered a demand for good, satisfying narrative fiction—the television equivalent of a 'good read'—when movies on television were restricted to a few very old films in very tired prints which had escaped the commercial cinema's embargo on its threatening rival. Single plays and adaptations which worked particularly well were given a number of productions. *Richard of Bordeaux*, for instance, a 1930s West End success written by Gordon Daviot, was produced five times before 1950 and, a little more surprisingly, Eugene O'Neill's *Mourning Becomes Electra* had been produced at least three times by 1955. For the record, and to show that it was possible, very exceptionally, to move in the other direction, it is worth establishing the history of *Dial M for Murder*. Written originally as a television play by the popular dramatist Patrick Hamilton and transmitted on 23 March 1952, it was adapted from television to the stage, achieving enough success in the West End theatre to be picked up

---

17 For a detailed account of the 1938 production of *The Ascent of F6*, see Jason Jacobs, *Early Television Drama: The Intimate Screen* (Oxford: Oxford University Press, forthcoming 2000).

subsequently by Hitchcock and Hollywood—where, of course, it became a monument of *auteur* cinema and forgot its humble origins.

Despite drama's importance for early television, however, there was some uncertainty about what exactly it was, or what it was for. In 1947, Val Gielgud, BBC Director of Drama, admittedly a self-confessed committed 'radio man', wrote in *BBC Quarterly:*

> It is probably true that once the television-receiver is as common a household furnishing as the present-day loud-speaker, the play broadcast in a single dimension will have as little chance of survival as the silent film, once the strains of 'Sonny Boy' had echoed round the world. But apart from the practical difficulties of supply and demand and economics, and subject to indignant correction from Alexandra Palace, I am not yet convinced that television drama is sure of its target. Does it aim to be more than a photographed stage play? Does it dream of competition with film? Or should its principal aim be that of *illustrating broadcasting*? For the practice and practitioners of televised drama there can be nothing but undiluted admiration. But looking forward into the future, it is perhaps not out of place to suggest that as far as any genuine theory of television is concerned, a question-mark is still the most appropriate symbol.[18]

Aesthetically and practically, the defining characteristic of early television drama was live transmission. Repeats, which were routine for major single plays (the Sunday night play was routinely repeated on Thursday), involved calling the cast and crew back for a second performance. Plays were transmitted live from the studio in real time, using a number of sets and sometimes more than one studio, with intervals to allow for regrouping or set changes which could not be accommodated within the flow of the action. Unplanned intervals to allow for a camera which had 'gone down' were commonplace. Film inserts into studio productions were possible and quite common. Even as early as the 1937 adaptation of R. C. Sherriff's *Journey's End*, a one-hour adaptation cut for continuity from the two-and-a-half-hour stage play ('the first time that an entire evening's programme has been filled by a single play'—*RT*, 11 November 1937), scenes from Pabst's *West Front 1918* (1930) were cut into the live drama. But film inserts were functional, barely qualifying the dominance of the aesthetic of live studio performance before they were absorbed into it.

Live outside broadcast transmissions direct from a current West End success were common before the war, and continued well into

---

18 Val Gielgud, 'Policy and problems of broadcast drama', *BBC Quarterly*, vol. 2, no. 1 (1947), 23.

the 1950s. In November 1938, the *Radio Times* claimed a first for a Basil Dean stage production of J. B. Priestley's *When We Are Married*:

> For the first time in the history of the theatre, a play with its West End cast, and given before an audience, will be televised direct from a theatre stage. By permission of Basil Dean, J. B. Priestley and the theatre lessees, viewers will see the entire performance direct from the St Martin's Theatre, London. (*RT*, 16 November 1938)

The programme ran from 8.30 till 10.40 p.m.

More common were outside broadcasts of scenes or a first act from a live theatre performance. These were mainly designed to relay the occasion, and presumably, from the theatre producers' perspective, to advertise the stage play:

> 7.45–8.20 p.m.: *Under Your Hat*. First night scenes from the Palace Theatre, London. By permission of Lee Ephraim, viewers will meet first-night celebrities in the foyer, will see Cicely Courtneidge and Jack Hulbert in their dressing rooms, and will witness the first act of the show. (*RT*, 24 November 1938)

These outside broadcasts crystallize the uncertainty of 'target' to which Val Gielgud refers, and the problem for a 'genuine theory of television'. Was it the function of television simply to relay theatre as a live social occasion into the home? Was this, along the lines of Cock's rush hour in Oxford Circus, what television did best? Was its role to serve other forms, its public service remit fulfilled by bringing theatre events and stage plays as abbreviated versions (like *Reader's Digest* abridged novels) to a wider public? Or could it have an aesthetic of its own? Discussions of a possible 'art of television' are much rarer in early television than they had been in early film, and the notion of service seems to have run much deeper than the notion of art. For television drama, the relay function performed by the outside broadcast of theatre occasions was consistent with the dependency on adaptation of original stage plays. Both are symptomatic of a powerful current of both practical, aesthetic, and cultural dependency which ran between early television and theatre, between television drama and 'real' drama.

This was reinforced by the institutional fragility of television within the BBC. For much of the immediate postwar years, television's horizons seemed to be pegged by institutional thinking and managerial authority to the achievements of radio. Even the Langham Group, based at Langham House, who were experimenting on the boundaries of an avant-garde television, seemed to be informed by the kinds of radiophonic workshops which were associated with the Third Programme. In cultural, social, and artistic terms, the Sunday night play on television was conceived as a continuation, with pictures, of the popular and successful Saturday night play on radio.

Writing in *BBC Quarterly* in 1948, Cecil Madden, very much more a 'television man' than Val Gielgud, nevertheless picks up some of the same doubts: 'Some people ask where television drama is going, whether it aims to be a photographed stage play, a competitor to the film, or an illustrated broadcast. The truth probably belongs somewhere between them all.'[19] Television's live transmission was celebrated from the very beginning as direct, spontaneous, authentic reality and, in drama, its place in the nostalgia of television is assured by the perpetuation of the legendary 'disasters' of broken cameras, trembling sets, tangled cables, even actors dropping dead on the set while the show went on. Apocrypha merges with nostalgia which merges with history to produce the 'buzz' of a television still living on the edge. The insistence on liveness, however, as an essential quality of the medium led to an adjustment of horizons involving an instrumental view of the medium, a general mindset which placed television in a dependent relationship to the other forms which it served. Television was a technology for relay and adaptation; the demand for a 'creative' television which spoke with its own voice, which as Jason Jacobs shows was always there,[20] struggled to be heard above the routines of production.

Adaptation and relay, then, were, for early television drama and for most of early television, more than simply a necessity forced on producers by the lack of suitable original material (although it must be the case that writers were slow to catch on to the possibilities): the service aesthetic seemed to define the horizons of aesthetic ambition. This is not to deny the practical experimentation and the heated debates about form which went on, but to place them within what seems to have been a more or less accepted dependency on a point of origin—the reality of the rush hour at Oxford Circus or the West End stage—which was located outside television itself. And for British television drama it was theatre, rather than cinema, which provided that elsewhere.

It is worth dwelling a little on this lack of connection between early television drama and cinema, because it may be one of the specific features of British television. By the early 1950s, the close relationship between the rising television industry and the faltering film industry was already established in the United States. Much of the programming was shot on film (a practice which has its origins in the need to transport programmes from coast to coast to accommodate the

19 Cecil Madden, 'Television: problems and possibilities', *BBC Quarterly*, vol. 2, no. 4 (1948), 225.

20 Jacobs, *Early Television Drama*.

different time zones), and the much celebrated live drama of the mid-1950s seemed like a preparatory school for the rising stars of the Method School on the route west from Lee Strasberg's New York Actors Studio to the big screen of Hollywood in which their fame would be made: James Dean, Steve McQueen, Kim Hunter, Rod Steiger, all appeared on NBC's Goodyear Television Playhouse or Kraft Television Theatre, or CBS's Studio One. In France, as John Swift tells us in his very useful account of the first twenty-five years of television, *Adventures in Vision*, the Paris service had established good relations with the film industry and relied for around 50 per cent of its programming on films, occasionally brand new films, and sometimes shown on television before their cinema release.[21] In Britain, on the other hand, though a number of foreign and/or 'old' films were shown on television—Swift lists *Panique* (Duvivier, 1946), *Open City* [*sic*] (Rossellini, 1945), *Un Carnet de bal* (Duvivier, 1937), *Les Enfants du paradis* (Carné, 1943–5), *Dr Caligari* (Wiene, 1920), *Blue Angel* (Sternberg, 1930), and *Birth of a Nation* (Griffith, 1915)—they tended to be shown as unprogrammed stop-gaps (few of them are listed in the *Radio Times*), and in appalling versions. A 1951 review in the *Listener* complains of the butchery of Rossellini's *Paisa* (1946): 'heavy cutting, undecipherable captions and commentary help so feeble that often it could not be heard' (5 July 1951).

Swift goes into some detail on the use of film on television, and limits its potential to fairly specific conditions:

the transmission of action recorded on film is not television in its true meaning. But it has three main uses:

(a) as a stop-gap between 'live' studio programmes, or as a substitute for programmes unexpectedly postponed or cancelled. Examples: Rain may stop play at the Oval or Lords. The sudden illness of a leading artist may cause postponement of a play or other programme. In such cases the commercial cinema film is generally used.

(b) as a 'convenience', such as continuity shots to link action (if necessary) between studio scenes. Also to establish scenes other than those in the studio . . .

(c) to bring to the screen something that can only be shown by film, including news—news of events, that is, taking place outside the range of the O.B. units, or where it is inconvenient for the O.B. cameras to operate.[22]

British television's resistance to the cinema film may, of course, be attributable to cinema's hostility to television. In the fragile ecology

21 John Swift, *Adventures in Vision: The First Twenty-Five Years of Television* (London: John Lehmann, 1950).

22 Ibid. 185.

which British cinema inhabited there was very little space for a negotiated settlement. Recent English-language films were simply not made available to a television which was increasingly seen as a dangerous competitor, and the practice of dumping unwanted films in unwatchable prints onto television was certainly one of the reasons why such material would only be used to patch up unprogrammed gaps in the schedule. But it is also worth noting that there were aesthetic reservations about cinematic style, and about the appropriateness of film to the conditions of reception and the forms of attention particular to television. John Swift again articulates these clearly:

It is doubtful if there exists a cinema film of any appreciable length that is ideally suited to the television screen. In the first place, the commercial film is made essentially for a mass audience, not a group in the sitting room. Secondly, because it is for a mass audience its tempo is much faster, with a quick-cutting technique that can be disturbing when viewed at home. Thirdly, there are certain differences, not appreciated by the layman, between television and film lighting, and what is suitable for the cinema screen is not always so for the television screen.[23]

Cinema, then, in a television of immediacy, did not simply represent the technologically or institutionally unattainable, but also the aesthetically undesirable. The suspicion directed against film was a quite conscious preference not only for immediacy as an essential quality, but also for a televisual style appropriate to the conditions of television viewing. A slow cutting-rate was not simply the product of studio technology, but came out of a considerateness for (and perhaps a certain pride in) the domestic viewer whose pleasures and aptitudes were distinct from the entertainments of the mass audience.

Theatre, and, to a lesser extent, radio, seemed to offer the possibility of such a style for television drama. The most obvious effect of this preference for theatre and radio over cinema is that British television drama tended towards the literate rather than towards the visual. The privileging of the word and verbal exchange over the image and visual style has frequently been remarked, and it forms the basis for much of the attack on so-called 'naturalism' which was initiated by Troy Kennedy Martin in 1964 in a famous article which will be discussed in subsequent chapters.[24] Significantly, Kennedy Martin calls for a television drama which takes its model from the formally inventive cinema of the French *nouvelle vague*—particularly Resnais—and breaks away from the model of theatre, even, it would seem, from

23 Ibid. 186.

24 Troy Kennedy Martin, 'Nats go home: first statement of a new drama for television', *Encore*, no. 48 (1964), 21–33.

the British new wave associated with the Royal Court Theatre in the 1950s.

It is worth insisting that the adaptation of theatre in early television drama was not simply a question of reworking scripts, but rather of capturing on television something of the nature of theatre performance. Television *relayed* performance, the live moment transmitted as it happened in the same blocks of continuous time as theatre. The studio was a performance space, full of the technology and techniques of mediation, but placing these technologies and techniques at the service of an ideology of immediacy. The limitations placed on *mise en scène* and editing as expressive devices, the restraint of style which comes to be associated with 'boring' naturalism, were not simply borne of technological constraint or imaginative failure; rather they belonged to the logical aesthetic of a technology whose essence was conceived in terms of immediacy, relay, and the 'live': 'The primary function of television is to transmit pictures as they are being made. . . . The *basic* attraction of the new medium is not so much the subject matter that it presents but the realization that whatever is happening is happening *at the time*.'[25] Whereas cinema, in the classical form described by David Bordwell,[26] subordinates the codes of time and space to narrative causation, television drama, in its formative stage, subordinated time and space to performance. The time, in particular, of early television is the real time—what Troy Kennedy Martin later calls the 'natural time'[27]—of continuous recording and live performance. Cinema constructs a narrative space and time governed by the economy of narrative causality and by the ability of the spectator to fill the gaps between cause and effect and to supply motivations for action through a system of learned conventions. Live television drama, constrained by continuous performance in real time, converts constraint into aspiration and develops an economy based on performance, designed to allow the performance to 'take its time'. This particular relationship between time, space, and performance is the specific characteristic of early British television drama, marking it off from the cinema and aligning it with theatre. Residual forms of this relationship seem to me still to characterize many examples of the single play, even when it is shot on, and labelled as, film. It also gives a specific importance to acting in television drama, an importance which has been remarkably neglected in criticism.

The values of live drama become clear in a 1964 article in *Contrast* by the director, Don Taylor:

25 Swift, *Adventure in Vision*, 11.

26 In David Bordwell, Janet Staiger, and Kristin Thompson, *The Classical Hollywood Cinema: Film Style and Mode of Production to 1960* (London: Routledge & Kegan Paul, 1985).

27 Kennedy Martin, 'Nats go home', 24.

Pictorially, we are limited by the demands of continuous or near-continuous performance, but we still have a fairly large degree of freedom to select what our audience shall see. I emphasize the question of continuous performance because it seems to me to be television's key advantage over film. The small screen, the small audience, the semi-darkness, all encourage a drama of high emotional and poetic intensity. The discontinuous film performance, even by the cleverest film actor, always suffers by comparison with a TV performance that really clicks. This seems too obvious to need amplification. In the emotion of a performance growing from scene to scene, new things are discovered about a part in playing it.[28]

Admittedly, Taylor's position on the values of continuous studio recording, articulated at a time when (and in a journal in which) the new drama was on the agenda, would not have gone unchallenged, and he himself goes on to bemoan the lack of a visual language of television, and to berate 'directors who put their actors in a box set, stick their cameras ten feet away, one in the middle and one on each side, and swing their lenses or zoom in when the actor says the shocking bit'.[29] Nevertheless, his position, seeking to preserve the traditions of early television as the ones which represent the specific and essential values of television drama, is an important one. The values are those of the captured performance, the ideology of a reality constructed in front of television rather than by television. The visual language which he seeks is one which will best serve the performance:

Our medium can communicate through word and image and sound, by using an intellectual argument, a poetic cinema, a pictorial composition, a lighting effect, a piece of music, or a mixture of all these things. The one thing that should be nailed over the desk of every writer and director in television is the statement that these things are servants, not masters. They are the tools of communication, not what is to be communicated.[30]

It is worth noting that Don Taylor's article was written in the same year as Troy Kennedy Martin's. The fact that Kennedy Martin makes a quite contrary plea for the centrality of the director suggests a debate within a transitional period, and the fact that Taylor was associated with the modernist work of David Mercer should prevent too simplistic a reading of his apparent division between the matter of expression and the means of expression. But the appearance of instrumentalism is characteristic of much writing about television

28 Don Taylor, 'Style in Drama (1): the Gorboduc stage', *Contrast*, vol. 3, no. 3 (1964), 153.
29 Ibid. 206.
30 Ibid. 153.

(both early and late), and seems to be tied to a kind of service economy in television aesthetics in which the function of form is to *serve* content rather than to *be* content.

Without the evidence of recorded programmes, it is extremely difficult to generalize, and there are limitations to how much can be extrapolated from the few recorded dramas of the mid-1950s and from the written evidence of secondary sources. Indeed, it is one of the characteristics of early television drama that there is no standard, not even the beginnings of a classical system against which norms and eccentricities can be measured. Like theatre productions, single plays were interpretations of an original—an original which could be reinterpreted by successive generations of producers and directors. There were debates—between those, for instance, who wanted to expand the limits of the studio by bringing in film extracts, and the purists who wanted to push towards greater depth by use of the close-up; between the 'one-camera technique' drawn from film, and the 'big-head method'. And there was scope for stylistic experiment, such as a 1939 attempt in a play called *Condemned to be Shot*, to shoot entirely from a first-person subjective point of view.

Technical constraints were clearly important, and changes in technology allowed shifts in style. Michael Barry, BBC Head of Television Drama, writes in *BBC Quarterly* of the arrival in 1952 of the variable lens camera:

> The variable lenses on these cameras broke through the shallow field of focus. They allowed the camera-man to compose in depth instead of restricting his clear vision to a narrow alley running at right angles before his lens. He was enabled also to reach in to observe detail without thrusting a bulky vehicle across the foreground of the other apparatus on the floor.[31]

The ability to pull focus and construct scenes in greater depth added considerably to the palette available to the director, but in a system of continuous performance in which mistakes could not be edited out, stylistic boldness must have been an indulgence to be used sparingly.

Given the centrality of time in continuous performance, editing style is of particular significance. As one would expect, the pace of editing is slow. In his account of early cinema, Barry Salt[32] has used Average Shot Lengths (ASL) as a measurement of style, showing that even in early cinema ASLs rarely went above twelve seconds, and stabilized around ten seconds in the classical cinema of the 1940s—even in the films of Wyler and Welles famed for their long takes.

---

31 Michael Barry, 'Shakespeare on television', *BBC Quarterly*, vol. 9, no. 3 (1954), 144.

32 Barry Salt, *Film Style and Technology: History and Analysis* (London: Starword, 1983).

For early television drama, the editing pace is rather different. Victor Menzies's 1955 production of *Richard of Bordeaux* has, by my calculation, an Average Shot Length of something around thirty-five seconds. It is admittedly at an extreme of theatricality, with long council discussions shot frontally in long shot, and a very sparse use of close-ups to cut into or break up the scene. The playscript, very definitely, is the thing. More daring is Rudolph Cartier's famous 1954 production of *1984*: imaginative in its construction of space and setting, and liberally interspersed with exterior film sequences, it still ends up with an ASL of just under seventeen seconds. An interesting case is that of a Rediffusion adaptation of Turgenev's nineteenth-century Russian drama, *A Month in the Country*, the first classic drama produced by commercial television in the first week of its operation in 1955. Directed by Robert Hamer, one of the few British film directors of the postwar period with claims to *auteur* status (*Pink String and Sealing Wax* [1945], *It Always Rains on Sundays* [1947], *Kind Hearts and Coronets* [1949]), the drama has an Average Shot Length of twenty-seven seconds, and is shot with very few close-ups, preferring a theatrical stage grouping. It is surely significant that Cartier, with a much faster cutting-rate, is working from a novel while Hamer is working from a stage play, the adaptation of theatre demanding a style which retains its theatricality in the organization of space and time. While the measurement of Average Shot Lengths may seem like a rather mechanistic way of measuring style, it is undoubtedly the case that a variation of only a few seconds in ASL makes a considerable difference to the 'feel' of a film or a drama. For the record, my calculation shows an ASL of around twelve seconds for a fairly representative sample of 1960s television drama.

It is worth pausing a little on Cartier's *1984*. Without making any claims for its typicality, it is the first recorded television drama available for viewing in the National Film and Television Archive, and it allows us to see what was possible in early television drama: both the constraints and the ways of turning constraints into a style. If television drama had *auteurs*, Cartier would be an early *auteur* of style: a refugee from Vienna in the late 1930s, he joined the BBC Drama Department in 1952. His background was in European cinema, and his work in television seemed to push against the boundaries of what was possible in the studio. The tracking shot along the platform of the vast railway station in his production of *Anna Karenina* (1961) seems to go about as far as you can go with a television studio setting and studio technology.

The visual style of *1984* [33] is not exuberant, and the settings have a sparseness of detail which is justified by the dystopian State which

---

33 A much fuller analysis of *1984* can be found in Jacobs, *Early Television Drama*.

they represent. Film inserts are used for exteriors—Winston (Peter Cushing) in the decaying prole quarters, Winston and Julia (Yvonne Mitchell) meeting in the countryside—but dramatic scenes are restricted to the studio. As soon as Winston and Julia have actually met in the countryside, we cut to the synchronized sound of the studio for the love scene, a scene which is conducted through dialogue in front of a fairly objective camera with all the flatness of light and the hollowness of ambient sound characteristic of the studio. The emphasis is thrown onto the words which are acted with a clarity of diction and a 'scriptedness' which are usually characterized, pejoratively, as 'theatrical'. Throughout the drama, the conventions of acting or 'actorliness' throw into relief the conventionality of the language of their love-making, giving it a rather distant quaintness for a retrospective viewing. (This, of course, is not a problem for television drama alone: theatrical acting in received pronunciation was always one of the characteristics of British film which drove audiences into a love affair with American stars.)

Most of the conversations take place in two-shot, the placing of the cameras producing quite strained set-ups in which two characters have to eat their lunch or drink their gin sitting side by side at a table instead of facing each other across the table. The scene is constructed frontally because, in the studio, it would be difficult to cut between the two actors in field/reverse field without getting the other camera in shot. Instead of cutting into the scene, the camera observes it from the front—like a viewer in the stalls. There are variations to this—in a conversation between Winston and Syme (Donald Pleasence) the camera pans between the two heads, and at moments camera angle is used to indicate a point of view between a sitting and a standing figure—but the characteristic disposition is frontal, viewing the action rather than cutting into it.

What seems striking about a number of the conversations is their length—a length which is emphasized by shooting in a single shot. Information is communicated by dialogue (somewhat wordy dialogue), and there is very little of the condensed economy of film in which the viewer is left to fill in the ellipses by deduction or by the conventions of narrative space and time. The domestic viewer, unlike the mass audience, seems to be addressed as someone who is not yet fully competent in the language, but needs to be spoken to slowly and with a very clear enunciation of ideas and connections.

And yet the scenes of Winston's interrogation have a real power. Partly this is to do with the acting of André Morell as O'Brien. A well-known actor on the English stage in the postwar period, Morell seems to adapt his performance to the small screen more successfully than other actors, detailing his characterization with what actors call 'business' (a little mannerism with his spectacles), but withholding expressiveness, minimizing the emotional 'signalling' which is characteristic of Peter Cushing, and allowing the camera to create an enigmatic power around him. It is not only the acting, however, which creates atmosphere: the shooting style of these scenes uses the limitations of the studio to produce tension, the same relentless shot of Morell's head against a black background dispassionately interrogating Winston (out of shot), and fading to black between each interrogation to signify the extension and repetition of time. The intensity and condensation of these scenes seems to operate on a different register from that of the wordy dialogues of 'real time' conversation.

It is difficult to write about a drama from 1955 like *1984* without a tone of condescension creeping in under the respect for its achievement, but it would be foolish to pretend that my interest does not have a trace of the antiquarian in it. Indeed it is worth considering how it could be that one can be completely absorbed by a Hollywood or British movie from the 1950s (*The Asphalt Jungle* [1955] or *Mandy* [1952]), or the 1940s (*Double Indemnity* [1944] or *It Always Rains on Sunday* [1947]) whose conventions of portrayal and acting have an even greater historical distance, and yet a television drama from the same period appears 'stagey' and remote. Partly, to be sure, it may be to do with the fact that we do not have a continuous history of the conventions of portrayal in television drama, and those monuments to which we do have access seem prehistoric, remnants of a bygone age barely recognizable as what we now mean by television. But partly also, it seems to me, it is to do with a drama whose roots are in the theatre, whose economy is looser than the tight economy of narrative logic, and whose grammar lacks the rhetoric of identification and involvement, point of view and editing, which we now rely upon for our experience and our absorption.

Having said that, it is important to note that in 1955 the transmission of *1984* produced such strong public emotion that questions were raised in the Houses of Parliament and indignant voices in the Press questioned the right of the BBC to expose its domestic audience to shock, fright, and horror. However wordy the dialogue, or stilted the acting, or frontal the scenes, or however much the walls of the set shook and the shadow of the camera boom intruded into the shot, the audience of 1955, sitting in darkened rooms with a low-definition image and 'boomy' sound, seem to have been sitting, white-knuckled, on the edges of their sofas and settees. The interest of *1984* is not simply as a relic of style, or as a monument of early television; it lies also in the social history of its transmission. Like the other 'terrifying' Cartier productions of the time, *The Quatermass Experiment* and *Quatermass II* (also scripted by Nigel Kneale), it points to a history of a subjectivity in which the conventions which we now find slow and distancing produced then an intense involvement, evoking terror and pity in an audience which was not yet schooled in home entertainment, and had not yet become immune to undomesticated television.

In some sense, *1984*, a recorded drama from 1955, marks the beginning of the end of early television. Where did change come from?

The most obvious answer is, 'from competition'. The arrival of Independent Television in 1955, the end of the monopoly and the introduction of competition did indeed shift the BBC in a number of very material ways. The audience was pursued much more vigorously, new programme formats were developed, programmes were bought in from the United States, and audience research grew in importance. At a less material level, too, the introduction of competition shook up the gentlemanly aesthetic and the homely domestic address of the paternalistic and patrician BBC. The shift in the tone of the *Radio Times*, the most obvious channel in which the terms of address are preserved, is almost immediate, and the first issue of the *TV Times* on 22 September 1955 bursts onto the scene with the very same mix of tabloid populism and aggressive entrepreneurialism which became familiar again with the promotion of satellite television in Rupert Murdoch's popular press:

> Television is at last given the real freedom of the air. The event is comparable with the abolition of the law that kept motor-cars chugging sedately behind a man carrying a red flag.
>
> Now it's the 'go' signal, the green light for TV, too—with no brake on enterprise and imagination.
>
> So far, television in this country has been a monopoly restricted by limited finance, and often, or so it has seemed, restricted by a lofty attitude towards the wishes of viewers by those in control.
>
> That situation now undergoes a great and dramatic change. Viewers will no longer have to accept what has been deemed best for them. They will be able to pick and choose.
>
> And the new Independent TV programme planners aim at giving viewers what viewers want—at the time viewers want it.

None of the dignified concern of Dinwiddie here, and no sense of the upstart treading warily in the presence of its elders and betters, but naked competition and aggressive consumerism—in short sentences and single-sentence paragraphs.

As well as competition, then, Independent Television (ITV) brought with it a change of class address. Although the class composition of the audience had already changed dramatically in the decade before ITV arrived (Briggs records a decline in the proportion of Class 1 television ownership between 1947 and 1954 from 48 per cent to 25 per cent, and a rise in Class 3 ownership from 16 to 59 per cent[34]), it was ITV which first addressed this new television public in the terms which it deemed appropriate.

In this new competitive context, drama could no longer maintain its secure place as an automatically self-justifying cultural good, but had to be seen also as a way of reaching and attracting an audience. The BBC had to respond very directly, in a way which Reith and his successors had resisted, to the demands of public taste as they found it rather than as they thought it ought to be. Although it was the BBC which eventually achieved what seemed to many to be a Golden Age in the 1960s, it was ITV which scared them into it. It was commercial television which initiated the original, live, and *popular* Armchair Theatre series in 1956, a series of live dramas, written specifically for television by writers like Alan Plater, Alun Owen, and Harold Pinter, which not only introduced the first 'school' of original television drama in Britain, but also attracted impressive ratings by scheduling the series immediately after the ratings 'chart-topper', *Sunday Night at the London Palladium.* Much more alert to the market, commercial television spotted the success of original drama in the United States in the mid-1950s, and in 1958 brought Sydney Newman from Canada to do the same for ABC Television's Armchair Theatre in Britain. The BBC poached Newman from ABC in 1963 to lead it into its Golden Age, and the rest is history.

It is worth noting, however, that when ITV opened in 1955, it continued rather than closed the privilege of theatre. Excerpts from *The Importance of Being Earnest* were shown on ITV's opening night, and though they famously brought the viewers *I Love Lucy* and *Dragnet*, they also brought a regular schedule of classic theatre. Under the heading, 'Classics Needn't Be Gloomy', the *TV Times* of 7 October 1955 published an interview with the theatre director, John Clements, introducing an International Theatre series: 'I believe that we can televise the kind of drama that appeals to an intelligent public,' says Clements, 'a really highly educated public in the theatrical sense.' By the beginning of 1956, Clements, now billed as drama adviser to Associated Rediffusion, was announcing a series of classics at the Saville Theatre to run throughout the year: 'Each is scheduled to run for roughly eight weeks in the theatre and, soon after, will be shown on ITV —with the same cast' (*TV Times*, 13 January 1956). The first play of the Saville Theatre series was Ibsen's *The Wild Duck*, to be followed eight weeks later by Sheridan's *The Rivals*. At the same time, calling on the history of a more popular theatre, the Granville Melodramas, a fortnightly series, was resurrecting popular stage melodramas of the nineteenth century such as *East Lynne* and *The Poor of New York*. The early ITV conceded little to the BBC in its love of theatre.

Every bit as significant as the arrival of Independent Television was the arrival of new technology. In 1948, BBC technicians at Alexandra Palace solved the problem of synchronization which had prevented the recording of television signals on 35mm. or the new 16mm. film. In an article in *BBC Quarterly* the following year, H. W. Baker and W. D. Kemp explained the system and the uses to which it might be put. It might be used, they believed, in four important ways: (a) to repeat important outside broadcasts; (b) to repeat drama productions, saving the time and expense of bringing actors back for a second performance; (c) to conduct post mortems on productions, allowing more informed discussions of where they succeeded and where they failed; and (d) to meet the 'demand for complete recorded television programmes of good technical quality and programme value in the Dominions, in the USA, and possibly in other countries where English is understood'.[35]

In December 1953, a feature in the *Listener* reports that General David Sarnoff was about to release a television picture-on-tape recorder, introducing reusable tape:

> General Sarnoff proposed two years ago that his scientists and research men should try to give him three presents to mark his fiftieth birthday in the electronic business: he suggested that one should be a television picture-on-tape recorder; another should be an electronic air-conditioner without moving parts; and the third should be a true amplifier of light.
>
> The first present is apparently ready . . . (*Listener*, 3 December 1953)

The invention of methods of recording television programmes on film or on tape did not simply add something to television, they changed its nature. They brought to an end its *essential* ephemerality, and transformed immediacy and liveness from technological necessities into residual aesthetic aims.

The change was slow to take effect. In the BBC, throughout the 1950s, recording was restricted, with a limited number of recording channels, and it was not until the 1960s that recording became routine practice. Since the 1930s, it had been common practice to repeat Sunday night's play later in the same week. Under the conditions of live transmission, such a repeat involved reassembling cast and crew for a second performance. With the introduction of transcription, and then tape, the second performance—and therefore the second fee—was no longer necessary. Understandably, Equity, the actors' trade union, and the other craft unions viewed this loss of earning

35 H. W. Baker and W. D. Kemp, 'The recording of television programmes', *BBC Quarterly*, vol. 4, no. 4 (1949–50), 236–48.

with concern, and their legitimate defence of their members' interests is one of the reasons for the slow introduction of recording as a routine practice.

But a more material, institutional interest was pulling in the opposite direction. Even before recording on tape was possible, Hugh Carleton Greene, then Assistant Controller, Overseas Services, later to be the Director-General of the BBC during the Golden Age of the 1960s, wrote an article in *BBC Quarterly* in 1952/3 titled 'Television transcription: the economic possibilities'. This article introduced into the official and public BBC discourse the terms of an international television market.

> Television transcriptions, whether kinescopes or specially produced films, are, for a variety of reasons, extremely costly. Only by breaking into the United States market could a television transcription service hope to make both ends meet. The potential earnings from the rest of the world will not, for some time to come, approach what, with the right sort of programmes, can be obtained from the United States alone.[36]

Interestingly, in his concluding paragraph Carleton Greene backs off from the language of the market and adopts the more traditional national, cultural, moral (and imperial) discourse of the BBC (and, notably, of Grierson):

> In television transcription this country has a potential means of enormous power for spreading knowledge of its way of life through the most intimate and immediate of all the senses, through the eyes of the viewers in all parts of the world. If the opportunity is not grasped by this country it certainly will be by others, particularly by the United States, and in Asia, by Japan. Things are moving quickly in the television world, and the chance, if missed, may be gone for ever.[37]

By the time of the arrival of commercial television, recording on film or tape was already well established. As well as introducing a more populist discourse to television, the arrival of the entrepreneurial independent television companies marked a new interest in the international trade in programmes. Early ITV companies not only bought in US programmes and formats, but, to offset the expenditure, they also sold them to an American market which was not yet as closed to the outside as it later became. The most successful sale in the

---

36 Hugh Carleton Greene, 'Television transcription: the economic possibilities', *BBC Quarterly*, vol. 7, no. 4 (1952–3), 217.

37 Ibid. 221.

early years was probably *The Adventures of Robin Hood*, shot on film, starring Richard Greene, produced by Sapphire Films for the ITPC (Incorporated Television Programme Company, later to form Associated Television), and sold to the USA as a series before ITV began transmission. A blatant public relations feature article in the *TV Times* of December 1955 revels in the new ITV's dollar-earning capacity:

> If you think that ITV is laying out large sums of money and drawing a revenue only from English advertisers, the news of the dollar-earning capacity of the shows will surprise you.
>
> *The Adventures of Robin Hood*, which had been sold to the United States, has brought to England a million and a quarter dollars—nearly half a million pounds.
>
> If that were the sum total of ITV's success in the tough American markets, it would still be a wonderful contribution. But there's more to hear yet. And even more to come later.
>
> *The Count of Monte Cristo* is not yet completed. But it has been presold to America for a large guaranteed sum. Then I hear that 'Theatre Royal' is also being syndicated over dozens of stations on the other side of the Atlantic.
>
> The actual return from these three shows is not known. But I would not be surprised to hear it was around a million pounds—all in much-sought dollars. (9 December 1955)

The terms now seem very familiar (and the success was short-lived), but it is still surprising to see how far back they stretch. By 1961, the BBC, slow to commit itself to the high-cost, high-risk strategy of shooting series on film for the uncertainties of foreign taste, had shown how far it was prepared to go to achieve international sales by recording its *Maigret* series simultaneously on Ampex tape, 16mm. and 35mm. film, using the cheaper techniques of drama for the production of a detective series for the international market.

The significance of the development of recording technology cannot simply be measured in terms of practical advantages, commercial benefits, or formal effects. What recording did was to lift television out of the ephemeral and give it a commodity form. The shift from direct transmission to recording turned television from use value to exchange value, re-forming even public service television as not only a cultural good but also a tradeable good. There had already been some exchange of films of important international events, but now what had been conceived as purely national and cultural production had the potential to enter the international market as a commodity. Much of the subsequent development of British television drama—the shift from single play to art film, the rise of the classic serial and Masterpiece Theatre, the shift to film technology and aesthetics—can be dated from the moment at which drama becomes simultaneously expensive, recordable, and marketable.

Like Ealing of the same period, television in the immediate postwar years was still driven by something of the enthusiasm of the amateur inherited from the prewar years, a cult of the amateur noted by none other than John Grierson as late as the 1960s:

> the cheapness of television's methods—the sometimes appalling and appallingly unnecessary cheapness of television's methods—drives it inevitably to what we can only in visual terms describe as amateur theatricals. But there are other factors involved. The medium itself is in some ways predisposed, and properly predisposed to the amateur.[38]

Much of the discourse of production which one can detect in the early writing—formal and informal—and in the reminiscences of the pioneers, the celebration of disaster, the informal working relations, the culture of the BBC canteen, the 'try it and see' attitudes, carried something of the 'wizard prang' about it, an extension of church hall dramatics which suggests a space which was not yet fully institutionalized. In many ways, this period parallels the experimentalism and lack of standardization characteristic of 'primitive' cinema as described by Bordwell and Burch. The significance of the late 1950s, with the arrival of competition and the technology of recording, was to install an increasing professionalism in the place of the enthusiastic amateur, and to begin the process of the institutionalization of the mode of production of television.

The transition which the 1950s began, however, may never have been fully completed. Within the terms of public service, competition and commodification did not finally eliminate the 'old' values of ephemerality, immediacy and the amateur (in the positive sense which Grierson implies), they simply placed them into contradiction with other values. The development of drama through the 1960s and 1970s was defined by often contradictory and sometimes conflictual relationship between the 'free' and unruly creative individual and the managerial needs of the institution. And in the 1990s, however much the new economic mandarins of broadcasting may want to sail on the tight ship of enterprise, they keep finding leaks.

Within the cultural and creative privileges of a public service television which valued originality and creativity and venerated the uniquenesss of the writer, television drama could never become a completed classical form in the Fordist mode achieved by Hollywood cinema. It lacked the industrial streamlining and the clearly

38 John Grierson, 'Grierson on television', *Contrast*, vol. 2, no. 4 (1963), 221.

demarcated divisions of labour which could standardize its production system and its practices within 'classical' rules. With the institutionalization of those contradictions between creativity and commodity, between national culture and international market, it could, however, begin the slow historical progress which would lead, in the 1980s and 1990s, to the virtual convergence of a British art cinema and British television drama.

3
The Making of the 'Golden Age'

L IKE 'serious drama', the idea of a 'Golden Age' of television drama is cloaked in perpetual quotation marks. Golden Ages only exist in retrospect. They are never lived as golden, but can only be constructed in memory from the hindsight of what came after. In television drama, the day-to-day experience of the people involved was probably much as professional life always is: a mixture of satisfactions and frustrations, victories and defeats, bureaucratic hassles and creative surprises, moments of excitement punctuating long stretches of routine. For the viewers, the experience was equally uneven. There were a lot of very dull plays and unremarkable evenings in the period between 1965 and 1975 identified as the Golden Age of BBC television drama, and for every Wednesday evening on which television lit a little fire with *Up the Junction* (1965) or *Talking to a Stranger* (1966) there were probably between five and ten evenings when the embers failed to glow. Nostalgia creates a past without rough edges which only exists in fantasy and desire.

The dangers of such nostalgia are clear, particularly when an unrecoverable and idealized past is used as a stick with which to beat the all-too-material present. There is, however, a sense in which the idea of a Golden Age may be meaningful: when it refers to that historical moment when one set of meanings and values is being replaced by another, when the traditions which stabilized a culture are beginning to be questioned and rewritten, and when creativity seems to transgress the boundaries of received good taste. It is out of such moments that Golden Ages have traditionally come (the Golden Age of Spanish theatre, of Elizabethan poetry and drama, or of the nineteenth-century novel), and while the ironic scare quotes point to a certain self-conscious hyperbole, it does seem that in the decade or so after 1956 British culture was indeed in a moment of historical transition in which values were being tested and rules rewritten. I want to argue that in the years after 1964 television drama became one of the key sites of this moment. Given the place to which television seems subsequently to have been assigned in cultural life— from the theoretically sophisticated 'distraction', 'indifference' or 'the everyday' to the mundane 'chewing gum for the eyes'—this in itself seems important to record. For many of us in the 1960s and 1970s, removed from what was happening in theatre either by geographical distance or by the taint of social exclusiveness, and with little to interest us in British film after 1963, television drama seemed to be one of the places in which surprises might occur and in which boundaries might be shifted a little. There were many dramas which confirmed the intimate strength of television as a dramatic medium, *Talking to a Stranger* being not the least of these. My interest in this and subsequent chapters, however, is in a few plays which seem to me to have tested boundaries in particularly resonant ways.

To introduce the argument, then, in somewhat schematic form: there is a familiar narrative according to which the revolution which happened in the British theatre in 1956, and more or less simultaneously in the English novel, found its way into British film in the late 1950s and early 1960s. With the help of the critic, Kenneth Tynan, the Royal Court Theatre production of John Osborne's *Look Back in Anger* in 1956 not only created a theatrical success but opened a breach in the culture through which the voice of a new generation could be heard—the voice of what the press dubbed the 'Angry Young Men'. The film production company, Woodfall, was created in 1959 by Tony Richardson and John Osborne (with the backing of Harry Saltzman and Cubby Broccoli) to capitalize initially on Osborne's theatrical successes and subsequently on the emergent voices in the novel—David Storey, Alan Sillitoe, Shelagh Delaney. Thus was created the British New Wave.[1] The conditions of British cinema in the international market in the 1960s, however, could not sustain an art cinema, and the New Wave cinema came to a remarkably abrupt end after the success of Tony Richardson's adaptation of *Tom Jones* in 1963: Tony Richardson went to Hollywood, and Saltzman and Broccoli went on to produce the James Bond films. And at this point, the narrative stops—the renaissance of British film runs aground, as it always seemed to do, on the harsh realities of the market. My argument is that the breach which was opened in 1956 and seemed to close in 1963 actually remained open in a place that very few 'serious' critics thought to look: in television, and specifically in BBC television drama after 1964.

Since the period after 1964 seems to lie at the heart of television drama's significance in British culture, I want to spend some time tracing the conditions which made this possible. This means rewinding a little to try to track some of the moments in the formation of a generation and the re-formation of postwar culture.

1 For a more detailed and historically nuanced account of this narrative, see John Hill, *Sex, Class and Realism: British Cinema, 1956–1963* (London: BFI Publishing, 1986).

The year 1956 was one of those pivotal years in recent British history which seems particularly rich in symbolic significance. The key historical events of the year were, of course, not simply symbolically significant but marked a turning-point in the political history not only of Britain, but of postwar Europe and its international relations. The Suez crisis, when 'Great' Britain tried and failed to impose its will on Egypt over access to the Suez Canal, was the first signal of a change after the Second World War in the distribution of power between the industrial nations and the resource-owning nations: a change, particularly in the Middle East, which would transform the global economy in the following decades. In international affairs, the lack of support for Britain's military solution (Britain and France sent in an invasionary force) was a signal that wartime alliances and the special relationship with the United States were now highly conditional and quite blatantly subject to economic self-interest. Britain and France were forced to withdraw from their 'disciplinary' invasion of Egypt by American opposition. On a more apparently symbolic level, both at home and abroad the historical event was heavy with significance: only ten years after 'we' had won the war our imperial tail was tweaked by Egypt—a nation whose only significance had seemed to lie in ancient pyramids, desert Arabs, and the accident that a modern European-built canal happened to pass through it. At least the granting of independence to India could be presented—whatever the chaos that was left behind—with some pomp and ceremonial dignity; but Suez was humiliation taken neat. Empire, and the long tradition of Palmerston's 'gunboat diplomacy', was ending not with a bang but a whimper. The confidence of the old order in Britain as an Imperial world power began to shake a little, and those who saw the possibility of a new order—Britain as modern nation—were not slow to notice the cracks.

Serious cracks, however, were not confined to the conservative and imperialist Right, but began to appear in the Left, too, in 1956. In April, in his famous 'secret speech' at the USSR Communist Party Congress, the Party Chairman, Nikita Khrushchev, denounced Joseph Stalin and acknowledged the 'mistakes' of Stalinist oppression. 'Uncle Joe' had had a place in British popular affections since the battle of Stalingrad, and for a significant part of the British Left it was really Stalin who had won the war and defeated fascism. The disclosure of the brutality of his regime was a surprise to the public, but the opening up of divisions within the Kremlin, which had become a kind of Vatican of infallibility for much of the embattled British Communist Party, shook as many certainties in the Party faithful of the Left as Suez was to do for the flag-waving patriots of the Right.

The troubles on the Left did not end in April. In October 1956, in the same month that British and French paratroopers dropped into

Egypt, Soviet tanks rolled into Budapest to put down the uprising of the Hungarian independence movement. From the point of view of the exercise of imperial power over insubordination, the only difference between British imperialism and Soviet imperialism seemed to be that the Soviets stayed until their objectives were achieved, the uprising was crushed and the leaders were 'disappeared'. Britain's moral authority to criticize the invasion of Hungary was, of course, silenced by its own shameful fiasco in Egypt, but the invasion liberated criticism from the section of the Left which had already become extremely restive about the way in which the British Communist Party had made uncritical loyalty to the Soviet Union an article of faith for Party membership. Cracks which had appeared in April became rifts in October, and many who still identified themselves with the Left split from the Communist Party to form what came to be known as the New Left.[2]

For the historical formation which I am trying to outline here, then, 1956 was the formative year, the year in which a generation came of age and entered the political sphere. The political events of 1956 crystallize the shaking loose of some of the certainties of postwar Britain on both the Left and the Right, not only widening the gulf of understanding between them but churning up the understandings and values within them. This is the immediate political context of the revolution in the British theatre which took place at the Royal Court Theatre, and it is the background for the still inchoate anger which found its expression in John Osborne's *Look Back in Anger*—inchoate because it is not yet clear whether the anger is motivated by personal fear of the feminine represented by Jimmy Porter's wife or political hatred of the England represented by her father (an ambivalence which became pervasive in the British New Wave).

More widely, 1956 was the year in which doubts about the strict economism of the Communist Party's interpretation of Marx and suspicions about the nature of the Soviet State finally took definitive shape in the New Left. These doubts and suspicions of Soviet orthodoxy now initiated a new analysis of the political which recognized the determinations of culture as well as, but distinct from, the determinations of the economic. Writers like Raymond Williams, Stuart Hall, Edward Thompson, and Richard Hoggart began to argue the importance of culture in the formation of class and identity, meaning by culture something other than the property of the cultivated elite— Raymond Williams's 'whole way of life'—and incorporating into

---

2 For the historical record, it is worth recalling that others remained within the Party to continue the debate, eventually forming the 'Eurocom' wing which identified itself with the social democratic tendencies of many of the European Communist parties, and which opposed from within the 'Tankies' who remained faithful to the Soviet Party line and the sequence of tank invasions with which the Soviet Union held the Eastern Bloc together.

the political what Williams, again, called 'structures of feeling'. Still Marxist, though not Communist, the logic of their position was to carry the political struggle into the arena of the cultural (the trick being not to disconnect it entirely from the economic), and to open debates about political culture and cultural politics. For many people, this transformed what it meant to be 'of the Left' in post-1956 Britain.

For those who were writing in the immediate context of 1956, it was a year in which currents which were already in the air began to take solid forms and find voices. For the generation which followed immediately after, 1956 was the year in which many of us encountered politics for the first time: a politics which meant something more complex than cheering for our wartime heroes and hissing at the villainy of our enemies. (Barely a teenager in 1956, my first political memories are of Suez—vaguely—and the invasion of Hungary—quite sharply.) It was the year in which a political culture began to materialize which was inclusive rather than exclusive, in which being political meant something more than membership of a party, in which politics was part of being an intellectual, in which being an intellectual meant being left-wing, and in which culture was at the cutting edge of redefinitions and rebellions. The political culture which culminated in the heady days of 1968 was born in 1956.

At least some of the generation which entered television in the mid-1960s had been exposed to this political culture. Most of them —writers, directors, script editors, even actors—came out of Oxford and Cambridge, the BBC's traditional recruiting ground. 'Oxbridge', because it saw itself as the elite institution where the culture was to be defended and handed on, was also the place where the cultural debates found their most concentrated form. Many of the new recruits to television were 'scholarship boys' and therefore the first members of their family ever to have the opportunity of going to university. (We hear very little in the nostalgia for the Golden Age about the 'scholarship girls' of whom Caroline Steadman has written.[3]) Because television was not yet one of the respectable professions—civil service, foreign office, the City—it was more likely to attract recruits who did not feel themselves to be part of what came to be known in the 1960s as The Establishment. A significant number of the new recruits to television had a class formation of nonconformity, a political formation of dissidence, and an educational experience of the cultural debates of the 1950s and 1960s. They came out of university with the idea that culture mattered, and that television as a popular form was an arena in which a difference might be made. Without wishing to see this sketch of complex histories congeal too

---

3 See Caroline Steadman, *Landscape for a Good Woman* (London: Virago, 1986).

easily into the convenient stereotypes of 'pop' cultural history, it is not difficult to detect how the political and cultural formation which began in 1956 might generate some of the political engagement which has come to be associated, rightly or wrongly, with the drama of the Golden Age.

The historical events of 1956 did not, of course, create a generation. They are simply the symbolic moments at which the fault lines of the culture become visible, and where the emergent discourses can be seen in sharp relief against the residual discourses of postwar common sense and consensus. The distinctive voice which emerged after 1956—in the theatre, the novel, the cinema and ultimately in television—was defined, in some part at least, by the established voices it was reacting against. As early as the end of the war, commentators were expressing some doubts that the values which had served Britain so well during the war—pluck, humour, and 'business as usual'—could be expected to produce a vibrant or challenging postwar culture. In one of his reports to the *New Yorker* in 1945, Edmund Wilson put it thus:

> Must we conclude that the articulate middle class that thought
> it was working for democracy and freedom is now almost
> completely dead, having failed in the time of its prosperity to
> create a lasting civilization; so that there is nothing left but a
> labouring and shop-keeping people, more and more equalized
> by the pressures of war services and wartime restrictions, over
> whom hangs a fading phantom of the England of the public
> school.[4]

The term which is most frequently applied to Clement Attlee and the government which he led after the 1946 election is 'decency', and, in the mythology at least, decency seemed to settle over the postwar period like a blanket—warm and protective, but a little suffocating. Even the great achievement of that first postwar Labour government, the Welfare State, came to be seen by many (particularly those who had least to gain from it) as the dead hand of the State regulating unruly lives and rationing our pleasures. Creative artists, in particular, found little to excite them in the ordered life and earnest concern of the new postwar society. In popular culture, bureaucracy became the whipping-boy of comedy, and Ealing Films made a genre out of the struggles of the self-regulating community against the interference of officious bureaucrats, centralized authority, and Whitehall. By the 1950s, a writer like Kingsley Amis, on his long march from the Left to the Right, could identify the Welfare State with the New

---

4 Edmund Wilson, quoted in Robert Hewison, *In Anger: Culture in the Cold War, 1945–60* (London: Weidenfeld & Nicolson, 1981), 2.

Barbarism, a barbarism which 'used to mean Hitlerism, but now it means the Welfare State and commercial television'.[5] Britain became the Nanny State—at least for those who had had experience of nannies. Lindsay Anderson wrote in 1957:

> Let's face it: coming back to Britain is always something of an ordeal. It ought not to be, but it is. And you don't have to be a snob to feel it. It isn't just the food, the sauce bottles on the café tables, and the chips with everything. It isn't just saying goodbye to wine, goodbye to sunshine. After all, there are things that matter even more than these; and returning from the Continent, today, in 1957, we feel these strongly too. A certain civilized (as opposed to cultured) quality in everyday life; a certain humour; an atmosphere of tolerance, decency and relaxation. A solidity, even a warmth. We have come home. But the price we pay is high.
>
> For coming back to Britain is also, in many respects, like going back to the nursery. The outside world, the dangerous world, is shut away: its sounds are muffled. . . . Nanny lights the fire, and sits herself down with a nice cup of tea and yesterday's *Daily Express*; but she keeps half an eye on us too . . .[6]

In both literature and theatre, the current of experimentalism which had followed the explosion of modernism in the interwar years, when even cultural conservatives like Eliot or Wyndham Lewis had had to find new forms of expression, seemed to have run out of energy. Modernism became a matter of form, dissipating into man-nerism (Christopher Fry) or hardening into classicism (T. S. Eliot). The new form in the literature of the postwar period was a return to a realism of an almost mundane restraint. A group of novelists and poets emerged—Kingsley Amis, Philip Larkin, Donald Davie, John Wain, Elizabeth Jennings, Thom Gunn—who came to be known as 'The Movement', a wonderfully undescriptive term which suited their refusal of 'isms' (except perhaps 'scepticism' shading into 'cynicism'). What the group shared, as Blake Morrison has described very well,[7] was a distance—either physical or spiritual or both—from the aristocratic culture of the post-Bloomsbury metropolis or the effete Oxbridge, and the cultivation of a sensibility which regarded 'provincial' as a positive term. Many of the writers subsequently became Oxbridge dons or metropolitan literary celebrities or both,

---

5 Kingsley Amis, *Socialism and the Intellectuals*, Fabian Society pamphlet, 1957.

6 Lindsay Anderson, 'Get out and push', in Tom Maschler (ed.), *Declaration* (St Albans: MacGibbon & Kee, 1957).

7 Blake Morrison, *The Movement: English Poetry and Fiction of the 1950s* (London: Methuen, 1986).

but the one who remained true to the end (in 1985) was Philip Larkin, a librarian in Hull.

The characteristic voice was one which treated strong emotion with suspicion. In his discussion of Donald Davie's poem, 'Rejoinder to a Critic', Morrison concludes,

> It was intensity of feeling, Davie asks the reader to believe, that led to the dropping of the atom bomb. The contemporary poet must counteract this catastrophic excess of feeling by eschewing emotion and rhetoric. Keith Douglas wrote during World War Two that 'to be sentimental or emotional now is dangerous to oneself and to others', and Davie's view is very similar:
> 'Alas, alas, who's injured by my love?'
> And recent history answers: half Japan!
> Not love, but hate? Well, both are versions of
> The 'feeling' that you dare me to . . . Be dumb!
> Appear concerned only to make it scan!
> How dare we now be anything but numb?[8]

In 1956, it was this voice of cool detachment and narrow horizons against which a new generation of writers, or at least a new element within the generation, began to express itself. It is the context of Jimmy Porter's much quoted cry of anger and disillusionment (or wail of frustration) against the 'Brave New-nothing-very-much-thank-you'.

> I suppose people of our generation aren't able to die for good causes any longer. We had all that done for us, in the thirties and forties, when we were still kids. There aren't any good brave causes left. If the big bang does come, and we all get killed off, it won't be in aid of the old-fashioned grand design. It'll just be for the Brave New-nothing-very-much-thank-you. About as pointless and inglorious as stepping in front of a bus.[9]

Pulling in another direction, however, it is also the context of Lindsay Anderson's plea for commitment in criticism in his influential 1956 article in *Sight & Sound*, 'Stand Up! Stand Up!':

> Our ideals—moral, social and poetic—must be defended, with intelligence as well as emotion; and also with intransigence. To look back (and around) in anger may be a necessary beginning: but as Jimmy Porter himself demands, 'The voice that cries out doesn't have to be a weakling's does it?' . . . I do not believe that humanism is exhausted; nor that we are without rebels capable of defending its cause. This is a responsibility to accept. (But responsibility is not conformism.)

8 Morrison, *The Movement*, paragraphs 43, 48, 107.
9 John Osborne, *Look Back in Anger* (London: Faber & Faber, 1957), 84–5.

> ... there is no such thing as uncommitted criticism, any
> more than there is such a thing as insignificant art. It is merely
> a question of the openness with which our commitments are
> stated. I do not believe that we should keep quiet about them.[10]

The significance of Anderson's appeal (borrowing its title, significantly, from a Methodist, nonconformist hymn) is that it was an
attempt to join the anger of Jimmy Porter (expressed even more
venomously in John Osborne's article in *The Times*, titled more than
a little provocatively, 'England, I Hate You') with the political engagement of the New Left. This is what seems to have left its mark on
the generation of new recruits who entered television in the 1960s,
transforming inchoate anger into political engagements of varying
forms and degrees, and converting the frustration of the Brave New-
nothing-very-much back into the possibility of a brave new world.

The generality of the writing which characterized the new generation of the theatrical and literary New Wave—in both the novel and
the theatre—shared with the writers of The Movement a suspicion of
modernist experiment, and rooted itself fairly firmly in realism. In his
survey of English culture since 1940, *Culture and Consensus*, Robert
Hewison makes the following point:

> The key point about the minor literary revolution of the fifties
> was that it had been in one sense a counter-revolution, a revolt
> against modernism and the obligation to be stylistically avant-
> garde. The shift in literature was in subject matter, a return to
> realism that allowed the rising generation to dismiss the stylistic
> inventions of their elders as elitist. . . . Kingsley Amis could argue
> (on the Third Programme): 'The adventurous path is the one that
> leads away from experiment'. Realism ensured a large middlebrow
> audience and, for both stylistic and political reasons, was the
> ruling mode for the new British cinema and television drama
> as it developed in the sixties.[11]

There were very substantial differences of class emphasis and commitment between the writers of The Movement and the Angry Young
Men but both identified themselves with an anti-aristocratic and
nonconformist form and matter of expression. The academic pro-
vincialism of The Movement became the working-class 'kitchen-sink'
drama of the post-1956 writers, and cynicism was elevated to anger;
but both were conscious of an audience to be addressed which went
beyond the cultural elites of Oxbridge and Bloomsbury.

---

10 Lindsay Anderson, 'Stand Up! Stand Up!', *Sight & Sound*, vol. 26, no. 2 (Autumn
1956), 69.

11 Robert Hewison, *Culture and Consensus: England, Art and Politics since 1940* (London:
Methuen, 1995), 117.

This attachment to realism was confirmed in the cinema. The tradition which began with Free Cinema—again, precisely, in 1956—in their programme of screenings at the National Film Theatre, converted the presbyterian and utilitarian documentary movement of Grierson into the more anglican and aesthetic tradition of Humphrey Jennings, but it continued to find in the documentary attitude a way of bringing the modern world alive. Lindsay Anderson, in particular, insisted on the poetry of cinema, but, in the documentaries of Free Cinema, it was a poetry of everyday life. The poetry of ordinary lives as they were lived by 'real people' became the measure of the realism of the New Wave which carried the torch of Free Cinema into the feature film, and it formed the distinctive voice and imagery of films like *Saturday Night and Sunday Morning* (1960), *A Taste of Honey* (1961), *This Sporting Life* (1963); even, though in a more complicated way, *Billy Liar* (1963). What was vibrantly new and alive in these films in the early 1960s was the shift in their subject matter, away from the decencies of the 'social problem' film and the petit-bourgeois communities of Ealing, to the gritty and grainy lives of the working class 'up North' where reality now seemed to reside.

In the late 1950s, however, other currents were stirring, cutting across and re-articulating the underlying attachment to realism. 1956 was also the year in which Colin Wilson published *The Outsider*,[12] a book which laid claims to defining this new generation with a title which proclaimed its allegiance to Albert Camus and a particular strain of existentialism. If to be young in 1956 was very heaven, to be existentialist was part of the kit. Existentialism, though it carried the prestige of philosophy, had the attraction of being accessible: it could be accessed through the novels of Camus or the plays of Sartre, contributing, in its popular form, a number of attitudes and postures to the post-1956 generation. In a more positive vein, the insistence on engagement, on the writer *engagé* making sense of an alienating world through personal commitment and action rather than through metaphysical speculation, gave an existential underpinning to the political dissidence of the new generation. It is precisely to this engagement that Anderson appeals in 'Stand Up! Stand Up!'.

The reverse side of this was that the world in itself no longer had a meaning, and its meaninglessness could best be expressed in a theatre of the absurd. Samuel Beckett's *Waiting for Godot* had lit up the London theatre in 1955. The theatre of the absurd in its continental version—notably in the work of Ionesco or Beckett—was a modernist theatre. Characteristically, it entered British theatre most distinctively, and brilliantly, in the work of Harold Pinter in a form in which its modernist experimentalism was cloaked in the disguise of

---

12 Colin Wilson, *The Outsider* (London: Victor Gollancz, 1956).

everyday, even 'kitchen-sink' realism. In plays like *The Caretaker* (1960) and *The Birthday Party* (1958) Pinter took the inanities of everyday speech and imbued them with a sense of absurd and indeterminable menace. In the television play which he wrote for ABC's Armchair Theatre season, also in 1960, *A Night Out*, we can see the limits to applying 'realism' as a blanket term for the television drama of the period: in this play Pinter pushes realism to the point at which meaning loses its terms of reference and shades into the terrors of the surreal.

The most enduring legacy, however, of Colin Wilson's version of existentialism is the romance which attaches to the outsider. The outsider alienated from a hostile world can only retain a sense of self through the refusal of consent. Non-conformity becomes heroic, and the individual's responsibility is to himself. The anti-hero may even refuse engagement: 'I'm out for a good time,' says Arthur Seaton in *Saturday Night and Sunday Morning*; 'All the rest is propaganda.' The significance for post-1956 culture of this neo-romanticism of the individual true to himself—its roots going back to the agonism of the nineteenth-century romantics—is that the individual invariably turned out to be male. In the dramatization of the hero's refusal of conformity, the agent of conformity equally invariably seems to be female. Marriage—which every woman wants—is the trap laid to ensnare the outsider, domesticating him, diminishing him, and emasculating him. (Interestingly, in the dramatization of this emasculation, watching television is one of the images of domestication —witness *Saturday Night and Sunday Morning*.) Jimmy Porter's speech about the loss of great causes is much quoted as the authentic voice of his generation. What is less frequently quoted is the beginning and end of the speech which lays disillusion squarely at the door of women:

> Why, why, why do we let these women bleed us to death? Have you ever had a letter, and on it is franked 'Please Give Your Blood Generously'? Well, the Postmaster-General does that, on behalf of all the women in the world. I suppose people of our generation aren't able to die for good causes any longer. We had all that done for us, in the thirties and forties, when we were still kids. There aren't any good brave causes left. If the big bang does come, and we all get killed off, it won't be in aid of the old-fashioned grand design. It'll just be for the Brave New-nothing-very-much-thank-you. About as pointless and inglorious as stepping in front of a bus. No, there's nothing left for it, me boy, but to let yourself be butchered by the women.[13]

13 Osborne, *Look Back in Anger*, 84–5.

As John Hill has shown, misogyny casts a long shadow over British film in the New Wave cinema.[14] Whether it be a dramatic device to materialize the inner conflict of the alienated outsider, or a sensibility of fear and loathing, or just a kind of forgetting, of rendering invisible, it is certainly one of the less attractive currents in post-1956 culture. It is not clear that young women in the 1950s and 1960s had any particular reason to celebrate the anger of the young men.

The 'kitchen-sink' tag hung around the neck of the new literature and particularly the new drama as a convenient journalistic label. Delivered with a slight wrinkle of the aristocratic, aesthetic nose, it spread a whiff of disdain across quite different works in different media—including, of course, television drama. If realism was the dominant, however, it was by no means the only key in which new work was written. It was given a twist by Pinter's encounter with the Theatre of the Absurd, and later, in the 1960s, it was rejected utterly in Peter Brook's and Charles Marowitz's versions of Artaud's Theatre of Cruelty. Both of these were important components of the new sensibility, injecting a shot of the irrational and the dangerous into the mundane rationalism of the drama of ordinary lives which surfaced in such plays as John Arden's *Serjeant Musgrave's Dance* (1959), or Edward Bond's *Saved* (1965), and in Brook's anti-Vietnam improvisation-based theatre piece, *U.S.*, performed in 1966 by, of all people, the Royal Shakespeare Company.

Most significantly, however, 1956 (yet again) also marked the British theatre's first face-to-face encounter with the theatre of Bertolt Brecht when the Berliner Ensemble visited London for the first time—just two weeks after the death of Brecht himself. This encounter transformed British theatre, stimulating a reinvention of theatre space and a recasting of the relationship between the spectator and the stage. So fundamental was it that what had been intended as a radical rejection of the illusionism of what Brecht called the Dramatic Theatre became part of the standard vocabulary of that theatre. Brecht's Epic theatricality, often stripped of its politics, became part of the new repertory of conventions designed to refresh rather than subvert the theatre of illusion. The laying bare of the devices of the theatre which Brecht had invoked as a new language of politics, far from calling the spectator to distanciated critical thinking and seeing the world as if for the first time, became part of the expectation of a more spectacular theatre. Brecht was good business for designers. Nevertheless, however formalistic many of the appropriations might have been, it is hard to conceive of British theatre—or British television drama—in the latter half of the twentieth century without the intervention of Brecht and his challenge to the 'natural'

14 Hill, *Sex, Class and Realism.*

and naturalizing space of realism. Dennis Potter is only the most obvious television dramatist to have absorbed the lessons of Brecht—almost to the point at which they disappear and become themselves 'natural'.

All of these formal counter-currents and cross-currents, then—Brecht, the Theatres of the Absurd and of Cruelty, as well as memories of modernist experiment and surrealism—cross and counter-cross the theatrical sensibility of the 1950s and 1960s, breaking up the homogeneity of realism and its association with the drudgery of the 'kitchen-sink'. For television drama, while the pull of realism and its accessibility was extremely strong, it is important to recall that the endurance of realism as an aesthetic form is precisely because of its adaptability, the very adaptability which makes it so difficult to define. Realism, historically, has been an extremely broad church, able to change colour to blend with its background, seldom binding itself with a programmatic manifesto, happy to transform the new currents it encounters on its way—naturalism, surrealism, the Absurd, Brecht—and equally happy to be transformed by them. The history of television drama, which comes into particularly sharp focus in the 'Golden Age', is a history of these encounters and transformations.

One final element, drawn again from the symbolic moment of 1956, should be added. 1956 was the year in which, in the USA, Elvis cut his first album for Sun Records (and entered his personal Golden Age); and in the UK, it was the year in which the Bill Haley film, *Rock Around the Clock*, was released. What this symbolizes is the arrival of the teenager, and the division of the world into a younger generation which screamed hysterically, tore up cinema seats, and dressed outlandishly, and an older generation which was doomed to be 'square'. The word 'teenager' was introduced to the language in the 1950s by advertisers who had identified a new market with free disposable income. What excited the teenagers and dismayed the 'squares' was the discovery that rock singers had bodies, that popular music was inescapably sexual, and that rebellion was fun.

Despite its acknowledgement that culture was a 'whole way of life' and not the property of an elite, the New Left was somewhat outflanked by the culture that was being embraced so enthusiastically by teenagers. They were as likely to be outraged by the commodification of entertainment as they were to be engaged by its rhythms, and where youth found new forms of excitement much of the Left found new forms of exploitation and cultural impoverishment. Jazz, traditional or modern, remained the music of choice for intellectuals *engagés*. It was not till the mid-1960s, when the Beatles began to write poetic lyrics and play with harmonies and Dylan played electric guitar, that popular music was claimed for 'serious' culture. When a traditional academic musicologist like Wilfrid Mellers began to write about the Beatles[15] and a conservative literary critic like Christopher Ricks wrote about Bob Dylan,[16] you could tell the fun was over.

The serious point I am making here is that, in the formative years of the Left's engagement with popular culture, teenagers seemed to be excluded from the new inclusive definitions. What writing there was from the Left about popular entertainment—Stuart Hall and Paddy Whannel's *The Popular Arts* from 1964 is the most import-ant example[17]—was clearly marked by a sense of responsibility: a recognition that education had a duty to address the popular arts as a way of encouraging discrimination and providing inoculation from the harmful effects of commodified forms. With an irony that was often recognized at the time, the early cultural studies inspired by new thinking on the Left continued the project laid out for a noncon-formist cultural conservatism by Leavis, and extended into popular fiction by Q. D. Leavis and Denys Thompson,[18] to guard against the debasement of commodified culture by teaching discrimination. More widely, the outflanking of the Left by a really *popular* Popular Culture points back to some of the tensions created by that sense of seriousness which always seems to walk hand in hand with com-mitment. Clearly, the critics on the Left were right about commodi-fication and exploitation, but in writing about the perils of mass entertainment there was always a danger of forgetting about the pleasures. This was not only a tension for cultural critics: in the liter-ature, theatre, and film of the New Wave, too, the angry young men were themselves inclined to be a little 'square' when confronted by even younger men and women coming up from behind with a very different formation and agenda. When Arthur Seaton proclaims the credo of a more hedonistic generation, 'I'm out for a good time. All the rest is propaganda', he is announcing a refusal of responsibility which it is the project of the rest of Sillitoe's novel or Reisz's film to punish.

In a sense, then, it is a kind of ethical seriousness, rather than simply formal realism, which seems to underpin the cultural move-ments associated with the 1950s and 1960s. This is what gives them much of their power and their value: the sense that these things

---

15 See Wilfrid Mellers, *Twilight of The Gods: The Beatles in Retrospect* (London: Faber & Faber, 1973).

16 See Christopher Ricks, *The Force of Poetry* (Oxford: Clarendon, 1984). Ricks's writing on Dylan originally appeared in a Dylan fanzine, *The Telegraph*, in the early 1980s.

17 Stuart Hall and Paddy Whannel, *The Popular Arts* (London: Hutchinson Educational, 1964).

18 See, for example, F. R. Leavis and Denys Thompson, *Culture and Environment: the Training of Critical Awareness* (London: Chatto & Windus, 1930); Q. D. Leavis, *Fiction and the Reading Public* (London: Chatto & Windus, 1932); Denys Thompson (ed.), *Discrimination and Popular Culture* (Harmondsworth: Penguin, 1964).

mattered and that theatre or literature or television drama could do something about them. But it seems important to point out that there were currents in the culture which left very little mark on the tradition of drama which emerged in television in the 1960s. Pop Art, which undermined commodification from within by a kind of ironic celebration, may have altered the house style of a few films and television programmes (Losey's *Modesty Blaise* [1966], the James Bond films [1962–] or the television pop show *Ready, Steady, Go* [1963–8]), but it made very little impact on the culture from which television drama took its dominant key. This is simply to place British television drama, in the Golden Age and beyond, in a very modern sensibility: a sensibility which has to be dissociated from any assumptions of television's 'essential' postmodernism.

This is not an attempt to trace influences or fix origins. It would be somewhat pointless to go off in search of the particular moments in particular texts which offer particular illustrations of culture at work. What I am trying to tease out are the 'structures of feeling' and the stirrings within the arts and within culture which seem to give some partial explanation of why particular kinds of drama happened at a particular time. Filtered through both the engagement *and* the romanticism of popularized existentialism, and driven by new definitions of what it is to be an intellectual and what it is to be political, television drama (and film and theatre) in Britain in the late 1950s and 1960s seemed to be formed out of a series of encounters between native traditions of realism and documentary and new continental currents: the Absurd, the Theatre of Cruelty, Brecht, existentialism, Italian neorealism, the French *nouvelle vague* in both its cinematic and its literary forms, even, in Troy Kennedy Martin's seminal article,[19] casting back to Eisenstein and Soviet montage. What emerges is not a series of new artistic movements, one replacing the other in rapid succession, but a system of translations in which the new language is translated into native speech and local dialects, and each is transformed by the other. Sometimes the relationships are quite direct— Potter and Brecht, or Mercer and the *nouvelle vague*—but often they are in the air, almost a common culture. And running through these relationships, a seriousness about values and about what television drama could do and should be: a European sensibility about the relative places of popular art and commodified culture. Although television drama in the period designated as a 'Golden Age' was emphatically British—even English—it belonged to a hierarchy of values in which art and quality were made in Europe and entertainment was American.

19 Troy Kennedy Martin, 'Nats go home: first statement of a new drama for television', *Encore*, no. 48 (March/April 1964), 21–33.

If this is the topography of culture in which the Golden Age germinated, there is, of course, a more direct history of development within television. Here, in total contradiction to what might be expected from all of the above, the breakthrough in original television drama happened in commercial television and its roots were in North America.

By the time Britain began its Golden Age of television drama in the mid-1960s, the United States had already had its Golden Age almost a decade before. Sponsored live drama written specially for television was winning top ratings in the network charts from *Marty* in 1953 to a quiet demise around 1957, demonstrating again that before the feature film became the chosen form of home entertainment there was already a strong demand for 'serious' dramatic entertainment. The sponsors were United Steel, Goodyear, Kraft, and Colgate, the writers included Paddy Chayevsky and Rod Serling, and the dramas were acted by the generation of actors associated with Lee Strasberg's Actors Studio who later came to define a particular realist moment in Hollywood cinema: Rod Steiger, Kim Hunter, and James Dean as well as Steve McQueen, Jack Palance, Jackie Gleason, and many others. The plays were small-scale, mainly one-hour 'situation dramas' in which character and psychology were the focus of interest rather than narrative action, the 'habitus' was lower middle class or working class, and the characteristic inhabitants were the damaged and confused, the walking wounded of the American dream. Writers like Chayevsky invoked Chekhov and Ibsen, but the most immediate resonances were with the Arthur Miller of *All My Sons* (1947), *Death of a Salesman* (1949), and *A View from the Bridge* (1955). They were popular dramas of serious purpose, and this, of course, would be their downfall. 'Seriousness' was not the ingredient which advertisers believed could best oil the wheels of commerce: US television was not meant to produce sober citizens, but happy consumers. By the end of the 1950s, having passed through the necessary period in purgatory to atone for the sins of the quiz shows, the networks were able to resume the real business of television, and live drama had been replaced at the top of the audience ratings charts by Westerns.

William Boddy has given an excellent account of the institutional pressures in a number of areas of television production in his critical and historical analysis of American television in the 1950s.[20] I do not intend to develop that analysis here, but it is important to establish the significance of the American 'moment' in the wider history of the development of television drama. American live drama drew on a native tradition of realist, left-wing, Popular Front theatre associated

20 William Boddy, *Fifties Television: The Industry and its Critics* (Urbana/Chicago: University of Illinois Press, 1990).

most particularly with the Group Theatre in the 1930s. The Group Theatre, in turn, drew on the Stanislavskian tradition of theatrical naturalism as it was brought to the Group Theatre by Harold Clurman, Stella Adler, and Lee Strasberg. This was a theatrical tradition which emphasized the 'truth' of the actor, and it was taken to its logical conclusion by Lee Strasberg in the Actors Studio, where the 'Method'—Strasberg's interpretation of Stanislavski's training method for actors—became almost a therapy designed to release the actor from the blocks which prevented total identification with the role, thus permitting a full, truthful, and courageous exteriorization of interior emotion. Such a style frowned on the contrivance of the theatrical and the stagey, and favoured the inarticulate expression of feelings not fully understood over the articulate expression of the classical school's 'beautiful lines spoken beautifully'. It was a style of acting which could have been designed for the close-up, and it was indeed in the films of Brando and Dean that it seemed to find its most perfect expression. But before that, US television's live drama had already built on this theatrical tradition, and played it on the scale of the television studio and the television screen: the very 'limitations' of the studio—the narrow field, the constricted sets, the lack of fluidity in the camera—gave power to the focus on acting and character. At their best—in *Marty* (wr. Chayevsky, for NBC's Goodyear Television Playhouse, 1953) or *Requiem for a Heavyweight* (wr. Serling, for CBS's Playhouse 90, 1956)—it was a style of drama which began to discover what might be specifically dramatic about live television, a style which sought to combine the immediacy of theatre with the intimacy of close-up film, giving a sense of dimension to 'small lives'. This located television drama in a tradition of naturalism as if it were its natural home, a location whose 'inevitability' provided one of the foundational debates for television drama in Britain in the 1960s and 1970s.

It was not entirely surprising that it should have been the relatively new commercial television which imported live original drama to British television: the commercial networks in Britain noted the North American ratings, recognized the populist appeal for its predominantly lower-middle- and working-class audience, and, particularly, had the same need as the American networks for some evidence of civic responsibility: something in the schedules which would rise above the 'lowest common denominator' entertainment which it was accused of encouraging, some fibre in the diet of game shows and imported comedies. In 1957, in the age when telecine and tape had brought an end to the literalness of live transmission and had given television a commodity form, the BBC had bought a number of 'live' Canadian dramas which had been shown in Canada as part of a twenty-six-week General Motors Theatre season. Howard Thomas of the ABC independent television company was impressed and invited their producer, a Canadian called Sydney Newman, to come to Britain to produce a series of live dramas for the commercial network. (In one of the little knots of history, Newman had worked for a time in the National Film Board of Canada, set up by John Grierson to carry on the spirit of the documentary movement.) Newman's remit was to take charge of ABC's Armchair Theatre series which had started in 1956, screening original plays on Sunday evenings imme-diately after *Sunday Night at the London Palladium*—one of ITV's top-rating shows.

Bernard Sendall, the official historian of the early years of ITV,[21] recounts the story that Michael Barry, then head of BBC Drama, took Newman to see *Look Back in Anger* at the Royal Court.

> That play, with its unusual worm's-eye view of society and its derisive radicalism, seemed to Newman the dazzling light on the road to Damascus; more accurately, it had come to sum up what he believed about the drama. He had developed the notion of 'agitational contemporaneity', and *Look Back in Anger* confirmed his ideas. An outsider in this country, he found both the country and its problems utterly fascinating. He wanted to make plain statements to the mass audience—statements falsified neither by sentiment nor by doctrinaire beliefs.[22]

Newman concentrated on building up a team of writers—Alun Owen, Alan Plater, Ted Willis, Harold Pinter, Robert Muller—who shared the vision of what television drama could be, and between 1958 and 1963 when Newman was 'poached' to be Head of Drama at the BBC, it was ITV which was at the cutting edge of contemporary and original television drama.

Armchair Theatre's achievement was to shake loose the metropol-itan, theatrical, and patrician codes which had defined the role of television drama in a public service system. Though it was rehearsed in London to accommodate the reality of actors' schedules, it was transmitted from ABC's studio in a converted cinema in Didsbury, Manchester. It benefited from the regional structure of the ITV net-work, and brought the same non-metropolitan perspective to tele-vision drama which had revitalized the theatre in 1956. Newman's insistence that the series would only use original material written for television made Armchair Theatre a decisive moment in the history of British television drama, and both he and Ted Kotcheff, the ambi-tious young director he brought with him from Canada, belonged to

---

21 See Bernard Sendall, *Independent Television in Britain*, vol.1: *Origin and Foundation, 1946–1962* (London: Macmillan, 1982), vol. 2: *Expansion and Change, 1958–1968* (London: Macmillan, 1983).
22 Ibid. 338–9.

a television culture which had no particular reverence for the classics of theatre and literature. The best of the writing which came to characterize Armchair Theatre belonged to the same school of 'naturalistic realism'—that is to say, a realism based on experience and environment—which had fuelled the new wave in the theatre and the novel, and would, during the lifetime of the series, fuel the new wave in film. Because it worked to a domestic scale, the new wave in television drama seemed to lend particular justification to the journalistic short-hand, 'kitchen-sink drama', and the tag stuck. Newman is quick to point out that Armchair Theatre, over his four seasons, included science fiction, comedies, crime thrillers, and a musical, and that it was not all gritty realism; but while a history of Armchair Theatre would celebrate its diversity, for the broader development of television drama its significance seems to lie in the incorporation into television of what was new about the new wave: non-metropolitan and non-patrician realism.

Newman is often referred to as a 'populist'. Sometimes, this means that he saw no contradiction between the terms 'popular' and 'culture', and could refer without aristocratic irony to a 'theatre of ordinary people'. Sometimes, it places him as a 'vulgarian'. In his very unpleasant account of Newman's arrival at the BBC in 1963, Don Taylor, the Oxford-educated, BBC-trained producer notable for his work with David Mercer, reveals uncompromisingly some of the cultural tensions inherent in the dawning of a new age, an age in which Newman emerges, dressed in skins, as the barbarian at the gates.

Sydney was not formally educated, and, frankly, knew little about the history or range of world drama. He also had a contempt for 'intellectuals'. . . . His own predilections in drama were quite clear. For hour after hour, he extolled to me the virtues of the American series, *The Naked City*, a New York cop drama with pretensions to dealing with Issues, and I could not, in many hours of patient and not-so-patient argument, convince him that drama was anything other than this kind of overplayed *Reader's Digest* seriousness, served up with all the sweaty melodrama characteristic of the American film industry at its lower levels. . . . I was in a group lunching with him the day after Philip Saville's production of *Hamlet* was screened. . . . It was clear that Syd didn't know the play, hadn't read it, and had seen it for the first time on screen. 'You know, it's a very exciting play', he said to the assembled company, while we all looked woodenly into our pudding dishes, or piled apple crumble into castles with our spoons. To put it brutally, I was deeply offended that the premier position in television drama, at a time when it really was the National Theatre of the Air, had been given to a man whose values were entirely commercial, and who had no more than a layman's knowledge of the English theatre tradition, let alone the drama of Europe and the wider world. It seemed like a conscious insult to the audience, the English people whom we were supposed to serve. In putting such a man in such a position, the BBC hierarchy were showing the deepest contempt for them, saying, we know what you slobs want, and this is the man to serve it up to you.[23]

It is worth quoting Don Taylor's naked snobbery at length lest there be any sense that there was wholehearted consensus within the new wave, or that the Golden Age represented peace and harmony throughout the land. Whatever Armchair Theatre had achieved, it did not resolve once and for all the tensions between the theatrical tradition and popular drama.

One of Taylor's objections to Newman, possibly the ultimate put-down, is that he 'industrialised the making of television drama'.[24] Whether or not we share the contempt, it may be that this lies at the heart of the shift which Armchair Theatre effected: the beginning of the end of the amateur. While Newman, almost for the first time in Britain, brought new original writing to television drama, the writers he developed most successfully were those who had a professional sense of the audience for which they were writing—an audience which had just been watching *Sunday Night at the London Palladium*. Interestingly, two of the most successful, Alun Owen and Ted Willis, went on to make their mark not in the single play but in the popular series: *Z Cars*, *Softly Softly*, *Dixon of Dock Green*. They were also writers who had a professional relationship to the medium, who tried to make a living by writing for television, and who worked in a more or less collaborative way with directors, producers, and even lowly script editors. And, like the poets and novelists of The Movement, they worked in the provinces, unaligned with the metropolis, and distinct from the generation of BBC writers for whom the BBC was a kind of finishing school for left-wing radicals.

While in criticism the writer continued to occupy the privileged place, in practice the writer's place began to be qualified by the fact that he or she was working in a television environment which looked more and more like an industry. This sense of the production team was extended by directors like Kotcheff who valued the opportunity that regional production offered to involve camera operators and lighting technicians actively and creatively in rehearsals, rather than bringing them in as hired hands at the last minute to implement the shooting script. Clearly the nostalgia of many of the memories of the

---

23 Don Taylor, *Days of Vision—Working with David Mercer: Television Drama Then and Now* (London: Methuen, 1990), 185–6.
24 Ibid. 190.

'team spirit' has to be handled with care, but it may indeed be that the crucial shift in Armchair Theatre—the 'industrialization' which Taylor disdains—was a shift from television drama as a reproduction of theatre or literature to television drama as a production of television in which creativity and technology were realigned.

Formally, Armchair Theatre expanded the space of live studio drama by shooting in depth with a moving camera. While individual directors in the BBC like Rudolph Cartier had already developed a more expansive style, Armchair Theatre seemed to adopt it as a house style. The opening shot of *Lena, O My Lena* (1960), written by Alun Owen and directed by Ted Kotcheff, is a long backward tracking shot opening up the studio into a full three-dimensional space with a movement which is reversed at the end of the play, creating a formal framing as well as a narrative closure. The objective was quite explicit: to use the camera as a way of breaking free from the stasis of theatrical space to the mobility of cinematic space. Viewed in retrospect, however, what is striking is not that the space which is created by this depth of field has become 'real' in the Bazinian sense, but that the studio has become fluid and expressive, freeing the actors within the space. There is a sense that the actors inhabit a space, rather than being constricted within a frame. Though they are only a few years apart, there is a considerable distance in televisual style between the scenes in *1984* in which characters sit awkwardly side by side at a table to conduct their conversations within the frame and the scenic disposition of actors in depth and in movement in *Lena, O My Lena*.

This could be interpreted simply as a liberation of the technology, a move towards the fluidity of narrative cinema. It seems to me, however, to be something more specific to the development of television drama. Crucially for notions of realism in television, what is created in plays like *Lena, O My Lena* is a performative space—a space for acting—rather than a narrative space—a space for action. The studio remains a studio, but the actors invest it with meaning. It is the actors who create a kind of reality: a reality which is watched rather than inhabited, a performed reality rather than the absorption into a narrative space driven by the logic of cause and effect and the fantasy of identification. Armchair Theatre's significance is not only that it introduced a new social space to television drama—the social space of class and region which it drew thematically from the New Wave in theatre and literature—but that it created a new televisual space in which the dramas of social relationship and social situations could be acted out.

Armchair Theatre, then, was a decisive moment in the passage of television drama from its dependencies on theatre and adapted literature to its discovery of its sense of identity. Probably more than any other form, television drama extended the social reach of the new discourses which had come into the culture in the mid-1950s. It may not have added any 'great plays' to the repertoire, and it produced many which were forgettable, but it expanded the range of what it was possible to be dramatic about in popular television. It provided a platform from which Sydney Newman was launched into the BBC, and operated as a training ground for many of the people who went on to become among the most innovative and influential writers, directors, and producers in the 1960s and after: Ted Willis, Alun Owen, Ted Kotcheff, Philip Saville, Peter Lukes, Verity Lambert, Irene Shubik. It also brought the new wave of actors to television, actors like Billie Whitelaw, Tom Bell, Peter McEnery. While it ran from 1956 to 1968, the 'golden years' were the years between 1958 and 1963 when Newman was in charge. Within the culture industries and in that particular period of capitalist culture, it seems that it was only a public service institution like the BBC which could provide the conditions for a longer tradition which was given the space and time and protection to evolve and diversify. Nevertheless, it is important to recognize that before Pilkington and before the recruitment to television of the 'scholarship boys', there was already an important current of drama which translated for a mass popular television audience the social commitment and serious purpose of 1956.

The Golden Age of television drama was ushered in, as golden ages often are, by an expansion in the economy: in television's case by the addition of a third channel, BBC2, in 1964. It was also associated, as golden ages often are, with a more liberal regime: whatever the contradictions of management, Hugh Carleton Greene's tenure of the Director-Generalship of the BBC from 1960 to 1969 does seem to have been marked by a greater sense of risk-taking—of testing boundaries and giving creativity its head—than any other regime before him and than most regimes which followed. The 1960s, of course, have the reputation of being a decade in which new social relationships were being forged, in which some of the restrictive senses of 'decency' were being eroded, and in which Britain became a little more experimental in its forms. Carleton Greene's job was to manage this cultural experimentalism in one of the central national cultural institutions. Managerially, this sometimes meant drawing lines beyond which the BBC would not go, but, culturally, it sometimes meant allowing lines to be redrawn. If nostalgia credits his period of office for its liberalism, and is prepared to forget the limits which were drawn, so be it: it was in the cracks between management and creativity that the possibilities of what television drama could do were tested.

But if the arrival of BBC2 is the immediate context and Carleton Greene's Director-Generalship is the agency, I want to argue that the particular shape and form of the Golden Age was legitimated, and even called into being, by a set of discourses which were embodied in the Pilkington Report which was presented to Parliament and made public in June 1962.

Royal Commissions have been the standard procedure for regulating and re-regulating public service broadcasting from the Crawford Committee in 1926 to the Peacock Committee in 1987. Typically, they are established with a membership drawn from what has come to be known as 'the great and the good' (a distinguished figure from the business world, someone from the church, a leading trade unionist, possibly an academic, maybe a writer, or a journalist, or a 'serious' celebrity). At the behest of the government of the day, they have been asked once a decade since 1946 to reassess the current state of broadcasting and the directions it could and should take. To enable the Committees to make their recommendations, they are expected to solicit opinion from as wide a range of sources as possible: professional broadcasters, interested parties (advertisers, for example), 'opinion formers', organizations which believed themselves to represent opinion (from the Women's Rural Institute to the Communist Party), and individual members of the public. Where appropriate, the Committees consider broadcasting systems from other countries, and commission reports on particular aspects of broadcasting. On the basis of this wealth of evidence, the Committees present a substantial report, plus appendices, intended to inform public policy. This is the mechanism by which broadcasting policy has been formed and transformed in the UK since the Crawford Committee Report recommended in 1927 that the British Broadcasting Company become a Corporation. The reports are not always followed by the government of the day to the letter: the economic liberalism of the Peacock Committee Report (1986) was watered down somewhat even by the economic libertarians of the Thatcher government, and Channel 4 did not match exactly the Open Broadcasting Authority the Annan Committtee (1977) had recommended. Sometimes the recommendations of the Committee are turned on their head: the recommendation of the Beveridge Committee in 1951[25] that commercial television not be introduced (a recommendation which had the support of the Labour Party) was overturned by a minority report which found favour with the new Conservative Government. Whatever the practical outcomes of the Reports, however, their discussions form a history of discourses about broadcasting in this century, and for television particularly their postwar progression— Beveridge, Pilkington, Annan, and Peacock—allows us to chart the ways in which television could be thought and spoken, and the positions it was asked to occupy in the national culture.

25 *Report of the Broadcasting Committee, 1949* (London, HMSO, 1951), Cmnd. 8116.

The 'Committee on Broadcasting' known as the Pilkington Committee had been established as a Royal Commission by the Home Secretary in 1960, under the chairmanship of Sir Harry Pilkington, to consider whether the third channel which had now become technologically feasible should be awarded to the BBC or to the commercial network of ITV. In some ways, the Pilkington Committee had a fairly straightforward task and, after the event, it seems unlikely that it would have recommended anything other than that it should be given to the BBC. Receiving its remit in 1960, however, five years after the introduction of commercial television, the break-up of the broadcasting monopoly and the arrival of competition for ratings, it was inevitable that it would become an end of term report, assessing the impact of the new arrangement and reporting on the good behaviour—or otherwise—of the two participants. Its language, therefore, was not simply the language of economic management, but was a language of values. It was these values as much as the practical arrangement which it recommended which provided the framework in which broadcasters operated for the next decade.

I want to quote at some length from the Report because, since it was its discursive intervention which seems to me to be crucial, it was not simply what they said that was important, but the way they said it.

Towards the end of the Report the Committee reviews its task, and recognizes that in order to make a recommendation about how a new broadcasting channel could be allocated, they had first to come to some conclusion about what broadcasting itself was for and how it had been transformed by the arrival of the age of television.

> We had . . . first to formulate a view on the purposes of broadcasting. The background to our thinking was the realisation that broadcasting will have profound and far-reaching effects; the working assumption must be that television in particular will be a potent factor in influencing the values and the moral standards of our society. *The burden of responsibility that this places on those to whom the services are entrusted is heavy.* The British Broadcasting Corporation and the Independent Television Authority have been formally charged with the duty of using this, the most influential medium of communication, as a means of disseminating information, education and entertainment. It is essential to the discharge of this duty that there should be presented, for listeners and viewers to choose from, the widest possible range of subject matter, treating as much as possible of the whole scope and variety of human awareness and experience. To do so, the broadcasters must not only reflect society; they must pick out and focus attention on that which is significant—*the best, because it is the best; the worst, so that we shall know it for what it is; the new*

and the challenging, because individual listeners and viewers should not be denied the opportunity of responding to them, and of judging them. At the same time, the broadcasters must care about public tastes and attitudes in all their variety in all kinds of programmes —in those designed to amuse and relax no less than in those that are demanding; *they must keep aware of them as they now are and of their capacity to change and develop.* This, we concluded, was the nature of the broadcasters' responsibility.[26]

Seen from the shores of a decade in which we have learned to wear our values lightly, and in which 'value' has come to be almost irredeemably associated with an economic metaphor, the discourse of Pilkington often seems to belong to another landscape, and the Committee's willingness to engage with questions of value in moral, and even scriptural tones ('. . . the worst, so that we shall know it for what it is . . .') may seem foreign, pompous, or simply quaint. But alongside the confidence of a discourse which knows where values lie, there is also an implicit recognition of the liberal contra-diction between an institution which cares about 'public tastes and attitudes' 'as they now are', but which also recognizes their 'capacity to change and develop'. Overwhelmingly, there is the sense that broadcasting matters, that the 'burden of responsibility' for broad-casters is 'heavy', and that it cannot be thought simply in terms of management, regulation, and (Adorno and Horkheimer's term) 'administrative rationality', but is the location where cultural—and moral—values are played out.

The viewer who forms the object of concern for the Pilkington Report is emphatically a citizen, one whose freedom to choose is a democratic right attendant with responsibilities, but who is not yet the 'sovereign consumer' who will emerge in the 1980s in the Report of the Peacock Committee, whose freedom to choose is the motor force of the broadcasting economy. Simply 'to give the public what it wants', to interpret the freedom of choice economically, was, for Pilkington, the ultimate abrogation of the broadcaster's burden of responsibility, the object of its most withering and most righteous anger, and it was one of the aspects of the report which made the greatest public impact and was the most hotly debated. The Com-mittee reported on a sense of 'disquiet and dissatisfaction' which emerged in submissions about the direction which broadcasting had taken since the arrival of competition.

Whereas the disquiet about television arose from 'sins of commission'—from the conviction that its capacity to influence

---

26 *Report of the Committee on Broadcasting, 1960* (London: HMSO, 1962), Cmnd. 1753, paragraph 1055, p. 285. My italics.

people was often misused—the dissatisfaction, the other main element made in the submissions made to us, arose from the 'sins of omission'—from the conviction that many of the best potentialities of television were simply not being realised. The theme common to nearly all those submissions which expressed dissatisfaction was that programme items were far too often devised with the object of seeking, at whatever cost in quality or variety, the largest possible audience; and that, to attain this object the items nearly always appealed to a low level of public taste. This was not, of course, to say that all items which attracted large audiences were poor, But in far too many the fact was to *produce a passively acquiescent or even indifferent audience rather than an actively interested one.* There was a lack of variety and originality, an adherence to what was 'safe'; and an unwillingness to try challenging, demanding and, still less, uncomfortable subject matter. It was put to us that, in television as elsewhere, one man's meat ought to be another's poison; that too often viewers were offered neither meat nor poison, but pap—because, presumably, though no-one much likes it, at least no-one will get indigestion. Against this, it has been said that in fact people watch these items; that the justification lies precisely in the fact that they are mass-appeal items. In a free society, this is what people freely choose; they do not have to watch; they can switch off. In short, by these tests, these items are 'what the people wants', and to provide anything else is to impose on people what someone else thinks they ought to like. Indeed, it has been held that, for this reason, it is not of great relevance to criticise television at all. We found this last a deflating thought.

. . . it seems to us that 'to give the public what it wants' is a misleading phrase: misleading because as commonly used it has the appearance of an appeal to democratic principle but the appearance is deceptive. It is in fact patronising and arrogant, in that it claims to know what the public is, but defines it as no more than the mass audience; and in that it claims to know what it wants, but limits its choice to the average of experience. In this sense we reject it utterly. If there is a sense in which it should be used, it is this: what the public wants and what it has the right to get is the freedom to choose from the widest possible range of programme matter. Anything less than that is deprivation.[27]

The democratic Left and the libertarian Right would still be picking over the contradictions of this position two and three decades later. In its privileging of the 'actively interested' viewer over the one

---

27 *Report of the Committee on Broadcasting, 1960,* paragraphs 17–18.

who was 'passively acquiescent and indifferent', Pilkington was continuing the desire which had been expressed in the BBC since 1927 for 'constructive listening' ('On the other side of the microphone the listener must recognize that a definite obligation rests on him to choose intelligently from the programmes offered to him'[28]), and the instructions and advice which had been offered in the *Listener* and the *Radio Times* on how to achieve it ('Try turning out the lights so that your eye is not caught by objects in the room'[29]). It also echoed in liberal form the appeal of the political avant garde in theory and practice for Brecht's 'active spectator' who had not left his brain with his hat at the door. For Pilkington, this imperative was tied to the moral responsibilities of citizenship, of a citizen who has the rights of choice but also the responsibilities of judgement.

Where television threatened judgement and an active citizenship most directly was in its natural inclination towards 'trivialization', the term which Pilkington used with greatest effect to beat the back of post-monopoly broadcasting.

> The criticism of triviality . . . was that trivial programming was a waste of the medium, and represented a failure to realise its potentialities. But the sin was not merely one of omission; too often, because it had positive results, it was also a sin of commission. Thus subjects billed as controversial sometimes avoided the controversy, and so served rather to reinforce than to disturb prejudice and complacency. Programmes which exemplified emotional tawdriness and mental timidity helped to cheapen both emotional and intellectual values. Plays or serials might not deal with real human problems, but present a candy-floss world. Bishop Cockin put it to us that such programmes taught that it was slickness which really counted, and that they had a more subversive influence than the portrayal of violence.

> Our own conclusion is that triviality is a natural vice of television, and that where it prevails it operates to lower general standards of enjoyment and understanding. It is, as we were reminded: 'more dangerous to the soul than wickedness'.[30]

Replete with sins of omission and commission, natural vices and wickedness of the soul, and slipping seamlessly between the submissions of the congregation and the judgements of the clerisy, the Pilkington Committee seems to stand as a kind of Testament within broadcasting history: brought down by the Elders from the mountain,

---

28 Quoted in Paddy Scannell and David Cardiff, *A Social History of British Broadcasting, vol. i: 1922–1939* (Oxford: Basil Blackwell, 1991), 371.

29 Ibid.

30 *Report of the Committee on Broadcasting, 1960*, paragraphs 101, 102, 34–5.

the tablets were inscribed with the values of the tribe before we were led astray (in the 1980s) by the seductions of the golden calf. While the scriptural tones have a certain self-conscious irony, the discourse which runs through the report leaves us in no doubt that the values and responsibilities which are being laid down for broadcasting are not simply cultural or aesthetic; they are profoundly moral. This is the burden of responsibility, and it cannot be fulfilled with material which is safe and comfortable. Broadcasting is serious, and to be serious it must be challenging, controversial, and even transgressive.

Much has been made of Richard Hoggart's membership of the Pilkington Committee, and there seems to be little doubt that the report resonates with his intellectual and cultural positions. Hoggart had been one of the group of writers who had formed the new definition of culture which emerged at the end of the 1950s. His book, *The Uses of Literacy*, published by Chatto & Windus in 1957, with Raymond Williams's *Culture and Society* (Chatto & Windus, 1958) and E. P. Thomson's *The Making of the English Working Class* (Victor Gollancz, 1963) are conventionally taken to mark the beginning of a new inclusive kind of cultural study which challenged the exclusive definitions which stretched from Matthew Arnold to F. R. Leavis and, with a different inflection, T. S. Eliot. Hoggart's book was probably the most popular of the three, and, as a kind of autobiography of a vanishing 'authentic' working class, it was also the most populist. It is a mark of the impact of the intervention which the new 'culturalists' made that Hoggart, in 1960 a Senior Lecturer in English Literature at the University of Leicester and in 1961 the founding Professor of the Birmingham Centre for Contemporary Cultural Studies, should be invited to join 'the great and the good' of a Royal Commission. What he seemed to bring intellectually to the Committee were all the contradictions implicit in the term 'Left Leavisism': a liberal recognition of the inclusiveness of culture which Leavis would have abhorred, coupled with a passionate desire to cultivate and preserve the 'life-enhancing' in culture and to cast out the tawdry—which Leavis would have approved. A phrase like 'the best, because it is the best; the worst, so that we shall know it for what it is' could have come directly from Leavis, even if the content of the two categories would have been rather different. Curiously, then, perhaps through the direct persuasion of Hoggart or perhaps because it was part of the climate of post-1956 culture, the Pilkington Committee Report came to represent an institutionalization of 'Left-Liberal Leavisism': Left in its extension of culture beyond the educated elite; Liberal in its recognition that entertainment could be excellent; but Leavisite in its hierarchy of values which preferred the challenging to the comfortable; and an awkward mixture of the three in its insistence that culture, even industrial culture, was serious. The Pilkington

Committee Report bears out Perry Anderson's placing of Leavis, and the values which are associated with him, at the centre of British culture in the period leading up to 1968.[31]

The Pilkington Committee Report, then, is crucially significant for the television drama which emerged in the mid-1960s in two respects. At the most material level, it allocated the third channel to the BBC, creating an expansion in public service broadcasting which led to a period of fairly intense recruitment. This recruitment happened at every level. Stuart Hood, a Marxist who had fought with the partisans in the north of Italy and who wrote some of the first published translations of Gramsci into English, was appointed Head of Programmes for BBC2. In television drama, Sydney Newman was poached from ITV. James McTaggart, one of the most innovative producer/directors in television, was brought south from BBC Scotland in Glasgow where he had begun to develop a new grammar of television drama with a production of Jack Gerson's *Three-Ringed Circus* (a production which joins the long litany of missing tapes). But perhaps most crucially, the BBC recruited a whole generation of young directors, writers, and script editors to staff the new service: a generation, new to television, formed in the culture of post-1956, who did not know what you could and, more importantly, could not do in television drama.

I have already suggested the significance of the fact that this new generation was recruited, as BBC recruits almost invariably were, from Oxford and Cambridge: scholarship boys, exposed to a post-1956 culture, who had been uprooted from their class and educated alongside the elite. In this they were significantly different from the slightly older generation of Oxbridge graduates who had formed the New Wave in cinema: that generation had come through the same elite educational route, but their own origins were already in the more traditionally privileged classes. The films which they made were made from outside the class which they represented: the working class had the romance of the Other. The new television drama, however, rooted itself in a particular experience of class from the inside, and it is notable how many of the dramas took as their theme the dislocations of class mobility: David Mercer's *Where the Difference Begins* (1961) and Potter's Nigel Barton plays (*Stand Up, Nigel Barton* and *Vote, Vote, Vote for Nigel Barton*—both 1965), are the most obvious examples, but it runs all the way to the first episodes of *Coronation Street* in 1961. It was a generational identity which seemed new to television, drawing on the culture of commitment and experiencing at first hand the contradictions of class. It is of course extremely

31 Perry Anderson, 'Components of the national culture', *New Left Review*, no. 50 (1968), 3–57.

dangerous to generalize, and there is a great deal of nostalgia for the revolutions which were planned in the BBC canteen: Don Taylor's sneering contempt for Sydney Newman should serve as a guard against idealizing a whole generation. But even allowing for mythology, it seems inevitable that this process of rapid recruitment from a highly educated generation which had grown up in a period when political engagement was almost a life style would have some kind of transformative effect within a national institution such as the BBC.

But if the material effect of the Pilkington recommendations was to create a space for these new recruits, the discursive form of the report was almost equally important in determining how the space might be shaped. In its insistence that television become serious and shun trivialization, Pilkington gave a licence to controversy. In giving broadcasters the double responsibility of caring about public tastes and attitudes 'as they now are' and of recognizing 'their capacity to change and develop', Pilkington seemed to be an invitation to test values, even if that involved crossing boundaries. The framework was established in which the contradiction between the desire of management to draw lines in the sand and the excitement of the young 'creative' recruits in crossing them seemed to be weighted in favour of transgression. Just as the later injunction on Channel 4 to be innovative came to function as a remit for experiment, so the moral discourse of Pilkington seemed to offer—albeit unintentionally—a remit to push boundaries to the breaking point.

In an introductory *Radio Times* article to the second series of the Wednesday Play in 1965 (the series which included *Up the Junction, Stand Up, Nigel Barton*, and *Vote, Vote, Vote for Nigel Barton*), Tony Garnett, then a young script editor, wrote:

> The series as a whole will have a personality of its own, and all the plays do have some things in common. Whether we are in the year 1865 or 1970, in a mining village or an Oxford College, with an aristocrat or an astronaut, we shall try to face things as they really are. We are not in the wish-fulfilment business. We will try to show the real hopes and conflicts of some ordinary—and extraordinary—people, honestly and directly.
>
> To tell our stories, we shall have to break a lot of old rules about what is permissible in television drama; and although we shall not set out to offend people, we may be provocative—but out of a compassion that comes from a concern for human beings. We invite you to join us tonight and hope you will be with us every Wednesday. (*RT*, 7 October 1965)

Up the Junction, with its open acknowledgement of back street abortion, may have offended many people and may initially have been denied its routine second screening. It was, nevertheless, transmitted and the producers and creative team eventually won their case for a second screening despite the nervousness of management. The 'great and the good' of the Pilkington Report may not have intended to write a radical charter, but they certainly made it easier for radicals to win some of the arguments. It is this charter, with all the contradictions of its theological language and its liberal aspirations, occurring within a particular cultural conjuncture and at a particular point in institutional history, which opens out the frame of possibility and the conditions of existence of a kind of Golden Age.

My argument, then, is that if the notion of a Golden Age of television drama is to resonate with something real which happened in the period after, say, 1964, it cannot be left simply to the coincidence of a few creative individuals and a liberal regime. Like all Golden Ages, it is rooted in the transformations and transitions of the culture. It acquired its enabling discourse in the Pilkington Report; it took its keynote from political sensibilities and generational impulses which had redefined British, European, and North American culture since the mid-1950s; and its aesthetics resonated with movements in the literature, theatre, and cinema of postwar Europe. This is not to deny the significance of individual creativity or a liberal regime, but it is to deny the Golden Age its coincidental nature. If it happened, it happened in a large context with all its complexities and contradictions. It is this large context which makes it reductive to think of television drama purely within the narrower context of television studies. From the 1960s, television drama became for a time a central component of British culture.

4
The Rush of the Real: An Aesthetic of Immediacy

WHEN Jean-Luc Godard announces the imminent death of cinema, he clearly cannot mean that films will cease to be made, or that multiplexes will be turned into parking lots, or even that audiences will abandon the cinema for some new distraction.[1] Rather, like Barthes when he somewhat more enthusiastically announces the death of the author,[2] Godard is signalling a shift in the system of privileges and values within the culture of modernity; a culture which, for much of the century, gave to cinema a central position both in mass entertainment and in modernism. The cinema which is dying is an ideal cinema which may only exist in the imaginations of cinephiles and cineastes. It is a *cinéma d'auteurs*, a cinema of masterpieces and monuments and *œuvres* which, in their particularity, stood out against the general, providing points of orientation by which the surrounding culture could be mapped and against which its shifting configurations of meaning and value could be measured. In his various accounts of the death of cinema—or in his account of its various deaths: the abandonment of silence, the distraction of entertainment, the failure to face up to the Holocaust—Godard reserves a very special place for television, and more generally for the absorption of cinema into *le paysage audiovisuel* (or, more generally, *l'audiovisuel*),[3] the spreading audiovisual culture of the late twentieth century for which television has come to be the emblematic form.

---

1 I am indebted to papers by Michael Witt and Michael Temple at the 1998 Screen Studies Conference in Glasgow for their discussion of the 'death of cinema' discourse in Godard's recent work. In particular I am indebted to Michael Witt's as yet unpublished article, ' "*Qu' était-ce que le cinéma, Jean-Luc Godard?*": An analysis of the cinema(s) at work in and around Godard's *Histoire(s) du cinéma*'. Revised versions of these papers and others appear in the 'Godard dossier', in *Screen*, vol. 40, no. 3 (Autumn 1999), 304–47.

2 Roland Barthes, 'The death of the Author', in Stephen Heath (ed.), *Image-Music-Text* (London: Fontana, 1977), 142–8.

3 *Le paysage audiovisuel* is the term which Godard uses in *Numéro deux* (1975). The term '*l'audiovisuel*' is the term used in a conversation between Serge Daney and Godard: see 'Godard fait des histoires', in *Libération*, 26 December 1988. Translated as 'Godard makes (hi)stories: interview with Serge Daney' in Raymond Bellour with Mary Lea Bandy (eds.), *Jean-Luc Godard: Son + Image, 1974–1991* (New York: Museum of Modern Art, 1992), 159–68.

As opposed to the ideal and imaginary cinema which Godard memorializes, the audiovisual space is a space of low differentiation or particularity: blockbuster succeeds blockbuster, monumental in its effects or its soundtrack or its box office receipts, but leaving no trace behind it; series follows series and each is consigned to quaint antiquity or consumed by amnesia. *Titanic* (James Cameron, 1997) inhabits the same sphere as *The X-Files* (Chris Carter, 1993–) or the Spice Girls, and each of them is subject to the same impermanence which makes them significant as phenomena without being substantial as works. (The impermanence is such that, in the interval between the time of writing and the time of reading, these references will have become irretrievably and embarrassingly dated.) To paraphrase Barthes, the birth of *l'audiovisuel* must be at the cost of the death of the *cinéma d'auteurs*.

The modernist longings of Godard's lament are echoed in Fredric Jameson's plaintive bemoaning of the lack of monumentality in television and video.[4] What Barthes might see as a liberating loss, a bringing into play of the Reader, Jameson sees as a waning of value, the dissipation of great works into the shifting sands of postmodern culture which deprive criticism and critique of the solid contour lines necessary for cognitive mapping. The monuments of cinema or literature form the foundation of a shared vocabulary of reference and judgement which may be debated or agreed, permitting the Leavisian dialogue by which we come to work out the values of the common culture: 'This is so, is it not?', 'Yes, but . . .'. Without this shared vocabulary, the dialogue slips into endless relativism in which the search for a common frame of reference is always contingent: 'Did you see . . . ?' The defining technologies of the audiovisual sphere— multichannel television and the videorecorder—are technologies which celebrate relativism under the name of freedom of choice. Claiming, in a parody of Barthes, to liberate the Reader from a culture dominated by monuments, these technologies and their economies turn Readers into Consumers: consumers ennobled with the promise of sovereignty. In this audiovisual space, criticism, rather than being the business of analysis—tracing the meaning and value of texts— becomes the business of description—understanding the phenomena by which consumption turns everything into text. Culture and politics begin to drift apart, lacking the points around which solidarities of judgement and experience can be formed. For Godard, as, implicitly, for Jameson, *le paysage audiovisuel* is the terrain on which difference

---

4 Fredric Jameson, 'Reading without interpretation: postmodernism and the video-text' in N. Fabb *et al.*, *The Linguistics of Writing: Arguments between Language and Literature* (Manchester: Manchester University Press, 1987), 199–223. Another version of this essay appears in Jameson, *Postmodernism, or, The Cultural Logic of Late Capitalism* (London: Verso, 1990).

and differentiation begin to dissolve and the particular is subsumed in the general. Under the more familiar guise of postmodernism, the audiovisual is the cultural terrain on which high modernism loses its bearings and stumbles into quandary and ambivalence.

> If the old modernising and monumental forms—the Book of the World, the 'magic mountains' of the architectural modernisms, the central mythic opera cycle of a Bayreuth, the Museum itself as the centre of all the possibilities of painting—if such totalising ensembles are no longer the fundamental organising frames for analysis and interpretation; if, in other words, there are no more masterpieces, no more great books (and if even the concept of good books has become problematical)—if we find ourselves confronted henceforth with 'texts', that is, with the ephemeral, with disposable works that wish to fold back immediately into the accumulating detritus of historical time—then it becomes difficult and even contradictory to organise an analysis and an interpretation around any single one of these fragments in flight.[5]

Telephobia may well be a necessary condition of cinephilia, and Godard's jeremiads may be dismissed as the grumblings of an ageing *gauchiste* who has lost his audience. And yet the ideal cinema which he memorializes belongs to a conception of art which it would be painful to abandon: art as that which goes beyond, which stakes out new territories of meaning, value, and experience, which refuses and subverts and transgresses, and which takes the audience where it has not gone before; a cinema, marked by the difference between this body of work and that body of work, creating around each communities of solidarity or dissent. The audiovisual space which Godard depicts—a space which is just as idealized and imaginary as his cinema—is one which dissolves the sticking points against which difference can be calibrated, and in which the cultural goods—now known as 'product'—are eased into consumption. In Jameson's critique, there is surely something grotesque about a libertarian Marxist memorializing the passing of a monumental culture which was erected, at almost every point in its history, on a system of elite groups, social exclusions and cultural contempts; *and yet* the levelling out of difficult unities, the absorption of hard works into a generalized culture fuelled by consumption, leaves little purchase for a conception of art which both aspires to commonality and makes a material difference. While it is hard, in other words, to conceive of Godard's mythic death of cinema and birth of the audiovisual space, or Jameson's passing of the age of monuments, as anything more than imaginary narratives, removed from the actual experience of

---

5 Jameson, 'Reading without interpretation', 208.

producing or consuming the diversity of cultural goods, *nevertheless* they offer us a metaphoric imagery which reminds us of a relationship between art and culture—'great art' and the possibility of a common culture—which still seems valuable as a counterclaim to 'post-utopian' or 'post-modern' accommodation.

The reason I am beginning this chapter with a detour through these narratives of dissolution is because I think that television has owned up too readily to the modernist case against it, has accepted too quickly its place in the generality of a phenomenological—rather than an aesthetic—audiovisual space, and has accommodated itself too easily to a version of postmodernism which is itself always already too easy. Underlying the arguments in this chapter is a belief that the history of television drama places it at the centre of aesthetic debates which were defining in late British modernism, and that there are plays and serials which came out of that tradition between the 1960s and the 1980s which had precisely that relationship between art and a common culture to which a politically informed modernism might aspire. At the very least, these plays and serials represent works which were not yet absorbed into the undifferentiated text of 'television itself' but stand out from the general flow of television as particularities which mark out difference, defining new possibilities of meaning and taking the audience where it has not been before. It seems important to recognize historically that these differences and particularities were once there in television in order that we can begin to detect critically the places where they are still active, resisting the assumption that 'in-difference' is the natural, essential condition of television and drawing a more careful map of the audiovisual space. This is not to resurrect a new monumental culture, or to suggest that television drama shared the epic ambition of *Ulysses* or the Ring Cycle; but to propose more modest monuments—memorials to a period when art fought for and won a place in the most public of spheres, establishing new communities of engagement in the audiovisual space itself.

My concern here is with the politics of form, and with the ways in which debates about form and politics in television drama connect with wider debates about modern and modernist culture. Some of this debate with respect to television drama has been conducted in quite formalist ways, assigning to form alone the determination of whether or not a work is 'progressive'. Elsewhere the debate has been marked by a discourse which is, at best, disingenuous, forfeiting complexity for accessibility; and, at worst, anti-intellectual, covering tough intellectual issues with a veneer of common sense or professional shorthand. What is at stake in the discussion is not simply one aesthetic style against another, or one set of artistic preferences against another, but the kinds of readings and meanings and subjectivities which forms enable or prevent—enable *and* prevent.

I want to begin from what has become a fairly conventional starting point, Troy Kennedy Martin's 1964 article attacking naturalism
in television drama, 'Nats go home: first statement of a new drama
for television', published in the theatre journal, *Encore*.[6] The title proclaims the polemical thrust of the essay, announces its banner-raising
claims to manifesto status, and issues its invitation to debate (though
if this was the 'first statement' we seem still to be waiting for the
second). The phrase 'Nats go home' in 1964 echoed with the call of
postcolonial struggles for independence, 'Brits go home': Kennedy
Martin and his allies in the BBC Drama Department (Jimmy
McTaggart, John McGrath, Roger Smith, Tony Garnett, Kenith
Trodd) as freedom fighters, shaking off the yoke of a colonizing power
and demanding self-determination. The naturalism which had insinu-
ated itself into television drama as if it belonged there is exposed as
foreign, an unwelcome alien which should instantly be sent back to
where it came from: the theatre. The fact that the article appeared in a
theatre journal which was associated with the theatrical New Wave
('The Voice of Vital Theatre'), rather than, say, in the short-lived
television journal, *Contrast* (1961–6), or in the BBC house weekly,
the *Listener*, suggests partly that Kennedy Martin was taking the fight
to the enemy, but more importantly that the debate which he invited
was not simply a local skirmish within the BBC, but was part of a
wider cultural battle for the definition of television drama and its
place in post-1956 culture.

Troy Kennedy Martin had joined the BBC in 1960, a little ahead of
the post-Pilkington expansion, but he was in many ways representative of that generation. Educated at Trinity College in Dublin, serving
his National Service in Cyprus, he began writing plays for the theatre.
He entered the BBC as a script editor on the basis of his television play,
Incident at Echo Six (1959). Characteristic of his generation, he was
sharply aware of the unexplored potential of television drama both in
popular drama and as an autonomous art form, and his career in the
early 1960s is marked by innovation not simply in his own writing
but in his attempts to push back the boundaries of form. In 1961,
he originated the series *Storyboard*, an attempt to develop the narrative form of television plays: 'To tell a story in visual terms: that, and
simply that, is the aim of *Storyboard*'.[7] In 1962, famously, he collab-
orated with John McGrath, another recent recruit from theatre writing, in the origination of *Z Cars*, the most popular new BBC series
of the early 1960s, an attempt to inject a measure of gritty Northern
realism into the crime series, moving it beyond the cosy benevolence

---

6 Troy Kennedy Martin, 'Nats go home: first statement of a new drama for television',
   Encore, no. 48 (March/April 1964), 21–33.

7 Elwyn Jones, introducing the series in *Radio Times*, 20 July 1961.

of the Ealing inheritance which was portrayed in *Dixon of Dock Green* (1955–76). And in 1964, again in collaboration with John McGrath, he co-wrote the six-part *Diary of a Young Man*, an extract from which is quoted in the 'Nats go home' article to exemplify his argument, and which indeed is one of the most formally adventurous pieces of drama from the period, employing an almost frantic editing which fully demonstrates the energizing possibilities of modernist montage on the small screen.

Like the *Cahiers du cinéma* group of critics-become-filmmakers of the French *nouvelle vague* in the mid-1950s (Jean-Luc Godard, François Truffaut, Eric Rohmer, Jacques Rivette), or like the British *Sequence* group in the late 1940s and early 1950s (Lindsay Anderson, Gavin Lambert, Tony Richardson), Kennedy Martin can be accused of using his article to promote a revolutionary need in television which, miraculously, he and his friends will come along to fill. But to take it any less seriously on those grounds is to miss the point. What seems striking from the hindsight of a much more pragmatic and en-trepreneurial ethos within television is that the underlying insistence of the article is not simply that television drama needs this or that practice, but that television drama needs a greater degree of theoretical elaboration and that that requires a greater degree of theoretical debate. Television drama, says Kennedy Martin, requires

> a working philosophy which contains a new idea of form, new punctuation and new style. Something which can be applied to mass audience viewing. Something which can re-create the direction, the fire, and the ideas which TV used to have. Something which can provide, for the first time, an area of theory, experiment and development which TV drama has never had and which it needs so badly.[8]

The significance of the article at the time of publication can be measured by the fact that it attracted responses from many of the luminaries of 1960s television drama—Sydney Newman (by then Head of BBC Drama), Michael Barry (former Head of BBC Drama), Dennis Potter (still television critic of the *Daily Herald*, but an aspir-ant dramatist), Tony Garnett (an equally aspirant actor about to become script editor), Ken Taylor (writer; later adapter of *Jewel in the Crown*), Philip Mackie (then producer with Granada). While many dissent from Kennedy Martin's prescription and prescriptiveness, there is a general assent to the call for some theoretical engagement with the nature of the beast. Whatever the limits of Kennedy Martin's theorization, it seems important to recall that there was a time when television drama sought to engage on its own terms, as a popular

8 Kennedy Martin, 'Nats go home', 21.

'mass' art, with aesthetic debates about form and the politics of form, and that it did so with the same sense of urgency which had animated new waves in theatre and in cinema. If there was a Golden Age on which we might look back in nostalgia, this was its animating spirit.

The central argument of Troy Kennedy Martin's attack on 'nats' and naturalism can be identified by an extended quotation:

> The common denominator in all 'nat' plays is that they tell a story by means of dialogue. Naturalism deals with people's verbal relationships with each other. When it deals with people's personal relationships with God, or with nature, or with themselves it does so by refraction through some dialogue style. When it deals with any of the abstracts—fear, impotence, hunger, hate, love or hope—it does so indirectly through symbols or again through dialogue with other people—wife, colleague, or even a stranger. Often these relationships become so strong that they overwhelm the original theme. The second common denominator is that naturalism works within a strict form of natural time—studio-time equals drama-time equals Greenwich Mean Time. Fades equal a long lapse of time, dissolves a short time and cuts immediate time. The third common factor is that this makeshift bastard born of the theatre and photographed with film techniques has brought two basic attitudes from these media which can now be seen to be destructive in television.
>
> ONE. Since naturalism evolved from a theatre of dialogue, the director is forced into photographing faces talking and faces reacting. The director faced with a torrent of words can only retreat into the neutrality of the two- and three-shot where the camera, caged from seizing anything of significance, is emasculated and only allowed to gaze around the room following the conversation like an attentive stranger. This enslavement of the visual element is too binding.
>
> TWO. Since naturalism visually evolved from Hollywood film techniques (no matter how far it has developed since then), there is still retained a deep-rooted belief that the close-up of an actor's face somehow acts subjectively on the viewer. We, therefore, get the spectacle of writer, actor and director all combining to somehow involve the viewer emotionally in a character's predicament by close-up writing, acting and shooting. This attempt to evoke subjective emotion similar to the Hollywood cinema of the 40s is on a direct collision course with the objectivity of the camera.
>
> The primary concern of the new drama must be therefore:
>
> • To free the camera from photographing dialogue
> • To free the structure from natural time, and

- To exploit the total and absolute objectivity of the television camera.[9]

Naturalism, of course, had been one of the slippery terms of aesthetic debate since the late nineteenth century, its boundaries with realism or, in certain contexts, with the avant garde, constantly subject to negotiation. What is complicated in the debate opened in television by Kennedy Martin, and pervasive in British aesthetic debate in cinema and theatre since 1956, is that the naturalism which is at stake lacks any clear definition and becomes a generalized term of disapproval. Such a fuzziness seems to dog naturalism, the term constantly slipping between, on the one hand, the French social and materialist naturalism inherited by Zola from the school of Naturalist philosophy of Comte, Proudhon, and Taine for whom human nature was always related to social, environmental, and hereditary factors; and, on the other hand, the theatrical naturalism of a human nature defined by individual psychology and experience associated conventionally with Stanislavski. It was the latter form of naturalism which gained high public profile when Stanislavski's system of actor training became Lee Strasberg's 'Method', and when the actors trained in Strasberg's Actors Studio became the new generation of Hollywood stars in the 1950s. Naturalism, in popular debate, has come to inhabit a generalized and undifferentiated space, sliding easily between one version which has its roots in an essential and subjective human nature and in the interior dramas of human psychology revealed in dialogue, and another which traces the origins of human nature, somewhat objectively, to inheritance and exterior historical social conditions. There are clearly connections between the two, the one providing the conditions of existence of the other—interior and exterior realities, the drama of the individual in society—but the specific contours and social commitments of Naturalism as a philosophical and aesthetic movement are often lost in the generality of disdain for a naturalism which has become simply a sloppy realism.

The particular aesthetic and cultural mix which is associated with the kitchen sink and gritty Northern working-class realism was perceived as a revolution in postwar British culture because it took its characters out of the drawing-rooms and their comfortable communities, out through the French windows, and placed them in a social context which was ordinary, determining, and characteristically hostile to the ideals of an emancipated and self-determining humanity. The social and physical landscape was no longer simply scenery, a background for social intercourse, but became a material force within the drama, setting the limits and pressures on action and psychology. In this sense, the mix did indeed have its roots in the

9 Kennedy Martin, 'Nats go home', 24–5.

avant-gardism which his contemporaries associated with Zola: 'We are looking for the cause of social evil; we study the anatomy of classes and individuals to explain the derangements which are produced in society and in man. . . . No work can be more moralising than ours, then, because it is upon it that law should be based.'[10] For Zola, his method was experimental in the scientific rather than the purely formalist sense: the 'experimental method' consisted in observing the material world closely and then analysing it scientifically by setting in motion an experiment, a narrative situation, to see what would happen, what actions and interactions would ensue and how human characters would develop and change and relate to each other. These experiments with characters in context were more significant for Zola—and more moral—than formal ingenuity. Rather than seeking a writerly experimentalism of form, Zola rooted his naturalism in the social responsibility and the objectivity of the report.

> I have said that the naturalistic novel is simply an inquiry into nature, beings and things. It no longer interests itself in the ingenuity of a well-invented story, developed according to certain rules. Imagination has no longer place, plot matters little to the novelist, who bothers himself with neither development, mystery nor denouement. . . . You start from the point that nature is sufficient, that you must accept it as it is, without modification or pruning; it is grand enough, beautiful enough to supply its own beginning, its middle and its end. . . . The work becomes a report, nothing more.[11]

Despite its good intentions, naturalism's refusal of good form in favour of 'scientific' responsibility and the refusal to manipulate the evidence, has, in both popular and critical discourses, earned it a bad name. Looseness of form and subordination of style have come to distinguish naturalism from achieved realism, and the idea of naturalism as nothing more than a negative—an absence of style, of craft, a form which is 'lapsed into' or 'transcended'—is recurrent in critical discourses about television drama both before and after Troy Kennedy Martin. 'The ingredients were much as ever: the rooms, the squabbles, and so on. Boring naturalism was transcended by two things: spot-on dialogue and humour.'[12] In the 1960s and after, in writing about television drama at every level, naturalism appears simply as bad realism, associated with sordidness, boredom, the kitchen sink— 'the rooms, the squabbles, and so on'—and marked by the absence

---

10 Emile Zola, 'To the young people of France' (1893), in *The Experimental Novel & Other Essays*, trans. Belle M. Sherman (New York: Haskell House, 1964), 57–106.

11 Zola, 'Naturalism on the stage', in *The Experimental Novel & Other Essays*, 123–4.

12 David Pryce-Jones, review in *Listener*, 8 April 1976.

of the saving graces of spot-on dialogue and humour. The dismay of the critics is repeated in the complaints of the audience against depressing stories and inconclusive endings, of which the following 1961 viewer's letter in *Radio Times* is a typical example (an example which also serves to remind us again of the social and domestic place which television drama once occupied):

> Once, the Sunday play meant a gathering of the family round the set. It was a regular occasion and any visitors who dropped in were expected to join the circle. Now, however, everybody seems to find something better to do than watch and listen to the morbid meanderings of neurotics and other unhappy people. The once pleasant family hour is as dead as a Dodo.[13]

The naturalist's preference for description as against plot, for reporting on nature and context as against a strong narrative line, results in dramas which meander and never quite reach a resolution. The articulation of alienating environment and individual psychology is conventionalized as neurosis and morbidity. The popular reaction against the conventions of naturalism in television drama echoes criticism of the form which has a much longer history: anathematized in the novel for its lack of form and in theatre for its lack of drama (Stanislavski regretted what he thought of as the occasional lapses into naturalism of the Moscow Art Theatre), naturalism quite easily becomes a stick with which to beat 'lazy realism' or stodgy writing and direction.

This is indeed the stick with which Kennedy Martin beats the form of television drama which had developed as an inheritance from conventional 'naturalistic' theatre. It is a drama of dialogue, of the psychologizing close-up, and of the flabby economy of natural time. It is a drama of the writer who adapts his or her theatrical imagination to the 'limitations' of the small screen. Interestingly, Kennedy Martin's attack neatly echoes the article, 'Une certaine tendance du cinéma français', with which François Truffaut had launched the *politique des auteurs* in 1953. In this polemic Truffaut denounced the writer-adapters of *la tradition de la qualité* in French cinema (represented by Aurenche and Bost) in favour of the director-artist-*auteur* who created pure cinema rather than adapted literature (Renoir, Tati, Bresson, Cocteau, Gance, Ophuls).[14] Like Truffaut, Kennedy Martin calls for a television drama which is ultimately created not by writers who write scripts for actors to speak, but by directors who integrate sound, lighting, editing and design into images and movement.

---

13 *Radio Times*, 2 February 1961.

14 François Truffaut, 'Une certaine tendance du cinéma français', *Cahiers du cinéma*, no. 31 (January 1954), 15–28.

'All this', he says, 'makes the new drama one hundred per cent a director's medium.' 'But the fact is', he adds,

> directors have been bogged down in their subservience to 'nat' photography and have ceased to have real creative energy. It is to be hoped that the great demands this kind of drama makes will stir some kind of response—and that their basic television thinking, which is reminiscent of Victor Sylvester's fox-trots being danced in the world of the Beatles, will be fragmented into something a little closer to the modern scene.[15]

Embedded within Kennedy Martin's polemic, then, is an implicit appeal for a *télévision d'auteurs*, and the directors he takes explicitly as his standard bearers are both the historic and the contemporary modernists: Eisenstein and Alain Resnais. The tools which the director of the new drama is to use are, somewhat confusingly, narrative and the objectivity of the camera. By narrative, I understand him to mean the narrative economy of editing which allows for the restructuring of time through condensation, ellipsis and juxtaposition. This economy of editing, in Kennedy Martin's account, takes its inspiration from the great directors of Soviet montage: Eisenstein is an explicit point of reference in the article. Like Eisenstein, Kennedy Martin imagines a montage which is not simply about joining strips of narrative time together end to end to form a continuity, but which is about juxtaposition and the clash of images and tempo, acting on the viewer in an almost physiological way.

By the objectivity of the camera I understand him to mean the camera's ability to analyse the event from the outside rather than simply to register an experience from the inside. In his insistence on the objectivity of the camera he makes a distinction between the television camera which is objective and the camera of classic realist cinema which 'evokes subjective emotion'. If I understand him correctly, this is an argument which defines the specificity of television drama by its capacity to place the viewer at some distance from the event, a critical distance which Brecht calls 'distanciation'[16] and which Laura Mulvey calls 'passionate detachment'[17]. Distance and objectivity, according to Kennedy Martin, are built into the apparatus, quite different from Hollywood cinema's absorption of the spectator into identification with the character's interior emotions and subjective condition. While it is not clear quite why this should be so (and there must be some suspicion that it is underpinned in Kennedy Martin's discussion by an assumption of technological determinism),

15 Kennedy Martin, 'Nats go home', 32.

16 See John Willett (ed.), *Brecht on Theatre* (London: Eyre Methuen, 1964).

17 Laura Mulvey, 'Visual pleasure and narrative cinema', *Screen*, vol. 16, no. 3 (1975), 18.

there seems no doubt that what Kennedy Martin is ultimately trying to do is to drag the debate about television drama—kicking and screaming if necessary—into the context of debates about modernism and into the possibility of a modernist rather than a 'boring naturalist' aesthetic and artistic practice. The fact that it was instead diverted into debates about some shaggy beast called 'non-naturalism' is one of the great blind spots of television criticism and aesthetics.

We will return to modernism—and the distraction of 'non-naturalism'—later. Here, I want first to pursue the connections between naturalism, realism, and 'immediacy' in the formation of the television drama aesthetic.

In his book, *Still Life in Real Time: Theory after Television*, Richard Dienst makes an argument that the truth claims of television depend less on systems of representation or conventions of portrayal and more on the fact of transmission:

> If these images rush to make a claim on reality, it rests on the fact of transmission—reproduction at a distance—not on the veracity of its representations. Perhaps it would be more accurate to say that the distance becomes part of the representation itself. A capacity of diffusion, its range and efficiency, preceded the development of anything like a televisual syntax or *langue*. Unlike cinema, which from the beginning constructed object-images using nineteenth-century industrial (or even preindustrial) techniques, television began by testing its ability to circulate the most ordinary expressions and stereotypes of a solidly, even proudly, corporate imagination, treated as raw data for the machine.[18]

In film, Dienst argues, 'the image appears in a here-and-now necessarily separate from the then-and-there of its actual production'. Television, on the other hand, in its formative stages before recording and in all subsequent stages which appeal to liveness, 'promises to revoke the Bazinian ontological distinction between the "natural" profilmic event and the inevitable "fall" into some kind of visual language'.[19] This is to give theoretical elaboration to Gerald Cock's early intuition that, on television, people would rather watch the rush hour in Oxford Circus than a Hollywood musical. It is also to suggest that not all moving images have the same relationship to external reality, but that film and television come under different regimes of representation and mediation, language and immediacy. Without suggesting that the sense of immediacy which was so important to

---

18 Richard Dienst, *Still Life in Real Time: Theory after Television* (Durham/London: Duke University Press, 1994), 20.

19 Ibid.

television in its formative stages could be regarded, quite literally—and quite impossibly—as an absence of mediation, it may nevertheless be the case that the fascination which television held out to its viewers was indeed embodied less in the re-presentation of its image or the 'good form' of its mediating language and more in the 'rush of the real', the sense of it happening now—before visual language had a chance to impose order.

The celebration of immediacy brings with it, then, a certain reluctance to submit the image to the mediation of good form, a mediation which might corrupt the innocence of its relationship to the real: 'You start from the point that nature is sufficient . . .'. The technologies of immediacy seem predisposed to the ethics and aesthetics of naturalism.

Historically, too, television's relationship to imagery is distinct from that of cinema—in a way which is almost too neat. As I suggested in the introduction, cinema spends the first thirty years of its existence with vision and no speech, and develops a highly elaborated visual rhetoric which survives the arrival of sound, determines the hierarchies of speech and image, and carries with it a respect for visual style, *mise en scène*, and the director. Broadcasting spends the first thirty years of its existence with speech and no vision, establishing different hierarchies between speech and image, and bringing a respect for the spoken word, the script, and the writer. Clearly, this is history with a very broad brush, but it does seem to hint at ways in which orders of meaning might have been established and internalized around specific hierarchies of word and image. The orthodoxy in early television that television is a 'writer's medium' assumes a hierarchy in which the image fulfils a service role in relation to script rather than functioning as a fully articulated discourse. The debilitating effect of the status given to the writer is the development of an instrumental view of television technology and style in which the writer is invited to use the medium as a neutral relay, to leave the technology to the competence of the experts and just get on with the writing.

> Too many writers at first acquaintance with television tend to become overawed by the mysteries of technique about which so much has been written. The producer should aim to liberate the writer from these entanglements—to encourage him to express his idea as he sees it and only at a later stage to begin to translate or reshape the work in terms of technical resources.[20]

What I am suggesting is that the 'naturalism' which Troy Kennedy Martin attacks influentially at the beginning of the period marked

---

20 Michael Barry (BBC Head of Drama, 1952–61), *Listener*, 7 July 1966.

out as a Golden Age—the 'naturalism' which becomes a constant complaint in television drama, spawning its even more indistinct Other, 'non-naturalism'—is in fact a tag attached to an aesthetic founded on immediacy. The historical importance of Kennedy Martin's polemic is as a marker of the end of innocence, the innocence of the image in all its immediacy and 'presentness' before the 'Fall' into the mediations of representation and '*langue*'. What is ultimately at stake is visual style, narrative structure, and a theoretical concept of the specific languages of television drama: all the accoutrements, in other words, of a *télévision d'auteurs*. The appeal is for a television drama conceived as a creative art, a late—and possibly great—twentieth-century visual art form.

What brings about television's Fall from the innocence of immediacy? Where is the serpent in the garden? It is, of course, film. Not necessarily cinema, which provides the model for Kennedy Martin's modernism, but film itself, the ability to record ending television's promise of the abolition of the ontological distinction between the pure event and 'some kind of visual language'. Already, with the introduction of recording and the possibility of *editing* narrative time rather than *mixing* real time, the aesthetic of immediacy (a.k.a 'nat') is no longer adequate to the possibilities of meaning in television drama. In the mid-1960s Kennedy Martin is writing at precisely the point at which the pressure from the new directors and producers of television drama is for greater access to film as a technology which would give them greater control of time and space within the image, and would get them out of the cramped 'naturalistic' style of the studio.

This, however, is not to say that immediacy—the force of presence and the rush of the real—instantly lost all its appeal and vanished with the dinosaurs of naturalism. Immediacy, or Kennedy Martin's 'naturalism', casts a very long shadow, and its roots in the aesthetics and poetics of television drama have proved to be very resilient. Rather I am suggesting that the interest of the Golden Age of television drama is precisely as a transitional moment in which two aesthetics clash: a moment between the 'pure' television drama of liveness and immediacy and a television drama which had begun the process of becoming film. It is this process which leads television drama on the path of convergence with an international art cinema which has itself become part of *l'audiovisuel*. It is also this clash of aesthetics (and ethics) which gives theoretical and historical importance to the idea of a Golden Age (even if all its plays do not live up to the mythology), and which gives it continuing significance for an understanding of television drama. It is as well to acknowledge also a kind of improper and irrational nostalgia for the moment of the loss of innocence, for the point just before television drama became mature, or entered what Noël Burch in the context of early cinema calls the Institutional Mode of Production,[21] bringing to a (perhaps) premature end the possibilities of a 'pure television' or of a television drama which did not wish it was cinema.

I want now to turn to the area of television drama—'serious drama'—in the 1960s and 1970s which seems to me to throw into sharpest focus some of the issues of form, language, art, and culture which I have been discussing, and which holds in most interesting tension the aesthetics of immediacy and the politics of form. It is not at all clear that Troy Kennedy Martin's call to arms did in fact produce the response from directors which he demanded, and television drama of the 1960s and 1970s continues to be marked and celebrated under the name of writers rather than directors. Much of it perpetuates the 'dullness' of representational innocence. Paradoxically, however, the area which came closest to becoming director's television, a *télévision d'auteurs*, was precisely the area which drew most from the conventions and the politics of Naturalism: the drama documentaries of Ken Loach and Tony Garnett. The drama documentaries with which they were associated in the 1960s and 1970s were indeed 'looking for the cause of social evil', studying 'the anatomy of classes and individuals to explain the derangements which are produced in society and in man'. Though Loach and Garnett might have resisted the notion that they were 'moralizing', they would no doubt have been happy to be producing reports on which laws might be based. In spirit and ambition if not in every aspect of its philosophy or form, Loach and Garnett can be placed in a Naturalist tradition; but—like Zola the novelist as opposed to Zola the theorist—while they may have built on the rush of the real and on the conventions of immediacy on which television's truth claims were founded, they did so in ways which did not, in any simple way, buy into innocence.

In a 1960 *Listener* review of a dramatized documentary series about the police made by the BBC Documentary Department, Hilary Corke articulates, apparently without irony, the political anxiety which was to pursue drama documentary in conservative opinion over the next couple of decades:

Drama or documentary?—the 'Scotland Yard' programmes fall uneasily between. Basically these are documentary, each dealing with some different aspect of the extremely complex activities of Scotland Yard. Unfortunately, it seems to have been felt, quite wrongly, that this would be insufficiently interesting in itself,

21 See Noël Burch, *Correction Please; or, How We Got Into Pictures* (London: Arts Council, undated), and 'Porter, or, ambivalence', *Screen*, vol. 19, no. 4 (1978/9), 91–105.

so little shots of drama are injected and these give the impression, that the police are incompetent or venal or both.[22]

Twenty years later, in 1980, the transmission of *Death of a Princess*, a dramatized documentary about the public execution for adultery of a Saudi Arabian princess, provoked a diplomatic incident which threatened Britain's trading relationship with the Middle East. In a speech to the Anglo-Arab Middle East Association following the incident, the then Foreign Secretary, Lord Carrington, said, 'The new formula of mixing fact with fiction, dramatization masquerading as documentary, can be dangerous and misleading.'

The formula was not, of course, new, and forms of dramatized documentary can be found in television and radio since the 1950s, in cinema since its inception, and in left-wing theatre in Britain and the United States since the 1930s. From Meliès's reconstructions of coronations and assassinations to post-revolutionary Soviet cinema's celebrations of the Revolutions of 1905 and 1917, early cinema dramatized events that it could not witness. In Britain, dramatized documentaries had been used in the various branches of the Documentary Movement, from the wartime propaganda of Humphrey Jennings's *Fires Were Started* (1943), to the dramatized instructional films on, for example, household budgeting, made by Ralph Bond for the Cooperative Society. In American theatre during the Great Depression, the Federal Theatre Project had developed the Living Newspaper which dramatized documentation about urban housing, farmworkers' struggles for unionization, the power industry, and even venereal disease. This was picked up by left-wing theatre groups in Britain, and developed by Joan Littlewood in her Theatre Workshop in the 1950s and 1960s. On radio, a crucial source for television genres, dramatized documentaries were a commonplace, and had been given a left-wing inflection in the 'radio ballads' devised by Charles Parker and Ewan McColl which dramatized (and mythologized) areas of working-class life and history: coal miners, lorry drivers, and the romance of male labour. Far from being new, drama documentary belongs to an important tradition in film, theatre, and broadcasting.

By the time of the Wednesday Play in the 1960s, conservative critics were probably correct when they saw it as an area which had been colonized by the left. The social responsibility of the 'documentary idea' associated with Grierson and Walter Lippman—the extension of democracy through social education in its most accessible form—was always liable to be appropriated by a politically motivated attempt to recover lost histories or to dramatize suppressed documents. As I have suggested in the previous chapter,

22 Hilary Corke, *Listener*, 2 June 1960.

the peculiar conjuncture in public service broadcasting produced by the Pilkington Report and the expansion of BBC2 opened a space in television drama in which social responsibility was particularly available for political appropriation and challenging reinterpretation.

In the beginning, however, television, in its dramatized documentaries of the 1940s, 1950s, and early 1960s, seems to have accepted the form 'in good faith' as part of its social responsibility to inform and educate a democratic citizenry. As early after the postwar resumption of television as May 1947, the form was being used in *I Want to be a Doctor* to dramatize medical training, perhaps to temper postwar idealism with documentary realism: 'At present many young men and women want to be doctors—far more than the medical schools can take. This programme shows what happens to the student who does gain admittance, and attempts to outline the tradition of medical teaching.'[23] In 1952, *Pilgrim Street*, a series of six 'documentary stories' produced by Robert Barr, was written—'with the cooperation of New Scotland Yard'—by Jan Read who had recently written the story for Ealing's *The Blue Lamp* (1950): 'The episodes themselves are fictional, but naturally they embody a great deal of incident from real life.'[24] *Can I Have a Lawyer*, a dramatized documentary on Legal Aid produced by Caryl Doncaster, who, with Robert Barr, maintained a close relationship with the genre throughout the 1950s, came with the following 'health warning' from the writer, Jennifer Wayne:

> One last word: don't expect a glossy picture of complacent well-being, welfare and dove-tailed planning. The impression may well be, sometimes, of an opposite kind: of frustration, inadequacy and helplessness in the face of injustice. I have tried to keep a balanced view and to do without spectacles of either rose or jaundiced tints.[25]

There were dramatized documentaries on bankruptcy, on the town vet, on a regional symphony orchestra, on a doctor struck off the medical list, on an epidemic in a small town, on the immigration service. Interestingly, in the light of later anxieties, these early programmes were more likely to be dismissed for their complicity as worried over for their radical tendencies. The reviewer in the *Listener* found *Pilgrim Street* 'shot through with primal dullness': 'there is the implied benevolence, the arm-patting reassurance that our police are wonderful; this series is stickied all over with it.'[26] Or Derek Hill,

---

23 *Radio Times*, 20 May 1947.

24 Ibid., 4 June 1952. (It is tempting to see *Pilgrim Street* as the link between *The Blue Lamp* and Dixon of Dock Green which began in 1955.)

25 *Radio Times*, 10 September 1954.

26 *Listener*, 26 June 1952.

also writing in the *Listener*, on a dramatized documentary on the immigration service in 1962: 'I don't suppose the series will dare suggest an immigration officer can ever behave unreasonably, can abuse his alarming power, can ever become anything less than a sagacious and trustworthy protector of society.'[27]

These information programmes appeared regularly on BBC until the end of 1962, and then seem to have disappeared as a clearly marked form. After 1962, there are isolated events of considerable importance—Peter Watkins's *Culloden* in 1964, the Ken Loach/James McTaggart *Up the Junction* in 1965, Peter Watkins's suppressed *The War Game* in 1966—before the Ken Loach/Tony Garnett *Cathy Come Home* appeared in the Wednesday Play series at the end of 1966 and established both a genre and, in a particular way, a *television d'auteurs*. It is the line which develops from *Up the Junction* (on which Tony Garnett was script editor) and, in particular, from *Cathy Come Home,* the line associated with the Loach/Garnett label—with the recovery of lost histories, with the exposure of social justice, with the 'causes of social evil'—which informs the debate about 'progressive realism' in television drama. This debate found its focus in a series of articles (including my own) published in *Screen* between 1975 and 1980.[28]

The focus of the debate, in brief, was the allegation made in Colin MacCabe's 1974 article, 'Realism and the cinema: notes on some Brechtian theses',[29] that 'the classic realist text . . . cannot deal with the real in its contradictions and that in the same movement it fixes the subject in a point of view from which everything becomes obvious'.[30] Since contradiction, in the Marxist (or Maoist) view, is the motor which drives history and produces change, to be an agent of change the subject (in particular, the revolutionary subject) must experience itself as being in contradiction, incomplete, out of balance, in order that the next step must be taken to progress towards a new position. The realist text, with its promise of plenitude and the restoration of order, offers the subject a secure equilibrium, a position of superior knowledge which allows it to misrecognize itself as, always already, a full subject removed from the struggle for meaning.

27 Derek Hill, ibid., 6 September 1962.

28 Colin McArthur, *'Days of Hope'*, Screen, vol. 16, no. 4 (1975/6), 139–44; Colin MacCabe, *'Days of Hope*: a response to Colin McArthur', ibid., vol. 17, no. 1 (1976), 98–101; Keith Tribe, 'History and the production of memories', ibid., vol. 18, no. 4 (1977/8), 9–22 ; John Caughie, 'Progressive television and documentary drama', ibid., vol. 21, no. 3 (1980), 9–35. These articles are reproduced as part of a section on 'History, politics and classical narrative' in Tony Bennett et al. (eds.), *Popular Television and Film* (London: Open University/BFI, 1981), 285–352.

29 Colin MacCabe, 'Realism and the cinema: notes on some Brechtian theses', Screen, vol. 15, no. 2 (1974), 7–27.

30 Ibid. 16.

The realist text, therefore, could not be progressive in the full revolutionary sense of the term. Its progressiveness was restricted to the social democratic reformist sphere, which depended on contradictions at the level of subject matter. 'There is', acknowledged MacCabe,

> a level of contradiction into which the classic realist text can enter. This is the contradiction between the dominant discourse of the text and the dominant ideological discourse of the time. Thus a classic realist text in which a strike is represented as a just struggle in which oppressed workers attempt to gain some of their rightful wealth would be in contradiction with certain contemporary ideological discourses and as such might be classified as progressive. It is here that subject matter enters into the argument and where we can find the justification for Marx and Engels' praise of Balzac and Lenin's texts on the revolutionary force of Tolstoy's texts which ushered the Russian peasant onto the stage of history. Within contemporary films one could think of the films of Costa-Gavras or such television documentaries [*sic*] as *Cathy Come Home*. What is, however, impossible for the classic realist text is to offer any perspectives for struggle due to its inability to investigate contradiction. It is thus not surprising that these films tend either to be linked to a social-democratic conception of progress—if we reveal injustices then they will go away—or certain *ouvrieriste* tendencies which tend to see the working class, outside any dialectical movement, as the simple possessors of truth.[31]

Even the protagonists in the ideological struggle might now be embarrassed by the absolutism of such a formulation, shot through as it is with its post-1968 discursive moment. From the perspective of the various 'new pragmatisms', it may appear simply—and quaintly—old-fashioned, and may be dismissed back to the nursery with a pat on the head. If we are to understand debates around the politics of realism, naturalism, and modernism, however, there is something at the core of the argument which goes beyond the moment: the argument between a politics of subject matter and a politics of subjectivity; between a politics which sought to effect change by unveiling 'the cause of social evil' but left the viewer secure in a position of superior knowledge, and a politics which threatened the security of the viewer's subjectivity, placing in jeopardy the stability of the subject itself and seeking to push it into movement. In the end the debate comes down to the competing claims to the high ground of 'progressiveness' of a politics of progressive form and a politics of progressive content.

---

31 MacCabe, 'Realism and the cinema', 16.

- Round 1: Colin MacCabe rejects the possibility of a truly progressive realism because its form is not adequate to the contradictions of the real.
- Round 2: Colin McArthur objects that its position on 'realism/naturalism' has disabled *Screen* from contributing to public debates about television programmes like *Days of Hope* (1975) which have acquired political importance as events. He contests the claim that a programme like *Days of Hope* cannot deal with contradiction, and cites, as example, the scene in which the urbane mine-owner instructs three Durham coal owners on the importance of the British way of winning assent through the processes of non-violent social democracy, while in the background the soldiers who have been brought in to quell any disturbance are engaged in violent bayonet practice. 'I am not sure', says McArthur, 'how such a scene fails to handle contradiction in MacCabe's terms.'[32]
- Round 3: Colin MacCabe responds:

  What McArthur here confuses is the narrative's ability to state a contradiction which it has already resolved, and the narrative's ability to produce a contradiction which remains unresolved and is thus left for the reader to resolve and act out. In other words while McArthur looks simply for contradiction in the text, we must look at how contradiction is produced in the audience. In the example McArthur cites, there is indeed a contradiction between what the mine-owner says and what the picture shows. But this is exactly the classic realist form which privileges the image against the word to reveal that what the mine-owner says is false. In this manner our position of knowledge is guaranteed . . .[33]

Not a knock out, but possibly a win on points.

This is, of course, to schematize as a gladiatorial contest a debate which seems to me to lie at the heart of critical approaches to television, constantly agitating within the question of how exactly television and television drama is to be taken seriously. At the academic level, it marks out the division between modernism and realism, and in both academic and professional discourses, it is the issue which informs the polemics against naturalism in television drama, and defines (or fails to define) the position which goes under the collective name of 'non-naturalism'. The 'nats' who are sent home by Troy Kennedy Martin are those who are content to dramatize content; the directors of the New Drama are those who seek through objective form to dynamize and agitate the subjectivity of the viewer. Or Dennis Potter:

32 McArthur, '*Days of Hope*', 143.

33 MacCabe, '*Days of Hope*: a response to Colin McArthur', 100.

I can now put more succinctly the case for non-naturalism in
television drama this way: Most television ends up offering its
viewers a means of orienting themselves towards the generally
received notions of 'reality'. . . . The best non-naturalist drama,
in its very structures *dis*orientates the viewer smack in the middle
of the orientation process which television perpetually uses.[34]

The animating spirit of the Golden Age, then, went to the heart of
debates in late twentieth-century modernism, and its polemical
gestures replayed many of the battles which marked out the territory
of modernism and its politics throughout the century. What is at
stake is the subjectivity of the viewer, and the capacity of forms of
representation and/or their contents to move that subjectivity on,
and take the viewer where she has not gone before.

If the McArthur/MacCabe debate about 'progressive realism'
and 'political modernism', and other debates about 'naturalism' and
'non-naturalism' reduce the positions to their polarities, it becomes
necessary to fill in the spaces between and restore some complexity
to the polarities. On the one hand, there is indeed a problem, as has
become so blindingly obvious, in a view of subjectivity which sees it
as passive and obedient, existing in a pure textual space outside the
social, waiting for form to throw it into contradiction in order that
it can move. Viewers, as well as being textual subjects, are also social
subjects, individuals with their own social histories and their own
experience of contradiction and injustice and their own utopian
imaginings. It is into these concrete histories and experiences and
imaginings that television programmes intervene rather than into
the abstract space of textuality. The conditions of progressiveness are
highly contingent, and cannot always be determined in advance
by the application of 'correct form'. Madeleine MacMurraugh-
Kavanagh has shown the extent to which the impact of *Up the
Junction* and *Cathy Come Home* may have had as much to do with the
way they were taken up in public and press discourses within a particular historical moment as it had to do with their form.[35] Texts do
their work in contexts.

On the other hand, there is an equally obvious problem in a view
which seeks guarantees of progressiveness in content alone. Being
moved to tears by heart-rending content does not *necessarily* involve
being moved on—the experience of a 'good harrow' may be its own
self-regarding reward. But neither does being moved to tears *necessarily* signify a reactionary and debilitating sentimentality; it may

---

34 Dennis Potter, 'Realism and non-naturalism', 'Programme of the Edinburgh
International Television Festival', 1977, 37.

35 See M. K. MacMurraugh-Kavanagh, ' "Drama" into "news": strategies of intervention
in "The Wednesday Play" ', *Screen*, vol. 38, no. 3 (1997), 247–59.

represent, in the heart of domesticity, the sudden painful glimpse of the experience of injustice in the world outside. At a more complex level, the progressiveness of Naturalism as a historical form has often been associated with its capacity to bring into public discourse elements (the working class, social injustice, homelessness) which had previously been excluded. This has a particular significance for television with its almost unique capacity to extend discourse, and it may be the case that arguments for progressiveness on television have to pay particular attention to this capacity. In an almost embarrassingly banal way, television's progressive function may indeed be to bring the world into the home in ways which sometimes escape the order of the institutional discourse—and sometimes don't. At the same time, within the more conventional and conservative forms of representation (whether they be naturalistic, realistic, or modernistic) the new elements of social discourse may enter the stage of public visibility as if they had always been there, adding to social discourse without transforming it or moving it on. Content which is innocent of form guarantees nothing—but neither does form alone. Rather than seeking guarantees and prescriptions, it seems more useful to look at how texts work and at the complex ways in which texts and contexts define each other.

To make this debate more concrete, I want to look a little more closely at *Days of Hope*, *Cathy Come Home*, and *Up the Junction*, three programmes which are generally held to come from the same stable but which seem to me to appear before us in very different colours.

I have written about *Days of Hope* before but let me restate and re-inflect the argument here.[36] *Days of Hope* was a four-part serial—six hours of television—which sought to narrate the progress of the working class in a series of formative moments between the Great War and the General Strike in 1926. The formative moments include: the pacifist movement during the war of 1914–18; the experience of colonial conflict in Ireland; the confrontations around mine lock-outs of the early 1920s; the formation of the parliamentary Labour Party and its relationship with the Labour Movement; and the culmination in the General Strike in which the Labour Movement, in the terms of the narrative, is 'betrayed' by its representatives in government and the unions. The narrative of class is condensed around the narrative of a family, the Matthews family: rural parents; daughter, Sarah (Pamela Brighton), married to a Christian Socialist, Philip Hargreaves (Nikolas Simmonds); and son, Ben (Paul Copley), whose progress from willing conscript to militant activist marks the learning process of the narrative. The narrative across the four episodes is triangulated around the conflicts between social democracy and

---

36 Caughie, 'Progressive television and documentary drama'.

political idealism represented by Philip and the increasingly militant class identification of Ben, political polarities which are mediated by sister and wife, Sarah. While Sarah herself is an activist, and increasingly sympathetic to Ben's position, her position in the family drama mediates between political debate and life experience. Writing in 1980, I argued that the family drama compromised the politics of the series; in retrospect, I would want to acknowledge that it may also complicate them.

For the sake of my argument, it is worth noting that the serial began life as a film script around the story of the mine-lockout, a script which could not find backers in the British film industry of the mid-1970s, but came to form instead the second episode of the television serial. This in itself says something about the relative centrality of television drama and cinema in British culture before the 1980s. Focused on Ben alone, this is the most narratively centred episode in the series, but the filmic quality—the production values, the lighting, the sound, the composition—is characteristic of the series as a whole, marking it out as a prestige production. Colin MacCabe objects that its 'conception of history . . . places *Days of Hope* firmly within the most typical of the BBC's varieties of artistic production: the costume drama',[37] but, again in retrospect, it may be worth complicating the political stigma which attaches to this. On the one hand, *Days of Hope*, preferring the politics of entryism to the politics of refusal, inserted into a highly conservative genre—the embryonic form of the heritage film—a class discourse which had previously been excluded and a class history which had been invisible, and used the popularity of the genre to secure an audience for political drama. On the other hand, by condensing it into a family drama it may have introduced this new discourse and new history as if it had always been there, yet another narrative of trouble in the family which transforms politics into melodrama. But on yet another hand which prevents this being an either/or problem, the introduction of the conflicts of family loyalties may have produced a view of politics complicated by everyday life experience and its complex attachments which escapes the simple abstractions of political idealism. All of the above now seem to me to be contradictorily true, each qualifying the other but not finally eradicating it in favour of one correct formulation.

At a certain level of form, however, the seduction of the film image still seems to me to be definitive for *Days of Hope*, placing it at a key point in the trajectory which leads from television to the art film. In my 1980 article I distinguished between what I then called the 'documentary look' and the 'dramatic look', and what I would now like to call the documentary gaze and the dramatic look. The slight

37 MacCabe, '*Days of Hope*: a response to Colin McArthur', 100–1.

change is partly based on an experience of misunderstanding in which the 'documentary look' was sometimes confused with the visual appearance of the documentary image rather than the look of the documentary camera, but I also want to emphasize the distinction between the fascination with which the documentary camera appropriates its object and renders it passive and the active look which is exchanged between agents of the drama. The dramatic look, that is to say, is the look which is familiar from theories of cinematic narrative, the rhetoric of the realist film: point of view, field/reverse field, eyeline match. It is the system of looks which orders narrative space, and gives the spectator a place within it in a process of quite literal identification: not only do I empathetically identify with the hero in the sense that I sympathize with him or want to be him, but I literally see the fictional world and the action through his point of view.

By the documentary gaze I mean the look of the camera which observes the social space and the figures within it. Whereas the dramatic look is cut into the narrative space, articulating it and us in the movement of the narrative, the documentary gaze stands outside, exploiting the 'objectivity' of the camera to constitute its object as 'document'. And whereas, in the classic paradox, the dramatic look creates its 'reality effect' by a process of mediation so conventionalized as to become invisible, the documentary gaze depends on systems of mediation (hand-held camera, loss of focus, awkward framing) so visible as to become immediate, apparently unrehearsed, and hence authentic. To paraphrase Bazin, in the age of the recorded image, immediacy can only be achieved in one way: through the mediations of artifice.[38] The documentary gaze is marked by the conventions of spontaneity and the appearance of being unrehearsed, and it is this which produces the 'immediacy effect' which constructs its object as somehow more authentic, more objective, than the characters who are subjects in the drama. The dramatic look inscribes the drama into experience; the documentary gaze claims that it is an experience of the real.

For a drama documentary like *Days of Hope*, then, two looks are in play, and they come to constitute a hierarchy. The rhetoric of the drama operates an exchange of looks between the characters, dramatizing their relationships, activating divisions between them and within them, putting them in doubt, giving them an incompleteness which can only be filled by the learning which they go through in the narrative. The dramatic look is reversible; characters look and are looked at; they are both in the play and in play. The documentary gaze

38 See André Bazin, 'An aesthetic of reality: neorealism', in *What is Cinema?*, vol. 1, trans. Hugh Gray (Berkeley/London: University of California Press, 1972), 26—'But realism in art can only be achieved in one way—through artifice.'

lacks this 'reversibility', in the sense in which Serge Daney uses the term when he identifies Antonioni's 1974 documentary on China, *Chung Kouo*, as the work of a *contrebandier* smuggling out in images the properties of the Chinese people.

> In the scene in *The Passenger* in which the old African chieftain grabs the camera and films Jack Nicholson, one can see quite clearly what is at issue: the sudden possibility of a *reversibility*, of the camera passing without a word from hand to hand to the great confusion of the scene and the actors. This, in China, was simply impossible.[39]

The rhetoric of the documentary, the fixed and fixing look, constitutes its object—the community, the social environment, the working class—as simply there, unproblematic, always already complete, 'extras'. Its objects appear as an unquestioned presence, functioning to locate the dramas of others—the subjects of the drama—but not themselves dramatized. Daney speaks of

> those for whom there exists no reversibility, no chance of becoming themselves '*filmeurs*', no possibility of participating in the image which is made of them, no hold on the image. Mad people, children, primitives, the excluded, filmed without hope (for them) of a reply, filmed 'for their own good' or for the sake of science or scandal: exoticism, philanthropy, horror.[40]

In *Days of Hope* the camera continually confirms the drama on the face of an extra (often a child) who is looking on silently, but the attention is then pulled back to the figures at the centre of the narrative and to their play of looks. This is the conventional order of a drama documentary form or of any naturalism which integrates the documentary gaze and the dramatic look: the subjects of the drama have points of view and reversibility of the look; the objects of the documentary gaze have reaction shots. The class which, in Marxist terms, is meant to be the subject of history appears in television history as the object of a gaze.

The problem is, exactly, one of integration. The two discourses, of documentary and drama, are integrated to produce a self-confirming system of images and looks, a self-authenticating discourse of truth. The problem for *Days of Hope*—and for naturalism of whatever hue—is that this integration can only be achieved by *failing* to dramatize the class which is supposed to be becoming the subject of its

39 Serge Daney, '*La Remise en scène*', in *La Rampe: Cahiers critique, 1970–1982* (Paris: Éditions Gallimard, 1983), 58–9. My translation.

40 Ibid. 59.

own history. To dramatize the working class itself and its contradictions would be to upset the order of hierarchies on which the conventions of realist narrative depend, and to produce a confusing reversibility, which, in quality television drama which is beginning to wish it was film, seems simply impossible.

The alternative model for drama documentary which proposed itself in the *Days of Hope* debate was *The Cheviot, the Stag and the Black, Black Oil* (1974). Directed by John MacKenzie, and scripted from his own stage play (or 'show') by John McGrath, the television adaptation brought together elements of recorded theatre (the performance by McGrath's 7:84 Theatre Company of the original stage version before an audience in the West Highlands), music hall (set pieces and songs), historical reconstruction of the Highland Clearances of the eighteenth and nineteenth centuries, and television documentary footage on the current working condition in the North Sea oil industry. The elements are not integrated to confirm and support each other, but are clearly separated out. *The Cheviot . . .* seemed to exemplify for drama documentary the 'separation of the elements' that Brecht recommends in his notes on his own opera *Mahagonny* when he attacks the integration of the Wagnerian '*Gesamtkunstwerk*':

> When the epic theatre's method begins to penetrate the opera the first result is a radical *separation of the elements*. The great struggle for supremacy between words, music and production—which always brings up the question 'which is the pretext for what?': is the music the pretext for the elements on stage, or are these the pretext for the music?, etc.—can simply be by-passed by radically separating the elements. So long as the expression '*Gesamtkunstwerk*' (or 'integrated work of art') means that the integration is a muddle, so long as the arts are supposed to be 'fused' together, the various elements will all be equally degraded, and each will act as a mere 'feed' to the rest. The process of fusion extends to the spectator, who gets thrown into the melting pot and becomes a passive (suffering) part of the total work of art. Witchcraft of this sort must of course be fought against.[41]

The Cheviot . . . seemed to achieve for television drama the same 'Brechtian' political form which Godard achieved for cinema, and which became in the 1970s the form with which critical theory—and, in particular, *Screen* theory—attacked the 'bourgeois realism' of the classic realist text. It was a form which, precisely, challenged the supposed 'passivity' of the viewer, depriving him of the points

41 Bertolt Brecht, 'The modern theatre in the epic theatre: notes on the opera, *Aufsteig und Fall der Stadt Mahagonny*', in John Willett (ed.), *Brecht on Theatre* (London: Eyre Methuen, 1977), 37–8.

of orientation, the conventions of classic narrative, and the self-confirming integrations which secured his position of superior knowledge. In the Brechtian terminology which became almost formulaic in the 1970s, the viewer could not simply consume meanings which were already integrated, but had to become active as a producer of meaning, working to produce her own understanding of the relationship between the elements of the drama. With the television version of *The Cheviot* . . . it was certainly the case that the risk which the theatrical production always ran of being overwhelmed by its own exuberance was tempered by the 'objectivity' of the documentary. The fairly conventional current affairs documentary account of the current oil industry—complete with interviews on housing shortage and safety regulations—produced a contemporaneity of history in the forms of everyday television which undercuts both the romance of a 'Celtic twilight' and the showmanship of the theatre. The collision of the elements—the montage technique familiar to Kennedy Martin and to the historic avant garde[42]—introduces a modernism to drama documentary which uses the conventional forms of television itself (costume drama, current affairs documentary) to produce a 'show' which was, at the same time, familiar to the audience in its separate elements and de-familiarizing in its montage. More than that, and more than Godard in the cinema, the 'show' remained a 'show', retaining its showmanship in the traditions of Brechtian theatre to produce television drama which was both politically didactic and entertaining. *The Cheviot* . . . , presented as a drama in the Play for Today series, still seems a unique achievement, one which came towards the end of a period when television drama was still exploring new possibilities of form and meaning, new ways of holding together the popular and the political.

Writing in 1980, *The Cheviot, the Stag and the Black, Black Oil* seemed to me unique to the point of isolation, the only model which could be held against the conventions which were becoming increasingly well-established in the drama documentary, giving the genre the status of what Peter Bürger calls 'expected shock'.[43] In contrast to the narrative and realist integration of *Days of Hope, The Cheviot* . . . seemed to provide an exemplary modernist practice of a drama documentary based on a radical separation of the elements. From a longer historical perspective, however, the experience of revisiting *Up the Junction* and *Cathy Come Home*—and using them as teaching texts in an unfamiliar context[44]—makes much clearer the

---

42 See Peter Bürger, *Theory of the Avant Garde*, trans. Michael Shaw (Minneapolis: Minnesota University Press, 1984).

43 Ibid. 81.

44 I am indebted to my graduate course at the Federal University of Santa Catarina, Brazil, for the realization that to confine *Cathy Come Home* to a British debate about realism was to miss the modernist elements in its construction.

connection between the modernist impulse which informs Troy Kennedy Martin's call for a New Drama and the early drama documentaries. To lump them together with the drama documentaries of the 1970s in a homogeneous genre unified under the authorship of 'Loach/Garnett' is to establish a continuity which smoothes out important historical discontinuities, and misses the complicated relationship between narrative forms of naturalism and montage forms of documentary in the early Loach/Garnett drama documentaries of the 1960s. To confine *Up the Junction* and *Cathy Come Home* to a debate about realism is to forget yet again the complex history which links the British documentary tradition to European modernism.

The opening thirty-nine shots of *Up the Junction*, a sequence lasting five minutes, have an Average Shot Length (ASL) of 7.8 seconds. The play opens with a studio close-up of a singer belting out a rather conventional 1960s pop song; it then cuts to a sequence of shots with an ASL of 9.5 seconds showing the industrial landscape of Clapham (railway train, smoke stacks, kids playing on wrecked car). The sequence ends with a shot which begins with a close-up of the sign for the Clapham Junction Railway Station, pans down to a street scene and zooms in on the three young women who form the centre of the drama. On the soundtrack, the pop song is still going on and the scene then cuts back to the dance hall in which the singer is singing. It continues with fragments of conversation (banal and 'typical' in the extreme) between the three 'birds'—Ruby, Sylvie, and Eileen—and the three 'lads'—Terry, Dave, and Ron—who are 'pulling' them. It is interspersed with two- or three-second shots in shaky close-ups and mid-shots of unidentified individuals and groups dancing, drumsticks hitting drums, a revolving glitter ball, and is marked by hand-held camera, spatial ellipses (conversations and looks directed out of frame with no answering reverse field) and temporal ellipses (Dave and Eileen, last seen in conversation, suddenly appear in close-up dancing). We also hear fragments of other people's conversation, presented in monologue form, 'little stories' of everyday life ('And there she was, reclining in a black nightdress . . .'). The scene is noisy and fast, never settling on any of the characters or their conversations for long enough for us to get a hold on them. The conversation does not express the individuality of the characters so much as their typicality, and like the image, it exists in montage fragments. Montage, then, is the dominant mode of the drama, a montage which continually cuts between the 'plot' of the central characters and the 'little stories' of the everyday into which their plot is inserted.

Let me add few more examples. Shortly after the dance hall scene, the couples separate out for their private encounters. There is a two-shot of Eileen and Dave embracing in a derelict building, silhouetted romantically against the evening sky as they kiss, framed in a window without glass with a giant crane at the edge of the image. The shot is held while the following non-diegetic monologue fragments are heard as voice-overs:

MAN'S VOICE: Once I had £800—just done a tobacconist's. Walked into a shop, all casual like. The salesman comes up to me immediately, 'Yes, sir.' 'I'll have that Triumph TR3 over there', I says. Took £725 out of my pocket. 'Sir', he says.
I drove away in that Triumph.

WOMAN'S VOICE: I want to be a nurse. Start my training this year in a hospital for children.

MAN'S VOICE: Got a terrible temper. I never start an argument with her in the kitchen in case she picks up a knife. I ask her to do me a hard-boiled egg and she does it soft.

MAN'S VOICE [*over an inserted still of a glossy magazine car advert with a man's hand holding it on a table*]: See this. Cost four thousand quid. I earn twelve quid a week. [*The shot cuts back to Dave and Eileen.*] Don't go far when you're used to a hundred nicker in yer pocket. I get a real ache inside me when I haven't driven for a long time.

The scene then reverts to Dave and Eileen's diegetic dialogue as they begin to make love in earnest. The married Dave assures Eileen that he does not love his wife because she had been with someone else before they met. She assures him that for her it is the first time. Their dialogue—the voice of the drama—exists at the same level of banal 'typicality' as the inserted monologues of the background voice-overs —the 'voice of the documentary'. The juxtaposition of voices places the dramatic voice of the characters in the context of the document-ary voice-overs of the 'non-characters'. The fact that 'background' and 'foreground' are not integrated, creates a kind of separation of the elements which complicates the conventional hierarchy of discourses.

There is an extended scene in the factory where a group of women talk about the minutiae of their lives and their relationships with men, again telling 'little stories' of married life, unmarried life, and the everyday experience of working-class women. (It is, of course, important that the play was written by a woman—Nell Dunn.) As the scene progresses we discover that the group of women includes the three central women characters, who also tell 'little stories' or react to the stories of the other women. Again, there is no obvious hierarchy between the foreground characters and the background characters, except, interestingly, at the level of acting where the background characters are played by actresses who belong more clearly to the category of 'character actress' rather than dramatic actress, and who *seem* therefore to speak more authentically from experience rather than from the script. What is striking about the scene, which runs for about eight minutes, is that it interrupts the narrative progression which has been established in the preceding scenes: the albeit very loose narrative progression which has established the relationships between the three couples and taken it to the point of romance (or at least sex) which will, a little further down the line, lead to the need for a back-street abortion. The narrative is suspended while women talk about men in a way which does not advance the dramatic narrative, but expands it with a kind of ethnographic narrative, documentary fragments which make the central narrative typical.

The narrative is interrupted even more radically by a six-minute sequence in which a 'tally-man' (an extremely unpleasant salesman who sells goods on credit to people who don't need them and then makes his profit on the interest of the loans) discourses on his life and opinions in a series of to-camera monologues, mock interviews, and dramatized episodes. He gives instructions on how to rip off the customers, expresses his contempt for them—and particularly for the blacks—interspersing a compendium guide to the tricks of his shady trade with oily references to his 'little bits on the side': 'I've had plenty of floozies in my time. I never mention my wife's name to them, though. I wouldn't. I think too much of her.' The scene has the same connection to the central narrative as the montage sequence of Clapham which opens the play: whereas that scene establishes a physical environment, this scene, using the same montage technique, establishes a moral environment. In Zola's terms, it is one of 'the derangements which are produced in society and in man', terrifying in its typicality.

What was taken at the time to be the central event of the drama, Ruby's abortion, is also made typical by the same technique: this particular abortion is contextualized by voice-overs and dramatic episodes recounting the abortion experiences of other unknown women which are played against or cut into a scene of Ruby, Eileen, and the friend who is to arrange the abortion walking in the park. In this scene, however, anticipating a technique much more developed in *Cathy Come Home*, the 'problem of back-street abortion' is addressed authoritatively by a male doctor's voice-over who supports his professional experience with statistical, documentary evidence.

What seems so striking, now, in retrospect, is the extent to which *Up the Junction* seems to be a very precise response, at one and the same time, *both* to Troy Kennedy Martin's polemical call for a rejection of naturalism *and* to Zola's polemical claims on its behalf. Following Kennedy Martin, it does indeed exploit the objectivity of the documentary camera; it breaks up natural time; it replaces a drama of conversation with a drama which is composed of dialogue and monologue fragments; and it initiates a new relationship between script and direction. At the same time, following Zola, it is a report on which law might be based; 'an inquiry into nature, beings and things'; a kind of experiment within an environment; and, perhaps most remarkable of all in retrospect, it 'no longer interests itself in the ingenuity of a well-invented story'. Although, as Madeleine MacMurraugh-Kavanagh has shown,[45] the press at the time seized on back-street abortion as the 'big story', and within the context of the time that clearly formed the core of the drama, watched now it is quite difficult to grasp the narrative centre of the drama. Is it the back-street abortion? Or the death of Terry? Or the relationship between Eileen and Dave which survives his imprisonment for petty theft? Or is it, indeed, the 'little stories' and 'reality fragments' which give these other narratives their social meaning? The 'elements' of the drama do not cohere in a final plenitude but play against each other; the dramatic and the documentary are separated out without the self-confirming integration which later in the development of the form became conventional. The narrative, such as it is, lacks the centred structure and the hierarchies which we have come to expect, and which characterize *Days of Hope*. The abortion, though horrific in its procedures and its risks, does not lead to melodramatic death and Ruby is restored to very rude health. The only death is Terry's in a motorcycle crash, and that seems to have been forgotten in the immediately following scenes, until it is memorialized sentimentally in the final 'funeral' montage. In the end, with the final shots of Ruby, Shirley, and Eileen going up West to do a bit of shopping with 'Sugar and Spice' (the Searchers, 1963) on the soundtrack, everything seems to be alright (a little like the final tracking sequence in Godard's *Tout va bien* [1973]), not because it has achieved the narrative resolution of 'good form' and brought the spectator to full knowledge, but because life goes on in its everyday disorder.

Most striking of all, perhaps, the documentary has nothing to gaze at—except smoke stacks, derelict buildings, and high-rise buildings: the physical landscape. The figures in the landscape speak. They do not simply hang around in the background, confirming that the drama is authentic with their silent reaction shots. They tell their stories, recount their experiences and act out their dramas. While some are heard only in voice-over or appear only as fragments, others appear and re-appear, peopling the narrative without playing a

45 MacMurraugh-Kavanagh, ' "Drama" into "news" '.

narrative role in it, but confirming by the way in which they inhabit the space that this is also their story. It is this absence of a strongly marked hierarchy between the documentary figures and the narrative figures, the documentary gaze and the dramatic look—a kind of reversibility of story-telling between drama and documentary—which greatly confuses the expectations of narrative order, and makes the form so full of possibilities.

A similar analysis could be offered of *Cathy Come Home*: the same montage principle governing the relationship between voice and image, documentary fragments on the soundtrack interrupting the emotional pull of the dramatic narrative. In *Cathy . . .* , however, there is a more journalistic sense of the message, a message given an urgency which seems to require a stronger central narrative and a greater authority for the documentary evidence. The documentary voices are no longer at odds with the image, as they are in the quite radical juxtaposition of the love scene in the derelict building in *Up the Junction*. In *Cathy . . .* the documentary fragments play a more ordered role; there is no danger that they might subvert the central narrative, rather they give Cathy's experience its sociological meaning. But the principle of montage still applies, leaving a gap which only the spectator can fill between the rational administrative approach to a social problem and the emotional devastation which that problem represents at the level of experience: the rationality of the documentary voice and the experience of the drama.

What seems so distinctive about both these drama documentaries when they are compared with the tradition which they found is the use of the voice as a montage element: either the non-diegetic voice of the voice-over 'reality fragments' or the diegetic voice of the 'little stories' which fill out the social space. Through the use of the voice, particularly in *Up the Junction*, typicality is dramatized rather than simply observed, the speakers are the subjects of a parallel discourse rather than the objects of an exterior gaze. While Colin MacCabe is clearly right when he points out that the contradiction which is, exactly, *contained* in the image in *Days of Hope* is a contradiction which has already been resolved, the montage of voice and image in *Up the Junction* puts levels of reality into play, breaking up the coherence and the authority of the image and pulling the narrative off-centre.

It is precisely this montage of sound and image which links *Up the Junction* to the modernist tradition in the British documentary movement, a tradition represented in television by the documentaries of the 1950s and 1960s by Denis Mitchell, and, in cinema, a particular tradition in documentary which stretches back through Free Cinema, Humphrey Jennings, *Night Mail*, to Cavalcanti and the experimentation with sound/image juxtapositions which he brought to the Documentary Movement from his experience of surrealist cinema in France. It also links into the modernist tradition through Eisenstein's writings on sound and image.[46]

In this connection, it may also be worth commenting on the technique of Nell Dunn's script for *Up the Junction*, which seems to depend on an ethnographic ear for fragments of the everyday, collecting her 'reality fragments' and 'little stories' like one of the part-time researchers for Mass Observation—and Mass Observation, too, through Jennings, Madge, and Harrison, had its roots in surrealism. From this perspective, the movement from *Up the Junction* to *Cathy Come Home*, the former written by a playwright whose political commitment is filtered through a surrealist ear for the strangeness of the everyday, the latter by an investigative journalist with a social purpose, replays the movements and tensions in the history of British documentary between poetry and sociology.

In one of his many denunciations of the naturalist novel in favour of the historical realism of Tolstoy, Balzac, and Scott, Lukács compares two horse-race scenes, one from Tolstoy's *Anna Karenina* and one from Zola's *Nana*. I have always found the comparison extremely useful in separating the concepts of realism and naturalism, and I want to quote it at length.

> We shall begin without introduction. There are descriptions of horse races in two famous novels, Zola's *Nana* and Tolstoy's *Anna Karenina*. How do the two writers approach their task?
>
> Zola's description of a horse race is a splendid example of his literary skill. Everything that may be seen at horse races is described precisely, picturesquely, vividly. It is really a small treatise on the contemporary turf. All phases of horse racing, from the saddling of the horses to the 'finish' are described with equal elaboration. The spectators' stands appear in the gorgeous colours of a Paris fashion show during the Second Empire. The world behind the scenes is just as elaborately described. The outcome of the race is entirely unexpected, and Zola not only describes that, but discloses the swindle behind it. But this skilful description remains merely an inset in the novel itself. The racing incident is very loosely joined up with the development of the plot, and could easily be removed. The only connecting link is the fact that one of Nana's many passing admirers is ruined through the exposure of the swindle.
>
> On the other hand, the horse race in *Anna Karenina* is an essential part of the plot. Vronsky's fall is a critical event in Anna's

46 See, for example, Eisenstein, 'Word and image', in *The Film Sense*, trans. Jay Leyda (London: Faber & Faber, 1968), 13–59.

life. Just before the races she had realized that she was pregnant, and, after some painful hesitation, had told Vronsky. The shock caused by Vronsky's fall gave her the impulse for the conclusive talk with her husband. Thus the interrelationships of the principal characters of the novel enter an entirely new phase as a result of the horse race. Here it is not merely part of the scenery, but a series of highly dramatic scenes, and a turning point in the development of the plot.

The entirely different functions of these scenes in the two novels are reflected in the very manner of their presentation. Zola's description is from the point of view of an *observer*. Tolstoy writes from the point of view of a *participant*.[47]

The quotation is taken from an essay whose title, in its original, translates as 'To narrate or to describe', and Lukács's constant complaint against Zola is that social problems 'are described only as facts, without exposing their origin', whereas in Balzac or Tolstoy we 'live' the problems through the experiences of the participants.[48] Whereas, according to Lukács, Balzac, Tolstoy, or Scott lived at a time when they experienced the historical transformation of their societies and condensed it into narration, Flaubert and Zola came after the revolutions of 1848 and lived in conditions of 'fully constituted, fully achieved capitalist society' which they could only describe as 'critical observers'.[49] Lukács is careful to make the point that there can be no such thing as 'pure' narration without description or 'pure' description without narration: the question is one of method and perspective. 'The descriptive method of the naturalistic school', he says, '. . . transforms people into still lifes',[50] whereas the method of realist narration makes them the bearers of historical change.

Lukács's historical and sociological analysis is complex and persuasive, and the comparison which he offers seems to me to be helpful in disentangling the slippery relationship between realism and naturalism. However, while it is historical in its analysis, it is formalist in its prescriptiveness—a crime of which Brecht accused him in another context[51]—chasing the shadow of a correct, 'progressive' form. While holding on to the distinction between naturalism and realism, I want to suggest, a little tentatively, that television in its immediacy has a

47 Georg Lukács, 'To narrate or to describe?' (*Erzählen oder beschreiben*, 1936). Translated as 'Idea and form in literature', in Lukács, *Marxism and Human Liberation* (New York: Delta, 1973), 109–10.

48 Ibid. 112.

49 Ibid. 115.

50 Ibid. 124.

51 Bertolt Brecht, 'Against Georg Lukács', in Ronald Taylor (ed.), *Aesthetics and Politics* (London: NLB, 1977).

technological and historical affinity with the descriptive method, with a metonymic relationship to reality rather than a metaphoric one, the 'objectivity' of its camera disposing it towards the observation of the real rather than the participation in it which the subjective camera gives to cinema. At the most simple level, the three-camera set-up of the 'live' studio drama allows for mixing between a variety of views of the scene but makes it difficult to cut into the middle of it and identify the look of the spectator with the look of the character. Hence the frontal compositions which I noted in *1984*, characters arranged in two-shot on one side of a table because the cameras cannot cut into the conversation in point-of-view shots without themselves being caught in shot. Similarly, the liveness and immediacy of pre-recorded television institutes an aesthetic which, as Dienst suggests above, depends on the 'fact of transmission' rather than on the elaboration of a metaphoric language. Television's formation in a technology 'innocent' of recording gives it the unique and specific possibility of exploiting its illusory capacity for the capturing of reality in 'unmediated' description, the 'rush of the real' in its untidiness, rather than the mediation and ordering of the narrative method.

Clearly, I am not suggesting that television is inevitably naturalistic, technologically determined into an essential immediacy which precludes the refinements of style, narrative, and visual language. Nor am I suggesting that drama documentary and naturalism are the only correct forms of television drama. What I am suggesting, though, is that the specificity of the televisual lies in the *possibility* of the immediate, and an aesthetics of immediacy has an affinity with naturalism as Lukács describes it, rather than with the classic realist narrative for which cinema has a similar affinity. At some level, the desire for the prestige and production values of the art film in television drama is a desire not to be television, or a desire, at least, to conceal the traces of the televisual in television. In general terms, the achievement of the drama documentaries of the 1960s and after is that they built on the specificities of the televisual, on its unique capabilities for the representation of the social real, and introduced a new form to twentieth-century art. They seem to me to have developed an *aesthetics* of immediacy which was grounded in the technological and historical specificity of television, but was articulated as an achieved form rather than a fact of nature, exploiting the illusion of the real for political ends. More specifically, however, the particular achievement of *Up the Junction* and, to a lesser extent, *Cathy Come Home*, and a decade later, *The Cheviot, the Stag, and the Black, Black Oil*, lies in the way they took the 'ground' of naturalism and 'unmediated' description, and crossed it with a montage of reality fragments, transforming it into a kind of modernism. The creative excitement of these particular drama documentaries lies in the transformation of forms and the complex politics of the everyday which they produce, rather than in the stylistic and generic refinements of later 'quality television'.

What I have tried to do in this chapter is to break up the homogeneity of drama documentary, and to suggest that, even within the Loach/Garnett tradition, there were at its inception other possibilities for the form, other directions it might have taken. More generally, I have tried to show that the categories which we have used in professional and academic discourses—naturalism, realism, modernism—are more unstable than we may have thought. In particular, I want to argue that the boundaries between certain forms of naturalism and certain forms of modernism are thinner and more permeable than the polemics have allowed. *Up the Junction* seems to me to sit on that boundary, and to confine it—and *Cathy Come Home*—to a debate about realism is sometimes to miss how strange and surreal that reality is in its construction. If by naturalism we mean the kind of convention-bound, conversation-led, and conservative form which Troy Kennedy Martin inveighs against, the tired naturalism of a theatre which has lost its drive and a television drama which is only derivative, then it was clearly necessary to sweep it aside to make way for the New Drama of the mid-1960s. What I am suggesting, though, is that an important section of that New Drama has its roots in a complex, critical, and dynamic naturalism, owing its characteristics to an aesthetics of immediacy which is unique to television and grafting onto it the aesthetics of montage which is the inheritance of modernism.

From the perspective of cultural history, it is interesting to compare *Up the Junction* with *Saturday Night and Sunday Morning* (1960): both from the early 1960s, both dealing with class, gender, unwanted pregnancy, and back-street abortion, both often lumped together into the catch-all category of 'gritty' British realism. I would argue that *Up the Junction* is a much more inventive work: it stretches the boundaries of representation and form more interestingly, and it deserves at least an equal place in the history of postwar British art and culture. It tells us something, however, about the relative status of cinema and television that whereas *Saturday Night and Sunday Morning* is accepted into the pantheon of British culture, revisited by succeeding generations, *Up the Junction* is locked up in the memory of the over-50s, revisited only on very special occasions and usually by specialists.

To come back full circle: Troy Kennedy Martin's article contains a Catch 22. *Up the Junction* and *Cathy Come Home* initiate the director's television which Troy Kennedy Martin calls for in the New Drama: a *télévision d'auteur*. They reject the boring naturalism which is derived from theatre and develop a form which is specific to television, and which probably only television could do in quite that way. While exploiting the resources of the 'objective' camera in the construction of the image, they maintain a dialectical montage relationship between sound and image, a relationship, which at the level of script, may owe something to an as yet fluid (and possibly equally dialectical) relationship between writer and director. The success (and 'scandal') of the first two drama documentaries in the school of Loach/Garnett give a new status to the director in television drama. But in inventing a *télévision d'auteur*, television drama begins the process which will lead it, passing through *Days of Hope*, David Hare, Mike Leigh, Jon Amiel on the way, out of television and into the cinema; or, more precisely, into Godard's audiovisual space—*le paysage audiovisuel*—where art cinema and quality television converge. The aspirations and desires of television to be filmic begin the process which leads to the death of television—or at least to the death of the televisual in television drama.

5

Art Television: Authorship and Irony

IN an account of classical Hollywood cinema which has itself become classic, David Bordwell, Janet Staiger, and Kristin Thompson open with the following brief definition of the characteristics of the classical:

> the principles which Hollywood claims as its own rely on notions of decorum, proportion, formal harmony, respect for tradition, mimesis, self-effacing craftsmanship, and cool control of the perceiver's response—canons which critics in any medium usually call classical.[1]

Bordwell goes on to describe the components of the Hollywood narrative in terms of 'devices' (the pan, the dissolve, the point-of-view shot, etc.); 'systems' (the logic of time, the logic of space, the logic of narrative causation); and, definitively, 'relations between systems'. The 'classical' cinema is defined by an ordered relationship between the systems which gives priority to narrative causation, and subordinates time and space to its requirements: 'In the Hollywood style the systems do not play equal roles: space and time are almost invariably made vehicles for narrative causality.'[2] What makes it classical is that it is rule-bound and systematic, following a system of conventions and proprieties, a common language shared by film-makers and spectators which makes it both familiar (and therefore legible) and flexible (secure enough to permit variation and difference within it). What makes it 'realist' is that the conventions are so thoroughly conventionalized as to become invisible, seeming to obey a law of nature rather than the techniques of rule-books and manuals. Representation is naturalized through an effortless familiarity and refreshed through acceptable difference. The priority which is given to narrative causation in the classical style implies an economic logic whereby those elements of space and time which are not necessary to narrative causation are cut out; the corollary being that those

1 David Bordwell, Janet Staiger, and Kristin Thompson, *The Classical Hollywood Cinema: Film Style and Mode of Production to 1960* (London: Routledge & Kegan Paul, 1985), 3–4.

2 Ibid. 6.

elements which are not cut out are invested with narrative significance: if a young girl coughs at the beginning of a classical narrative
(*Mildred Pierce* [Curtiz, 1945], say, or *La Bohème* [Puccini, 1896]) we
know that she will die of tuberculosis before the end.

The Hollywood system did not become classical by accident. It was
learned in the 1910s and 1920s as the most effective way of ensuring
continuity across the division of labour in an increasingly mobile
industry, and of streamlining and standardizing the production of
mass art along the industrial lines of a Fordist model. The genius of
the system was to take a model which was designed to ensure that each
product was *exactly* like the other (like cars off a conveyor belt) and
inject into it the unexpectedness of art, achieving a particular balance
of repetition and difference which allowed enough repetition to
guarantee that the experience the audience got was what it had paid to
see (the guy getting the girl, order disrupted only to the extent that
it could be restored) and enough difference to guarantee that you
would get it this time as you had never got it before. The audience
had a 'good experience' based on a play of confirmations and denials
of expectation, the economic balance of the representational system
assuring the economic returns of the industrial system.

In such a model, the individual worker was ultimately at the service
of the system, his or her creative individuality valued as a component
of product differentiation (where that was appropriate), but strongly
discouraged from asserting itself as a value independent of the system
in a way which might endanger the balance. In his list of factors which
might motivate and justify the conventions of the narrative representational system (verisimilitude, genre, intertextuality), David Bordwell
includes artistic motivation: the system allowed Sternberg his artistic
composition, Hitchcock his fancy editing, or Ophuls his crane shots,
but trouble ensued when artistic motivation threatened to get out of
control (Orson Welles, Von Stroheim, or Eisenstein in Hollywood).
Artistic motivation was valued as a flourish within the system, bringing with it the prestige of art in a way which might appeal to what were
thought of as 'specialist audiences', but approval was quickly with-
drawn if the flourish which was meant to decorate the narrative began
to obscure it or to pull it out of equilibrium.

Television drama, at least in its historic single-play forms, is a resol-
utely non-classical system. While this statement may seem relatively
uncontentious, I am not sure that its implications either for criticism
or for the formal determinations of television drama are always fully
absorbed. The logic seems to go like this: television drama belongs to
television; television belongs to popular culture; therefore, television
drama must belong to popular culture. Television drama is then
called to account within debates about both realism and authorship
which have their origins in certain 'classical' precepts associated with

the study of popular culture, precepts in which television drama's participation is complex and specific. In this chapter I want to pursue a rather different line, starting from the somewhat heretical position that television drama is not only not 'classical' but that it is not always 'popular' either; or at least that its relationship to the territory of the popular is almost always a negotiated one. Somewhat tentatively, to signify this negotiated relationship I am proposing the term 'art television'. What I mean by this is an area of television which occupies an analogous position within television to that occupied by the postwar European art cinema (particularly in the period 1946–80), a position which in each instance breaks up the homogeneity of the apparatus—'cinema itself' or 'television itself'. The analogy is not intended to be precise in every detail—'art television' and 'art cinema' each have their own pressures and limits—but there are similarities in their ways of being 'non-classical' and in the values which are assigned to them. I also have a particular interest throughout the book (following from my argument at the end of the previous chapter) in tracing the ways in which the *art television* of the 1960s and 1970s is absorbed into the audiovisual space of the *art cinema* of the 1980s and 1990s: the birth of the British art film may have been at the expense of the death of art television.

The status which is given to the artist is decisive (and not just in film or television) in discriminating between classical and non-classical systems. In very broad terms, the investment of primary value in creative freedom, the 'shock of the new' and unconventionality (in both artistic form and life-style) is characteristic of romantic and non-classical discourses. While classical discourses value the 'wit' of a well-turned convention, the re-articulation of the familiar, or the ability to invest the 'rules' with the appearance of freedom, non-classical discourses celebrate the romantic agonism of the artist-rebel who transgresses rules and conventions. In the non-classical value system the balance swings in favour of the individuality of authorship while in classical systems more weight is attached to the proprieties and niceties of genre. The primacy attached to art as an expression of self, then, is not an absolute; it is a historical rather than a natural criterion. For criticism (again, not just in film theory), the changing place of the author has been central to twentieth-century critical theory, the business of new modes of critical inquiry being, like the business of new philosophical inquiries, to find new ways of approaching meaning and value when the creator who previously anchored meaning—in the world or in the text—is removed from the centre of creation.

It has become a commonplace of television studies that, whereas in classical cinema authorship is invested in the director who turns a screenplay into images and who animates the conventions of genre, in television drama the status of '*auteur*' has historically been accorded —as a matter of routine as much as of critical theory—to the writer who creates *ab nihilo*. It is quite generally accepted that this reflects a hierarchy of script and image, a hierarchy which, in its turn, reflects the privilege given to theatre as the cognate form which brings prestige to television. If the system of classical narrative is founded on the articulation of repetition and the animation of the familiar, the power which the non-classical system yields to the writer, the power to invent the new out of her unique experience—to say it the way she feels it— swings the balance in favour of difference, with repetition confined to a functional role depending on the extent of the writer's desire to reach the popular audience or her willingness to risk unpopularity.

I have tried to show earlier the way in which the Pilkington Report of 1962 gave a licence to writers, script editors, producers, and directors to be controversial, to 'push the boat out' and take audiences where they had not been before. All of this served to enshrine in television drama notions associated with art rather than entertainment or popular culture: more precisely, an art which is provocative and moves us on, but which is *nevertheless* situated within a popular medium for a mass audience. In such a context, the authority of the author is protected by the flag of 'creative freedom' which can be waved at the first signs of political or institutional 'interference'. The institution of television itself, a public service institution within a pluralist liberal democracy, belongs to the belief system which pays tribute to creative freedom, and interference can only be justified for special reasons: national security, or, reluctantly but increasingly, offences against public taste—or, of course, money. The most honoured writers in 'serious' television drama (the most 'serious' writers) are those who invent new forms of expression, bringing cultural prestige to television by preventing it from being routine, by preserving the rough edges of the non-classical, by being 'original' rather than 'conventional'.

At the same time, the writer is clearly not released from all constraints, and many writers will feel that the respect for the artist is more ideological than actual. Institutionally, she is subject to the usual pressures and limits of money, power, and status, and participates in systems of privilege and ranking familiar from cinema: not all writers are great artists; the same distinction might be applied between 'author' and 'jobbing writer' as that between '*auteur*' and mere '*metteur en scène*'—and with the distinction comes a certain power, a freedom of manœuvre which allows the truly creative artist to rewrite the rules.

All of this is the routine disposition of post-romantic 'capitalist culture'. The distinctive constraint which faces the author or writer in television drama, however, is the power which is conferred on the viewer by his or her ease of access to the control button: the ability to switch on or switch off or switch over. It is in this sense that television drama as 'art television' involves a complex negotiation between art and the popular, a negotiation which is always a negotiation with a viewer who can find something else on another channel without even leaving his seat.

I am not then proposing a new theory of television authorship, nor am I particularly hostile to the notion that, with all the qualifications of context and collectivity, some authors, even in television, are indeed creative and imaginative artists whose intentions are more or less realized in works of art. What I am interested in is the ways in which this affects the forms which television drama takes, and the forms of reading and understanding which it encourages and discourages; the ways, that is, in which the author is structured into the complex weave of forms which determine the conditions of possibility of meaning and subjectivity. I am interested, in short, in the kinds of question which Foucault proposes about authorship (though I do not propose to address them all here):

> No longer the tiresome repetitions:
> 'Who is the real author?'
> 'Have we proof of his authenticity and originality?'
> 'What has he revealed of his most profound self in his language?'
> New questions will be heard:
> 'What are the modes of existence of this language?'
> 'What does it come from; how is it circulated; who controls it?'
> 'What placements are determined for possible subjects?'
> 'Who can fulfil these diverse functions of the subject?'
> Behind all these questions we would hear little more than the murmur of indifference: 'What matter who's speaking?'[3]

All of this has implications for the boundaries of form in television drama, and for the ways in which it organizes meanings and possible subjectivities. In a non-classical television drama which is accorded the status of art and which has an investment in the creativity and inventiveness of its authors—whether they be writers, directors, or producers—the unexpected comes to be expected: originality carries a higher premium within the system than conventionality. This has two consequences. On the one hand, art television, like art cinema, is less bounded by generic conventions. It relies less on an iconography

---

3 Michel Foucault, 'What is an author?' [1969], in John Caughie (ed.), *Theories of Authorship* (London: Routledge & Kegan Paul/BFI, 1981), 290. Foucault's last question returns to the question from Samuel Beckett's *Texts for Nothing* which he had used as an epigraph for his essay, 'What matter who's speaking, someone said, what matter who's speaking.'

of meanings which is already in place and which has become meaningful through repetition, and more on the articulation of meanings whose force lies in their difference and originality. Difference and originality are often not properties of the meanings themselves, but of the formal prisms through which they are refracted, a refraction which enables us (or forces us) to see reality *as if* for the first time as we have never seen or experienced it before. This is the familiar territory of 'estrangement' and 'distanciation' elaborated by Brecht,[4] and it is important to recall that for Brecht (as for the Russian Formalists who influenced him) estrangement is not the exclusive property of modernist or formalist experiment but is central to the basic functioning of art. It is what art is for: a 'realism' which is not fundamentally generic in its form, relying on classical rules and hierarchies, but which covers ways of seeing and experiencing the real which are both diverse and dynamic.

On the other hand, to say that the unexpected is expected is to say that it has become conventionalized. One of the key determinations of television is its repetition—week in, week out, same time, same channel, same theme tune to ease the programme into familiarity—a repetition which absorbs difference with astonishing rapidity. After a few episodes, the bizarre is routine in *Twin Peaks*, the blurring of generic conventions is conventional in *Hill Street Blues*, and zip pans, zooms, and unsteady Steadycam are no longer disorienting in *NYPD Blue*. Difference rapidly becomes acceptable, and the provocation of the Wednesday Play becomes a little less provocative. The 'repressive tolerance' of the system does not necessarily imply an institution which seeks to repress (though it sometimes does), but rather a system whose repetition and availability seem constantly to normalize, drawing difference into acceptable limits. The outrage of the avant garde seems out of reach of television. And in any case, the possibility of an outrageous avant garde is always qualified, again, by the fact that the control button is within easy reach of the outraged viewer.

These two contradictory poles seem to me to be the boundaries within which the author works. On the one hand, she is endowed with at least the trappings of creative freedom and is expected to deliver the unexpected. On the other hand, the unexpected is bounded not only by the repetition of the system and the restraint of the institution, but also by the tolerance of the viewer. Since it was probably access to a large, diverse, *and relaxed* audience which got her writing for television in the first place, it does not require a repressive institution to put limits on her creative freedom or her outrageous invention. This is not meant to be a pessimistic scenario in which nothing is possible because it will all end up the same: there is plenty of evidence of

4 See John Willett (ed.), *Brecht on Theatre* (London: Eyre Methuen, 1964).

inventiveness, and some of well-targeted outrage. What it proposes is a model of authorship in television drama which is familiar from most areas of art: an author who makes conscious choices of form and meaning, aware of the limits of the system, the institution, and the language; who is invested with freedom and honoured for creativity, but whose freedom is constantly qualified by calculation: how much or how little difference can the system take in this context and at this time?

The status of the artist/author in non-classical 'art television'—an author who is expected not to be bound by conventional expectations—has a bearing on the nature of realism in art television—a realism which, similarly, shakes loose conventionalized norms and proprieties. Art television allows us to talk about realisms and modernisms in a different way, and suggests some relationships between 'non-classical realisms' and 'non-auteurist authorship'. Academic discourse has frequently been guilty of promoting simplified oppositions which polarize 'realism' and 'modernism'– oppositions which come to form an orthodoxy not because they are adequate to their complex objects but because they are teachable. The critical language of television practitioners, too, has reached for the easy shorthand of 'naturalism' and 'non-naturalism'. This is not to say that the ground which was contested under the name of realism was not of considerable historical and political importance; rather I want to argue that once we move beyond the highly conventionalized order of a classical system, firm category definitions become more difficult to sustain, and quickly reach the point of redundancy and reductionism. It is precisely because it is so unstable that realism has been so enduring, absorbing the brunt of each attack by taking on the shape and hue of its surroundings.

The terrain of realism, in other words, cannot be contained within a single definition, but is continually fought over by contending aesthetics, each informed by its own ethics and its own politics. In his eloquent and ethical arguments for a morality of realism in cinema, André Bazin gives his support to those forms which use their artifice to restore ambiguity to the world, giving back to the image its continuity in time and space through depth of field and the long take.[5] In a manner directly contrary to the classical form of Hollywood narrative, he praises Rossellini for refusing to subjugate the real to the requirements of narrative causality: a stone is just that; it is not a stepping stone to something else.[6] Reality is already meaningful, and

---

5 See André Bazin, 'The evolution of the language of cinema', in *What is Cinema?*, vol. 1 (Berkeley/London: University of California Press, 1971), 23–40 at 35–6.

6 See André Bazin, 'In defence of Rossellini', in *What is Cinema?*, vol. 2 (Berkeley/London: University of California Press, 1972), 93–101; see also 'An aesthetic of reality: neorealism', in *What is Cinema?*, vol. 2, 36.

the artist who describes it as it is with rigorous truth is to be preferred to the story-teller who manipulates it for the sake of a good story. While recognizing cinema as a narrative art, the ethics which underpins his aesthetics is a naturalist one. Unlike the aesthetics of the drama documentary, however, which capitalizes on television's immediacy to build its descriptions of the real, Bazin seeks to minimize the corrosiveness of technical mediation by means of the conventions of illusion.

Lukács, on the other hand, arguing from a materialist and sociological conception of art rather than from the idealist perspective of Bazin, proposes a narrative realism which condenses historical movement in individual dramas.[7] His argument against the descriptiveness of naturalism, like Marx's critique of idealist philosophers, is that it only shows the world as it is and not as it changes or how it might be changed. Literature provides in condensed symbolic forms the narrative of larger historical processes, taking the tumult of history and allowing us to grasp it as it might be experienced by participants in its essential and determining conflicts.

And to broaden the spectrum almost to breaking point, Brecht, engaging directly with Lukács, argues against the formalism which prescribes a realism achieved by purely formal means to be consumed passively by readers, and proposes a realism which presents its spectators with real problems and real contradictions demanding real solutions through an active and critical engagement.

> With the people struggling and changing reality before our eyes, we must not cling to 'tried' rules of narrative, venerable literary models, eternal aesthetic laws. We must not derive realism as such from particular existing works, but we shall use every means, old and new, tried and untried, derived from art and derived from other sources, to render reality to men in a form they can master. We shall take care not to describe one particular, historical form of a novel of a particular epoch as realistic—say that of Balzac or Tolstoy—and thereby erect merely formal, literary criteria for realism. We shall not speak of a realistic manner only when, for example, we can smell, taste and feel everything, when there is 'atmosphere' and when plots are so contrived that they lead to psychological analysis of character. Our concept of realism must be wide and political, sovereign over all conventions.[8]

Following on from the previous chapter, then, I want to suggest that the 'classic realist text' and the reductive polarizations which

---

7 See particularly, Georg Lukács, *The Historical Novel*, trans. Hannah and Stanley Mitchell (London: Merlin Press, 1989).

8 Bertolt Brecht, 'Against Georg Lukács', in Ronald Taylor (ed.), *Aesthetics and Politics* (London: NLB, 1977), 81–2.

have characterized much of the debate about television drama, though they may have made it teachable, have also presented a formalist impasse which seems to follow Troy Kennedy Martin (and before him, Lukács, and after him, Dennis Potter) by locking discussion into perpetual oppositions between 'good form' and 'bad form', in which form is always already constituted as 'realism' or 'modernism', 'naturalism' or 'non-naturalism'. In the discussion of *Up the Junction* I tried to show the ways in which the naturalism of drama documentary was crossed by modernist montage. This seems more characteristic of a non-classical dramatic narrative than the generic realism associated with classical forms. In discussing the complex modalities through which television drama attempts to grasp the real and to make us see it differently, it seems more useful to think of crossings and impulses than of already constituted forms and stable conventions; or of an unstable and shifting equilibrium of repetition and difference, familiarity and the unexpected, modernist aesthetics and realist ethics; or of a spectrum in which the logic of narrative causation exists in different relationships to the logic of space, the logic of time, and, crucially I think, involves new logics of characterization and performance. The question, then, is not of assigning a work to a category, but of exploring the various equilibriums and shifting relationships which characterize it, placing it within a spectrum of possibilities of meaning and subjectivity.

In this respect, it may be useful to consider television drama in relation to what Bakhtin calls 'novelistic discourse'. The work of Bakhtin has been 'taken up' in television writing. Appeals to the 'carnivalesque'—torn out of the historical context in which Bakhtin placed it—have become part of the routine vocabulary of a criticism which attempts to legitimize popular culture in terms of 'resistance'.[9] Much less attention, however, had been paid to Bakhtin's work on genre, and, in particular, to his use of the concept of a 'novelistic discourse' to develop an approach to narrative which is historically resilient precisely because it is responsive to social, cultural, and technological changes within society. The 'chronotope'—the specific organization of time ('*chronos*') and space ('*topos*') within the work or within the genre—is at the centre of Bakhtin's tracings of the changes within genres and the boundaries between them. 'The chronotope', according to Michael Holquist and Katerina Clark, 'both defines genre and generic distinction and establishes the boundaries between the various intrageneric subcategories of the major literary types.'[10]

---

9 See, for example, John Fiske, *Television Culture* (London/New York: Methuen, 1987); particularly Chapter 13, 'Carnival and Style' on *Rock 'n' Wrestling*, music video, and *Miami Vice*.

10 Katerina Clark and Michael Holquist, *Mikhail Bakhtin* (Cambridge, Mass./London: Harvard University Press, 1984), 280.

In his return to classical Greek narrative, for example, Bakhtin distinguishes three spatio-temporal regimes which, he argues, still leave traces in contemporary narrative: romance 'adventure time', the 'adventure time of everyday life', and 'biographical time'. In the ancient romance, the initial event (boy meets girl) and the final event (boy marries girl) are separated by a series of events which have no causal relationship and no natural location, and which, though they impede the relationship between the boy and girl, do not change it. The characters do not grow; the chronotope is 'characterized by a technical, abstract connection between space and time, by the reversibility of moments in temporal sequence, and by this interchange-ability of space.'[11] In the adventure of everyday life, on the other hand, the characters are affected by the events (however fantastic) that befall them, and the progression of change fixes the order of events, giving a materiality to space as the scene of transformation and metamorphosis: 'Space becomes concrete and saturated with a time that is more substantial.'[12] Biographical narrative, the most complex of the three, the most various in the chronotopal forms it takes, and the most influential on the later development of the novel, places character at its centre, organizing space and time around it, variously tracing time as a spiritual or intellectual journey through a symbolic landscape, unfolding character through a series of acts and deeds, or tracing character through the different components of domestic and public life: family life, conduct in war, memorable sayings.

Each of the three basic chronotopes which Bakhtin describes has resonances for later forms of the novelistic, and particularly for the generic forms of popular narrative. More generally, though, his discussion of these chronotopes exemplifies the way in which the shifting organization of space and time can be used to chart change in the novelistic discourse in its various historical forms. Just as Bakhtin, somewhat scandalously, traces the rise of the novel back to the romances and adventure narratives of Hellenistic Greece, so it may be useful, if equally scandalous, to think of film and television narratives as specific twentieth-century extensions of the same novelistic discourse into new media, new technologies, and new forms of transmission and reception. While many of the popular genre narratives of classical cinema may share the characteristics of the adventure narrative in which time and space are substantial insofar as they serve the narrative transformations, the television drama I am discussing seems to me to be associated much more characteristically with a biographical time which places character at its centre and subordinates space and time to its logic.

---

11 M. M. Bakhtin, *The Dialogic Imagination: Four Essays*, ed. Michael Holquist, trans. Emerson and Holquist (Austin: University of Texas Press, 1981), 100.

12 Ibid. 120.

This freeing of time and space from the economic logic of narrative causation seems central to the narrative form of television drama. While historically it has sometimes exposed it to accusations of naturalistic formlessness, the centrality of character demands an organization of time and space which will allow the materiality and complexity of characters to emerge in all their idiosyncrasy. The camera gives sufficient time and space to characters to allow them to reveal their eccentric particularity because while these eccentricities may pull the narrative 'off-centre' they also demonstrate its reality. Its truth claims are based on the particularity of visible detail rather than on the generality and naturalized invisibility of convention. It is this which makes acting so important in understanding how television drama works because if narrative time and space are organized around character the visual elaboration of this 'chronotope' is organized around performance. The respect for theatre cannot *simply* be dismissed as an institutional desire for respectability, nor is the theatricality of space and time confined to the technological restrictions and conditions of possibility of early, live, studio productions. It is a continuing characteristic of television drama that it is cut to the measure of character, but always of character as revealed in performance. The 'chronotope' of performance is designed to give space and time to the material and particular details which will situate the dramatic narrative as a drama of the real rather than simply a narrative fiction.

In the best traditions of public service broadcasting and in the traditions which formed the generations of 1956 and 1968, the canonical line of British television drama seems characteristically to place the real in the social. Characters are not simply interesting as individual psychologies as they might be in a purely or principally psychological realism, but they function, in the Lukácsian sense, as points of condensation for the social and the historical, and what connects them to the social is the space in which they circulate. Space, that is to say, is not simply the space of narrative action but is the contextual space of social history; it is not simply at the service of narrative but is the point of contact to a reality outside the narrative, there in its own right and giving the narrative its social significance—its 'seriousness'. This does not of course mean that all dramas are documentary dramas or Naturalist reports on the state of the nation, but it does imply, in Bakhtin's terms, that the spiritual or intellectual journey of the biographical time takes characters through a space that is social and historical, a space which functions not simply as background but as the material context which gives their journey meaning. It is this space which seems to locate the 'seriousness' of 'serious drama'.

As Bakhtin suggests, biographical narrative is marked by its flexibility, and its chronotope is subject to all kinds of variation. In television drama, space appears in the form of the almost allegorical landscape of Potter's *Pennies from Heaven* or the symbolic landscape of his *The Singing Detective*; or as the historical space of *Days of Hope* which takes historical documentation as its reference; or as the everyday of *Up the Junction* guaranteed as real by its immediacy; or as the highly mediated and coolly ironic space of Trevor Griffiths's *Country*; but in each of these forms, space not only leads in to the demands of the narrative, but also leads out, in mediated or immediate ways, to a social which exists independently of the story and is taken to be real in a way that makes the fiction matter.

This offers a way of approaching television drama within the variable forms of a novelistic discourse centred on character. There is also, however, an organization of space and time which may be more specific to television as an apparatus—may indeed be its specific contribution to the development of the novelistic discourse. This is an organization which depends less on narrative form and more on the disposition of transmission and reception: the space and time of viewing—a specific chronotope which involves an everyday space and an interruptable time. However much I may want to resist the generalities of 'television itself' as an essentialism which seems to block off other ways of thinking about 'serious drama', the space and time in which television itself is viewed seems to exercise a level of determination which is both specific and insistent in all forms of television. Whereas the architecture of cinema and the rituals associated with going to it seem designed to make the feature film precisely into a *feature*, a textual event, the time and space of television always seem to pull its texts back into the everyday: the better the image becomes the less necessary (and more perverse) it becomes to watch with the lights off; the viewing space is also the living room; the time of everyday living is always liable to interrupt the time of viewing. Even when the phone does not ring or when commercials do not break into the flow, the *possibility* of interruption seems significant for the forms of attention we bring to television and the kinds of pleasure we expect. What is determining is not the fact of interruption but the possibility, and the way in which everyday space seems to remind us of viewing as interruptable.

It is important not to exaggerate here, or to essentialize. Some programmes, some channels, and some broadcasting systems are more 'interrupted' than others, and, in some sense, an interruption which is expected ceases to be an interruption and becomes part of the pattern. It is part of the fascination and difficulty of thinking about television itself that it is open to so many different forms of attention, and an over-emphasis on interruption can lose sight of that diversity. Some programme forms are more designed for interruption than others, and commercial breaks in watching a feature film on television are quite different from breaks in watching a chat show. Watching television drama probably comes at the 'feature film' end of the spectrum. It is also worth observing that though television may be specific in the interruptability of its time, it is far from unique. Think, for instance, of popular theatrical melodrama of the nineteenth century and the continual interruption of the narrative line by songs, displays, tableaux, or 'turns'; or of the short serialized narrative forms of the early popular press; or of the form of radio sitcoms of the 1950s and 1960s. Equally, there are traditions of oral narrative and of theatre (Kabuki, Katakali, Mystery Plays, even the comic interludes in Shakespearean tragedy and the architecture of his theatre) for which the organization around interruptable time, everyday space, and a consequently intermittent attention would be quite familiar. And even for the novel, closure at a single, uninterrupted sitting is the exception rather than the rule. Clearly, within popular forms of culture it is the concentrated, condensed, and closed narrative form of the feature film that is out of line, a rupture within a generic tradition of the popular novelistic discourse from which television's specific forms of interruptability are more continuous. And where the chronotope of everyday space and interruptable time becomes determining is in the forms of subjectivity and identification specific to television.

Given the centrality of issues of identification in film theory, questions of subjectivity and identification have been mysteriously lacking in television theory—or, where they appear, they often seem to have been imported lock, stock, and barrel from film theory. Here, I want to draw attention to Beverle Houston's article, 'Viewing television: the metapsychology of endless consumption',[13] which seems to be one of the few serious attempts to theorize television subjectivity. In it Houston attempts to relate the familiar interruptions of television narration to questions of desire and consumption. While her emphasis on consumption is based on an experience of American commercial television rather than of British art television, nevertheless common to both, in varying degrees, is the promise of television as constantly available, an availability which derives from its 'endless flow' and can be accessed at the touch of a button even when the set itself is off. This flow, argues Houston, evokes a different form of subjectivity from that of the specularity of cinema, suggesting instead 'the first flow of nourishment in and from the mother's body'.[14] The flow of nourishment, then, is, for Houston, the formative figure for a psychoanalytic, or 'metapsychological' account of television's promise of full subjectivity, just as the mirror figures for the specular

13 Beverle Houston, 'Viewing television: the metapsychology of endless consumption', *Quarterly Review of Film Studies*, vol. 9, no. 3 (1984), 183–95.

14 Ibid. 184.

subjectivity of cinema. But, just as the intervention of the cut motiv-ates the desire to see and projects the cinematic Imaginary into the Symbolic, so interruption for television marks the impossibility of the promise of endless flow.

The work of the symbolic, of the American television institution, in articulating this technical and imaginary possibility is to break it, interrupt, withdraw by separating the text into saleable parts, breaking up the promise of coherence and wholeness into short sessions, as it were, constantly jerking us out of the dream of coherent signifieds into the world of the endless play of signifiers. The symbolic reproduces this imaginary in discrete, regulated entities—small, discontinuous, easily consumable like the bits of information on a computer screen, like the items in the supermarket, like the small, framed and mirrored segments of the glass-skinned skyscrapers that offer us gleaming reflections of our lives from moment to moment in the high-income, high-tech regions of the American urban environment. TV offers, not access to an imagined coherence of a subject and a signified, but instead an extremely intense miming of the sliding and multiplicity of the signifier.[15]

Here again, there is a danger of essentializing television by normal-izing and universalizing the American experience. I have argued in the first chapter that British public service broadcasting, and art television in particular, offer a differently structured experience, and regulate subjectivity in less playful ways. What I want to retain from Houston's argument, however, is the decisive shift from the metaphor of spatial-ity as defining for the cinematic imaginary—an imaginary sustained by the image and threatened by the cut—to a metaphor of temporality in television's promise of endless flow—an endlessness continually denied by interruption or threatened by interruptibility. The shift from the irreplaceability and loss imposed by the cut to the possibility of resumption always held open by interruption suggests something of the difference of television, and the inappropriateness of a theory of subjectivity which takes the cut as the defining moment of desire. That familiar figure of cinematic theory, the Symbolic Father—*Nom du Père*, figure of the Law, administrator of knowledge and prohibition —seems to command less authority for television theory than the Symbolic Mother—providing, nourishing, invisibly mediating.

There is a distinction, originating in Freud and developed by Lacan, between 'need', 'demand', and 'desire'.[16] Needs can be satisfied

15 Houston, 'Viewing television', 185.

16 See J. Laplanche and J.-B. Pontalis, *The Language of Psycho-Analysis*, trans. Donald Nicholson-Smith (London: The Hogarth Press and The Institute of Psycho-Analysis, 1973), 481–2.

by the adequate object (food); demands, while aimed at an object, are addressed to others (the demand for love disguised as a need for food); but desires have no real objects, cannot be satisfied, and exist only as fantasy (the desire to be reunited with the Mother, the desire for plenitude and unity). Desire has been the definitive figure for the fantasmatic identifications of cinema. It seems to me that for television, interruptability and the possibility of resumption (the old BBC caption when a programme was interrupted by technical breakdown: 'Normal service will be resumed as soon as possible') structure subjectivity and identification quite differently, occupying a different structure of interruptable time and everyday space, with a different relation to fantasy, and motivated much less by desire, loss, and lack. Television's relation to the everyday seems much more determining than its relation to fantasy, and this limits, or at least complicates, the explanatory force of a psychoanalytic discourse whose terms are founded on the metaphor of the Oedipal moment of lack, castration, and desire. For cinema, the motivation which the cut institutes at the level of the movement from frame to frame in continuity editing is foundational for subjectivity, producing an intensity of identification which may be the specific contribution of cinema to novelistic discourse. On the other hand, what television adds to the history of novelistic discourse, its distinctive contribution, is founded on flow and the interruptability of everyday space and time. In many genres of television, as has been observed quite frequently,[17] this has resulted in a segmented narrative form built on the principle of interruption, organizing expectation and attention into segments and a multiplicity of plot lines as a way of compensating for interruptability. Where this is less commonly the case, as in the single play, art television, and 'serious drama', the mark of the everyday seems to lie in forms of attention and subjectivity which do not depend on fantasmatic identification, on losing oneself in identification with the narrative space, but offer instead a relaxed detachment, the possibility of a space of engagement which is also a critical one. 'The spectator is an examiner,' says Benjamin in 'The work of art in the age of mechanical reproduction', 'but an absent-minded one.'[18] Although he was writing about early cinema, he might have been even more to the point if he had been anticipating the age of electronic transmission.

This seems to me to give television drama an affinity with forms of irony. Just as, technologically, documentary drama plays on an affinity with naturalistic forms which depend on the appearance of

17 See John Ellis, *Visible Fictions: Cinema, Television, Video* (2nd edn.; London: Routledge, 1992).

18 Walter Benjamin, 'The work of art in the age of mechanical reproduction', in *Illuminations*, trans. Harry Zohn; edited and with introduction by Hannah Arendt (London: Harper Collins, 1982), 241.

immediacy, so the particular conditions of an art television—an author endowed with creativity and a viewer endowed with relaxed detachment—seem to produce an affinity with irony. Benjamin's 'absent-minded examiner'—also translated as a 'distracted expert'— seems to be echoed (probably quite directly) in Brecht's desire for a spectator who watches with the combination of engagement and detachment familiar to the aficionado of boxing—caught up in the conflict but able to assess the finer points.[19] The time and space of television seem to provide the conditions of existence for such an engagement. The interruptability of time works against the relentlessly goal-oriented classical narratives which Bordwell, Staiger, and Thompson discuss in *The Classical Hollywood Cinema*; the 'everydayness' of space works against the fantasmatic identification with the narrative space which one experiences in the cinema. While neither may produce precisely the 'estrangement effect' which Brecht promoted in the theatre, they seem to me to produce the conditions for the detached engagement of irony. Rather than the abstract figure of the interpolated subject, ideologically seduced in the narrative, which seems to dog film theory, art television seems to imply a viewer conceived to be intelligent, and possibly critical, 'reading' an author conceived to be intentional, and possibly creative.

I want to illustrate this through a discussion of *Dreams of Leaving*, a Play for Today written and directed by David Hare and produced by David Rose for the BBC Regional Drama unit at Pebble Mill, Birmingham. It was transmitted in January 1980, billed as a 'film for television'. Hare is interesting for my argument in a number of ways. His earlier play, *Licking Hitler* (BBC, 1978), was the first occasion in which a writer had been allowed to direct *on film*. David Rose, who had been the original producer of *Z Cars* and was to become the Channel 4 Head of Fiction who initiated Film on Four, allowed a drama, the action of which was confined to a country house and would normally have been shot on tape in the studio, to be shot on film—*and as film*—by a writer who had never directed before. 'The result', according to Peter Ansorge,

> was a film that looked completely different from the normal BBC 'Play for Today'. The majority of the films shot for television during this period did not really question the tradition of neo-realism. Often they looked and felt like documentary, with the minimum use of artificial light and the emphasis on a moving camera tracking through real locations. Hare and his lighting cameraman, the late Ken Morgan, approached *Licking Hitler* in a completely different way. They turned the interior of a real stately

19 See Bertolt Brecht, 'Emphasis on sport', in John Willett (ed.), *Brecht on Theatre*, 6–9.

home into a film studio. Each shot was lit according to the style of 1940s cinema. They high-lighted the contrast between light and shadow; the actor's face was often surrounded by darkness in order to convey an emotional effect. For the first time in a BBC film the camera did not move, apart from one long tracking shot towards the end. As in the stillness of 1940s British cinema, a classical style powerfully dominated the action. The movement away from television and towards cinema had begun.[20]

David Hare is interesting, then, as a limit case, marking the point at which the transformation of art television into art cinema gathers pace. His work after *Dreams of Leaving*, though commissioned by television, is conceived for cinema exhibition. (It is worth noting that the actress who featured in both *Licking Hitler* and *Dreams of Leaving*, Kate Nelligan, also made her future career in film. At the risk of allowing personal judgement to intrude, neither seem to me to have lived up in their work in cinema to the promise or distinctiveness of their television work.) Hare is also interesting from the point of view of authorship: a writer whose credentials came from theatre, but who worked in television as a writer/director, and as a writer/director who *composed*, in collaboration with a lighting cameraman, for film. The films place an emphasis on style and *mise en scène*, rather than script, to produce meaning; Hare functions like an *auteur* who creates meaning with images rather than a *littérateur* who illustrates his script with pictures. *Dreams of Leaving*, photographed this time by Mike Williams, continues and extends the cinematic style of *Licking Hitler*, shooting in a multiplicity of real locations, but it seems to me to offer an even clearer illustration of the workings of an ironic detachment.

The published script of *Dreams of Leaving* gives the following book-jacket description:

> In the early 'seventies a young man comes to London to make his name in journalism and to savour the opportunities, personal, cultural, sexual, the metropolis has to offer. He meets a girl who appears to embody them all, who moves with easy assurance through the worlds of pop, public relations, art galleries, photography and modern dance, with a promiscuity whose reflection in her personal life becomes inescapable. David Hare follows the award-winning *Licking Hitler* with a film which explores with sometimes painful insight the human cost of a modern way of life.[21]

---

20 Peter Ansorge, *From Liverpool to Los Angeles: On Writing for Theatre, Film and Television* (London: Faber & Faber, 1997), 99.

21 David Hare, *Dreams of Leaving* (London: Faber Paperback, 1980).

This rather banal promise of a tale of yuppies *avant la lettre* should be read in conjunction with two comments made by Hare. The first, from a pre-transmission interview with Michael Billington in the *Radio Times*:

> This film is an attempt to put something serious about sex on television. There's a lot of smut on television but hardly anything about the real variety of people's sexuality. I wanted to write something which a mass audience would recognise as a situation in which they'd been. And to deal with the impact of sex on people's lives.

While one may raise a quizzical eyebrow about Hare's sense of the 'mass audience' and what experiences it might recognize, the comment suggests a writer seeking to expand the discourse of television, to take the audience where it has not been before, but nevertheless conscious of a negotiation with both audience and television. The second comment comes from the text of a lecture given at King's College, Cambridge, in March 1978, and reproduced in the published script of *Licking Hitler*: 'For five years I have been writing history plays. I try to show the English their history. I write tribal plays, trying to show how people behaved on this island, off this continental shelf, in this century. How this Empire vanished, how these ideals died.'[22] There is no reason not to assume that *Dreams of Leaving* continues this historical project, even if it is very recent history. The tragedy and disappointment of people's lives—their dreams of leaving—are lifted out of banality and made historical: the reality of people's sexual, emotional, and psychological encounters are made to matter not because they are individual and unique but because they are social and representative.

The narrative of *Dreams of Leaving* is structured around a set of encounters between William (Bill Nighy) and Caroline (Kate Nelligan). There are six major encounters:

1. The newspaper office at night.
2. Begins at the gallery where Caroline works, and moves to William's room for a sexual encounter that does not happen.
3. Begins at a press conference for the rock group to which Caroline is, in some probably drug-related way, attached; progresses through scenes in a hotel corridor, the band's office, and William's room; to end in Andrew's room.
4. A dance centre where Caroline is rehearsing.
5. Caroline's flat.
6. Springfield Psychiatric Hospital to which Caroline has been committed with 'long term damage'.

22 David Hare, *Licking Hitler* (London: Faber Paperback, 1978).

There is also a telephone conversation, a brief meeting in a Chinese restaurant, and a scene in which Caroline watches William in the newspaper office, he only becoming aware of her presence as she disappears out of the door. The emphasis in each encounter is on Caroline's elusiveness, an elusiveness associated with the instability of her identity. He does not know who she is and nor, by extension, do we. Her ultimate confinement with long-term mental damage gives us the security of knowing that she did not know who she was either: 'I was glad she was mad', says William. Caroline is that familiar figure: the unknowable woman who becomes the mad woman in the attic.

The narrative opens with an expository sequence which establishes William's move from country to town, his employment on Fleet Street, and his search for girls. It closes with an epilogue which places William in 'mature' domesticity with a wife and two children—and a regretful but distant memory of Caroline.

Importantly for the historical project, there are a number of scenes from which Caroline is absent and which do nothing to advance the narrative of William's increasingly desperate attempts to 'know' her, but whose purpose is to place that narrative of individual psychologies and sexualities in its precise historical and cultural context: Fleet Street, the 1970s popular music scene, drug culture, a press conference on Britain's entry into the EEC, a meeting with Caroline's mother which serves only to expose the deep racism of the English suburbs after Enoch Powell.

The main encounters within the narrative have a supposed temporal continuity (more or less), but may cover a number of locations which makes that continuity seem less continuous. The narrative is marked by ellipsis, moving from scene to scene, location to location without causal connectives or logical necessity. Interestingly and surprisingly, in Bakhtinian terms its organization of time and space echoes some of the features of the chronotope of the romance adventure time in which the initial event (William meets Caroline) and the final event (Caroline is catatonic and William is happily married) are separated by a series of events which have no causal relationship and no natural location. The chronotope is, as Bakhtin describes it, 'characterized by a technical, abstract connection between space and time, by the reversibility of moments in temporal sequence, and by this interchangeability of space'. While the characters undergo experiences, they do not seem to change: William is almost as naïve and cynical at the end as he was at the beginning, and, more alarmingly, the implication is that Caroline's 'madness' was always already latent in her elusive sexuality and protean identity. The 'real variety of people's sexuality' which Hare set out to write about seems to come back in the narrative form to essentialisms of male and, particularly, female sexuality which are not available to change. Authorial intention and good will are no guarantee of meaning and values.

What holds this disparate narrative together is the commentary provided by William's voice-over, which recounts retrospectively the memory of what happened seven years ago—'So it began, that very strange summer'—and allows him to reflect on it from hindsight. Even his 'present' domesticity is contained within his own explanatory voice-over. Though William's is the privileged discourse through which the viewer comes to understand what is at stake in the story, the voice-over is simultaneously marked by a banality which undermines his status as a point of knowledge: 'I mean, I think a marriage is refreshed by affairs.' In the final lines, however, William is given some kind of qualified redemption: 'Our lives dismay us. We know no comfort. We have dreams of leaving. Everyone I know.' Echoing the title of the play, these lines give it its retrospective significance, reintroducing something of the biographical narrative with its journey through a socially symbolic landscape to a point of recognition. This repeats the strategy of *Licking Hitler* in which Anna (Kate Nelligan), the 'innocent' from the Home Counties exposed to the emotional inarticulacy and violence (and Scottishness) of Archie McLean (Bill Paterson), is given a closing voice-over from hindsight which retrospectively and surprisingly explains the wider significance of the story, and places it in history. What is important for *Dreams of Leaving* is the ambivalence which in the end lets William off the hook of his own cynical innocence, and reveals him also as a silent and complex sufferer, affording him an easy redemption for his sexuality which is not available to the 'mad' Caroline.

William's control of the narrative is qualified by ironic distance. William is not aware that this is a history play. His discourse can make no comment on the significance of the historical and cultural context of which his story is representative. Whatever exemplary historical significance the events may have can only be seen from a hindsight which is not William's. It is available to the spectator through a discourse which is not William's, but is contained in those references to what are assumed to be the 'tribal' experiences and defining political moments of England in the 1970s: trendiness, cynicism, sexual adventurousness; national identity at the point of entry into Europe; and English chauvinism as expressed through 'genteel' racism. This historical discourse takes place, as it were, behind William's back, or over his head: a nod of recognition between author (writer/director) and viewer, an ironic superiority which allows us to know more about what is going on than William does. Although it is apparently William who tells the story, we do not see the story from William's point of view, but from the point of view of a superior knowledge which is able to see the inadequacy of William's understanding. We do not identify with William so much as contemplate him: the relationship of knowledge is not an identification between viewer and fiction but an ironic contemplation shared between viewer and author.

This is reinforced by the same cinematic style which Peter Ansorge describes in *Licking Hitler*. The image is not 'cut to the measure of desire' (Laura Mulvey's phrase again). The spectator is rarely invited to identify with the narrative space through the look of a character (with the notable exception of the first meeting between William and Caroline in the newspaper office which is filmed in tight point-of-view structure). More characteristically, the viewer is invited to contemplate the image as an aesthetic object: Kate Nelligan's 'to-be-looked-at-ness' (Laura Mulvey again) is justified by the careful lighting and composition of the image rather than motivated by the desire of the cinematic voyeur. Paul Willemen makes a similar point in his 'Letter to John', a reply to an article by John Ellis on pornography:

> Whereas images in classic narrative cinema (e.g. Boetticher or Capra) use the frame as a mask, arty compositions . . . emphasize the frame, and, in so doing, also stress that the look of the viewer is co-extensive with that of the camera, that the two looks are one. In that way, they achieve an increase in their 'to-be-looked-at-ness' in terms of an increase in aesthetic effectivity while at the same time retaining the naturalization of the frame as mask for a contiguous and homogeneous diegetic world. Such images, directly analogous to fetishes, stress the presence of an organizing 'I' which uses (directs) the camera's look to circumscribe and organize the field of vision, thus denying autonomy while acknowledging the presence of the viewer's look, making it present and absent at the same time.[23]

Characteristically in *Dreams of Leaving*, the look is less strongly marked as someone's look, stitched into the narrative space, and more strongly marked as an aesthetic and aestheticizing look, composed by someone outside the fiction: Kate Nelligan back-lit in the viewing room or the living room, or posed against paintings by Rothko, Mondrian, or Lichtenstein is there as an aesthetic object offered to a contemplative view more than as a sexual object to be looked at voyeuristically.

What I am suggesting is that, in both style and narrative structure, *Dreams of Leaving* works against a close identification between viewer and character, freeing the viewer from the fictional space and allowing him to *watch* television without being lost in it. If there is an identification it is with the author who frames both the discourse and the image, authorizing the narrative and contemplating it from a position of superior knowledge. It is this form of identification with a

---

23 Paul Willemen, 'Letter to John', *Screen*, vol. 21, no. 2 (1980), 55–6.

discourse which knows the narrative from the outside which seems to me to produce the conditions for detachment and irony.

But having said that, it is important to avoid the pop postmodernist line that if it is ironic, it is unassailable. For the record, *Dreams of Leaving* seems to me to perpetuate a romance of sexuality which leaves all the bits in the usual places, looking refreshed in cinematic style. Detachment and irony are not inevitably critical nor are they a protection against ideology, and irony is as likely to invite complicity or to refresh ideology through wit and whimsy as it is to produce a critical distanciation. Its affinity with irony does not automatically make 'art television' progressive, any more than documentary drama is automatically a 'progressive realism'. In her discussion of parody, Linda Hutcheon borrows a term from E. M. Forster to talk about a ' "bouncing" . . . between complicity and distance'.[24] The irony of 'art television', where it is present, can best be conceived as a complex and variable relationship between complicity and distance, bouncing the viewer between the security of a superior 'knowingness' and the 'difficulty' of critical engagement. The ways in which the relationship works to produce meaning and value is a matter of judgement and analysis.

Irony, then, is a broad category, a sensibility or form of engagement rather than a genre. For Trevor Griffiths it takes the form of 'critical realism'. In an interview with John Tulloch, Griffiths distinguishes his work from that of the 'naturalists':

> I think critical realism accepts that it is a convention, a literary convention, or a filmic convention; and naturalism on the whole doesn't allow its practitioners that degree of self-reflexivity and self-consciousness about what they're doing. . . . They actually believe, I think, that reality . . . is an unproblematical concept, that somehow your job as an artist is to set up a window on the real world, and allow the audience to see the real world through that window that you've introduced into their lives. Now, I suppose that nobody actually practices naturalism quite that way. I mean they'd be crazy if they did. But that passes for theory quite often, when you push people. Whereas I think what I do is construct scenes which are fictions. . . .
> *Performance*, the deployment of performative skills in the realization of meanings and values of the text, is absolutely key to my work. My texts cannot be done by non-actors.[25]

24 Linda Hutcheon, *A Theory of Parody: The Teachings of Twentieth-Century Art Forms* (London: Methuen, 1985), 32.

25 Quoted in John Tulloch, *Television Drama: Agency, Audience and Myth* (London: Routledge, 1990), 161.

Griffiths's work—much more than David Hare's—tends towards the 'classical' end of the spectrum, relying on the re-articulation of familiar conventions, its ironic contract with the viewer depending in different ways on recognition of generic norms. Although he quite correctly distinguishes his work from naturalism, in many ways his plays seem to belong to the class of drama which Troy Kennedy Martin inveighs against in his attack on the 'Nats': they are dialogue based; they rely on script rather than image to make their meanings; they are theatrical rather than cinematic in their form; and they depend for their success on the 'classical' skills of actors performing the parts which are written for them. They are 'well-made plays', and it is no coincidence that one of Griffiths's great triumphs was a new translation of Chekhov's *The Cherry Orchard*, which was performed in both theatre and television. Where Griffiths's realism becomes critical is in the appropriation of conventional forms of theatre and television for political meanings and values. His translation of *The Cherry Orchard* was intended to rescue the most familiar of twentieth-century plays from its accretions of middle-class respectability and, precisely, to defamiliarize it:

> For theatregoers . . . Chekhov's tough, bright-eyed complexity
> was dulced into swallowable sacs of sentimental morality. . . .
> Translation followed translation, *that* idiom became 'our' idiom,
> that class 'our' class, until the play's specific historicity and
> precise sociological imagination had been bleached of all
> meanings beyond those required to convey the necessary
> 'natural' sense that the fine will always be undermined by
> the crude and that the 'human condition' can for all essential
> purposes be equated with 'the plight of the middle classes'.[26]

The act of translation is posed as an act of critical defamiliarization, of making the natural strange. In a similar way, *Absolute Beginners* (1974) opportunistically appropriates the form of a BBC costume drama series, *Fall of Eagles*, about the fall of the European dynasties at the turn of the century to dramatize the intense political debates surrounding the formation of Bolshevism, embedding the difficulties of dialectics in the popularity of the costume drama. *Bill Brand* (1976) was an eleven-part serial for Thames Television about the life, loves, and politics of a new Labour MP, a kind of soap opera of the political and the personal in which stories of Brand's family relationships, his relationship with his lover, his intrigues within the Labour Party, are interspersed with political dilemmas and debates: again a strategic embedding of the political within the popular.

26 Trevor Griffiths, introduction to *The Cherry Orchard* (London: Pluto Press, 1978), p. v. Quoted in Mike Poole and John Wyver, *Power Plays: Trevor Griffiths in Television* (London: BFI Publishing, 1984), 153.

One of the most interesting examples of Griffiths's critical realism and his ironic use of conventional form is *Country*, transmitted as a BBC Play for Today in 1981. Here Griffiths takes that most traditional of English theatrical forms, the country-house melodrama, and uses it to explore the resilience of the land-owning class despite its apparently decisive defeat in the first postwar election in 1946. Beginning on the day of the election and culminating in the realization of the landslide Labour victory, the play is a narrative of dynastic succession, using the occasion of a family reunion to celebrate the golden wedding of Sir Fredric and Lady Carlion (Leo McKern and Wendy Hillier) to choose Sir Fredric's successor as chairman and chief executive of the family brewing firm. The usual family intrigues are there, but the succession is complicated by the fact that the obvious successor has been killed in the war, and of the two remaining direct descendants, one, Philip (James Fox), is effete, decadent, and homosexual, and the other, Virginia (Penelope Wilton), is female, outcast, and a radical socialist, her radicalism formed in the experience of the Spanish Civil War. The comprehensive defeat of the representatives of the ruling class in Parliament, however, focuses minds wonderfully. Philip renounces his decadence and his homosexuality and assumes control, demonstrating his business acumen by introducing a prototype carbonated beer which will keep for ever ('weasel piss' says one eccentric old dodderer) to replace the traditional real ale. Virginia departs, denouncing the family for its cynical self-interest.

> 'One day—soon, I hope—there'll come a banging at your door. It'll be the people. And because they're English, they'll probably give you a third class rail ticket to Dover or Southampton when they ask you to leave. Personally, I would not object if they followed the example of Spanish peasants, and garrotted you in your beds. Because I feel, were there a God, he would want you to suffer—for the suffering you cause.'

The play ends with Philip and his father watching the hop-pickers celebrate the great victory of 'their' Party—Attlee's Labour Party—and 'their' class—the working class. They celebrate around a bonfire on which burns an effigy of the capitalist class. 'Is it a funeral?' asks the aged and confused Sir Fredric. 'I rather think it is, father,' replies Philip. 'But they have not yet noticed that the grave is empty.'

Country, like *Dreams of Leaving*, is a filmed drama, but unlike *Dreams of Leaving* the film style is unobtrusive and self-effacing, the camera placed at the service of the actors and the script. There seems to be a clear division of labour between writer and director, and Richard Eyre's direction is highly effective but not self-regarding. It may be significant that Eyre's reputation was built in the theatre. The final climactic scene of the dinner party at which Philip takes command is a scene in the theatrical sense, absolutely precise and economical in writing, direction, and acting. At its centre is a short speech by Philip which takes its power from the timing and restraint of James Fox's acting:

> 'It may not entirely have slipped your notice, gentlemen, that today—Thursday 26th of July—the people of this country have declared war on us. This whole discussion may already be obsolete. Before the year's out, we may all be living in the West Indies on such capital as we've been able to muster from the expropriation of our resources that the socialists have been elected to effect.
>
> The ship's sinking, gentlemen. That's water round your ankles.'

The actors speak highly literate lines, lines which have been *fashioned* by a writer rather than disguised as the natural exchanges of everyday, immediate discourse. The values of the scene are dramatic rather than cinematic, its dramatic fascination coming from the rituals, gesture, and language associated with the exchange of power. If the scene is theatrical, it is so in a sense which carries no pejorative undertones.

The play (and the term 'play' seems much more comfortable here than with *Dreams of Leaving*) is ironic in a number of ways. Mike Poole and John Wyver identify quite clearly the functioning of ironic distance within the text, and its motivation:

> There were dangers. A lavish production (the budget was £400,000) and the eminent cast could easily swamp the text's critique and offer little more than a celebration. Griffiths wanted to present the precise *texture* of his characters' lives, and to achieve both a sociological accuracy and the sense of a concrete world, inhabited by believable beings. But he also saw the necessity of a critical, ironic distance from them, and this is achieved through the character of Virginia, through certain filmic strategies and through the subtle stylisation of performances. Virginia is introduced taking photos of the Carlion estate, a device which establishes the idea of the families and their tribal rituals being dispassionately watched by the viewer. References to observation occur throughout the text. These are complemented by director Richard Eyre's handling of the cast and of the camera. For his employment of movement, of framings and the placing of characters within environments always contributes to, and never undercuts, the meanings of the script. As Griffiths says, there is 'the sense of real life being lived, real space being occupied and yet a very cool, detached and mobile camera seeing them from another point of view'.[27]

27 Poole and Wyver, *Power Plays*, 163–4.

The tribal rituals are offered up for contemplation from an ironic distance. As well as Virginia's structural place in the narrative as outcast and observer, Philip's elegant cynicism, given edge by James Fox's highly sophisticated and stylized performance, places him in superior detachment from the intrigues, a detachment which turns out, in fact, to be the familiar mask of aristocratic authority. Virginia and Philip very precisely play out the bouncing of complicity and distance: Virginia's passionate hatred of her class is in dialectical tension with the suave and ironic complicity of Philip's charm; the one denounces capitalism, the other demonstrates why it will survive.

Perhaps the most striking ironies, however, are not textual but intertextual. By setting his play in the country house, Griffiths is occupying one of the prime locations in which the little dramas of the English ruling class have been played out not only in theatre but also on television (from *The Whiteoak Chronicles* through *The Forsyte Saga* to *Brideshead Revisited*). More than that, as Poole and Wyver show,[28] *Country* is a fairly close 'translation' of one particular country-house drama, one of the most successful plays of the interwar years when the genre was at its height: Dodie Smith's 1938 West End hit, *Dear Octopus*. Also set during the celebration of a golden wedding, also involving a fashionable son who is required to get married and a daughter 'with a past', and with a number of parallels in characterization, Dodie Smith's play is a light-hearted celebration of the family as an institution, 'the dear octopus from whose tentacles we never quite escape'. As in his work on Chekhov, Griffiths's translation here is designed to expose the real meaning of class which the country-house drama takes as natural. In the ultimate insult, he links the 'charm' of the ruling-class family at play or in its rites of succession to the rituals of sophisticated criminal power associated in yet another popular form with that other Great Family: Cosa Nostra, the Mafia. The family name in *Country*, Carlion, is a sly, but fairly obvious reminder of the Corleone family whose dynastic saga is recounted in the various episodes of *The Godfather*. Beneath the quaint family rituals of the English country house lie the will to power and the survival instincts of the gangster.

Griffiths's consistent ironic strategy, then, is double-edged: he exploits popular form for the stories and conventions which made them popular, and, at the same time, he turns them against themselves to expose the meanings which the conventions have naturalized or concealed. He plays difference off against familiarity, placing political analysis in the gap between the two. Where his irony seems to me to differ fundamentally from David Hare's is in authorial presence. Whereas Hare's authorship is insistent in the *mise en scène* through an

---

28 Poole and Wyver, *Power Plays*, 161–2.

aestheticization of the image which becomes almost self-regarding, and in a complicity between author and viewer which goes over the heads of the characters, Griffiths's authorial voice recedes behind the voices of his actors. Griffiths crafts the lines, but it seems to be the actors who put ideas into play, materializing a complex dialectics in their words and their relationships. Both offer an ironic detachment, and both might be described by the term 'critical realism', but where Hare seems to invite a knowing complicity, Griffiths seems to me to offer more successfully an analytical and critical distance.

The point of this comparison, however, is not to rank Hare and Griffiths on a scale of ironic value, but rather to show the discriminations which need to be made within the category of ironic forms. The kinds of television drama for which I am proposing the notion of an 'art television' are distinguished by the respect which is given to writers (or writer/directors) as creative artists who are imaginative, purposive, and conscious of the intentions which motivate their work. When such a writer is confronted by a viewer whose specific conditions of viewing—everyday space and interruptable time—seem to dispose her to contemplation rather than identification, it seems appropriate that forms will emerge which build on that specificity. Television drama seems to me to occupy a space which is designed for relaxation, and to depend on an image which is scaled to detachment. Relaxed detachment can result as easily in sleep or in the choice to change channels as in critical engagement and this is the negotiation in which the creatively 'free' artist has to engage. By 'irony' I am trying to describe forms of relaxed detachment by which the viewer may be intellectually or emotionally engaged; or better still may be intellectually *and* emotionally engaged. These forms of detachment are by no means to be confused with distanciation, subversion, resistance, or political progressiveness, though some or all of these may be in play. Irony carries no guarantees of value, but it may be the condition in which values are put in play, and in which the viewer exercises her creativity. It is, again, one of the conditions of possibility of meaning and value in television drama. No discussion of distance, irony, and detachment, however, can be complete without some discussion of modernism.

6

Modernism; or, Not 'Non-naturalism'

I can now put more succinctly the case for non-naturalism in television drama this way: Most television ends up offering its viewers a means of orienting themselves towards the generally received notions of 'reality'. The best naturalist or realist drama, of the Loach-Garnett-Allen school for instance, breaks out of this cosy habit by the vigour, clarity, originality and depth of its perceptions of a more comprehensive reality. The best non-naturalist drama, in its very structures disorientates the viewer smack in the middle of the orientation process which television perpetually uses. It disrupts the patterns that are endemic to television, and upsets or exposes the narrative styles of so many of the other allegedly non-fiction programmes. It shows the frame in the picture when most television is busy showing the picture in the frame. I think it is potentially the more valuable of the two approaches.

And it reminds the viewer, even as he lurches with a growl towards the off-button, that he is at least watching a play, A Play, A *Play* . . .

Dennis Potter[1]

One of the more curious characteristics of critical thinking about television drama is the status which has been given to a 'non-term'—'non-naturalism'. While the history of aesthetics is littered with 'neo-'s and 'post-'s which express some re-articulation of the properties of an original (neo-classicism, post-romanticism), I can think of no other term of a similar status which simply expresses a negative, defining something only by what it is not.[2] More problematic still, the 'naturalism' which 'non-naturalism' is not is itself an extremely shaky term, and in television drama particularly its roots lie in polemics

1 Dennis Potter, 'Realism and non-naturalism', in 'Programme of the Edinburgh International Television Festival' (1977), 37.

2 Though 'non-naturalism' is shared with theatre criticism, which also boasts 'non-text-based theatre'.

and generalized dissatisfaction rather than an engagement with the history of forms and culture. Dennis Potter, in the quotation above, slips easily between naturalism and realism, quite happy to collapse together two terms which have had a history of disagreement since the nineteenth century. 'Non-naturalism', then, is a shorthand founded on a shorthand. More than that, since I can think of no context in which anyone—critic or professional—has ever referred to 'naturalism' in television drama as a term of approval, something to be achieved rather than a mark of failure, 'naturalism' is already a negative. 'Non-naturalism' becomes a kind of double negative, cancelling out the negativity of 'naturalism' and turning itself into a positive. Not only a shorthand, then, but a sleight of hand. Television criticism seems to have bought into this system of shorthands, rescuing 'naturalism' from itself in the form of 'progressive realism' or erecting a canon of the 'non-naturalistic' (which, curiously, does not include 'realism') with Dennis Potter at its head. 'Naturalism' is an easy target, that which we do not like, and 'non-naturalism' is the stick to beat it with.

What makes this shorthand even more curious is that there is a readily available term with considerable currency in critical discourse which seems to do the same work as 'non-naturalism', albeit in a more complex and necessarily historical way: the term 'modernism'. Television criticism, however, seems to have avoided this term, instead drawing a map of television with naturalism/realism at one 'serious' pole and postmodernism at the other 'playful' pole, and 'non-naturalism' as the name of the gap between them, a territory without a real name. Modernism, which played such a large part in transforming the ways in which we think about cinema, theatre, or the other twentieth-century arts, seems to be surrounded in television drama by an awkward silence.

This silence may, of course, be less awkward than strategic. Modernism in twentieth-century culture enters public discourse trailing clouds of the elite, the experimental, the difficult. It is associated with a 'high art' which historically has excluded television. For Dennis Potter, a professional writer for television as well as a creative artist, to identify himself with modernism would be not only to identify himself with 'high art' but with a form of 'high art' which threatens to be both difficult and exclusive. Since the attraction of television is precisely its inclusiveness, its ability to attract the popular audience, television dramatists have preferred to appeal to their audience in the soft tones of non-naturalism or the macho terms of anti-intellectualism rather than aligning themselves with the more stringent demands of modernism. At this level, the silence is a matter of public relations and marketing, using unexceptionable generality to dissociate this brand of drama from the negative connotations which might suggest that this week's Wednesday Play was going to be difficult—as opposed to simply controversial. At a more unconscious level, this may be accompanied by a professional disdain for theory which is quite familiar in television, and sometimes in artistic practice more generally, in which artists pour contempt on theoretical labels—and on the theory which gives them meaning—leaving the business of critical categorization to the critics while they get on with the business of creativity. Fair enough. What seems to have happened in television criticism, however, is that the critics themselves have agreed to participate in the same silence around theory, allowing a 'non-term' to persist instead of subjecting it to critical scrutiny. Again, there may be strategic histories to this: what attracted us to television studies was popular culture, and we have developed an instinctive suspicion of the association of television drama criticism with elite culture. Better to keep one's critical feet firmly planted in the security of the popular. There may even be a desire to put a protective ring round the term 'modernism', which, in film studies, had come to be identified with the political and revolutionary radicalism of Godard and Brecht in opposition to 'bourgeois realism'. In film studies, modernism became the aesthetics of Marxism. Television drama seems to raise the confusing possibility of a 'bourgeois modernism', familiar to literary criticism but foreign to the criticism of popular culture.

The cause for concern in all this—a concern at the way in which 'non-naturalism' has become institutionalized in professional and critical discourses—is that it seems to represent a devaluation of the critical currency of television drama, removing it from the mainstream of contemporary cultural debate. 'Non-naturalism', like the rouble, is a soft currency with little exchange value outside television drama and no purchasing power in the wider economy of art and culture. It accepts the relegation of television drama to the margins of the culture, and adopts a parochial language befitting its status.

In the second instance, 'non-naturalism' is a formalism, defining its object by techniques and devices and avoiding questions of representation and subjectivity. If the term has a use, it is indeed to describe certain techniques of formal stylization: techniques which are called on to 'jazz up' television drama but which seem to require no theoretical reflection. It may indeed be useful to distinguish between works in which non-naturalistic devices are used formalistically to brighten up a conventional narrative, and works which are imbued through and through with a modernist sensibility. Since Brecht, non-naturalistic devices in theatre and drama have become the new convention, the accoutrements of modern theatrical design, but these devices, separated from the political culture in which Brecht worked, are as likely to refresh tired old ideologies as they are to demand new and critical forms of engagement. It may not be necessary to proscribe the term 'non-naturalism', but it is necessary to restrict its meaning and to avoid confusing it with a theory, a coherent aesthetics, or an epistemology. 'Non-naturalism' seems to breathe most easily in an atmosphere of 'non-theory'.

I have suggested in the introduction to this book that one of the things which gives television drama its seriousness within an understanding of British cultural history is precisely that it is one of the places where modernism can be traced in British art in the second half of the twentieth century, and that, more globally, it represents a particular and complex intersection of modernism with the popular. This intersection allows us to think about certain areas of television drama through modernism, and, at the same time, to think about modernism in more complex ways by refracting it through television drama. In the previous two chapters, I have tried to show the ways in which currents associated in different ways with modernism—montage, detachment, distraction—have crossed and transformed some of the forms of television drama often lumped into the categories of realism or naturalism. I have even suggested that the particular disposition of time and space in the viewing of television may give it a particular aptitude for that 'relaxed detachment' which a modernist like Brecht saw as a precondition of the critical spectator. In this chapter, I want to address modernism more directly as a formal and critical category, and to rescue it from the generality of 'non-naturalism' by looking at some of the particular questions it poses for television drama.

My insistence on the term 'modernism', then, however qualified and complicated it may be within the specifics of television, is to allow me to claim a place for television drama in the understanding of the wider culture, and to give it a wider historical frame of reference within aesthetics. This is to say that it seems more important to me to situate *The Singing Detective* as one of the significant works of twentieth-century British modernism than to canonize Dennis Potter as not a naturalist. At the same time, it may be useful to distinguish—even within Potter's work, for example—between the modernism of *The Singing Detective* and the more instrumental use of non-naturalistic technique in some of the plays which preceded and followed it.

Troy Kennedy Martin again:

Editing for involvement on television is all, and when the editing of different objects (as opposed to the same object from different angles) is fully developed then editing becomes absolute.
Its sudden acceleration shifts viewers' responses into a different key. Even wild editing of random objects reveals this: Look—an

eggshell—a piece of wood. Look—a cloud—a running man—a foot. Whose foot? A telephone—a girl's dress folded—with buttons—an unmade bed—a hair on a pillow—a man's face. Look—the man has a wart on his nose—with hair on it. A shadow—a what?—something—a boom in shot—check curtains blowing—a catch on the casement—open.

This kind of montage can stimulate a very personal kind of meaning like pictures seen in the fire. Developed in the right direction, this personal meaning can disturb the emotions. This is a restatement of Eisenstein's portmanteau rule that a picture changes its meaning in relationship to what precedes or follows it. Thus two pictures having separate meaning when put together create a third and different meaning. Real montage demands total viewer interest and if it is good enough obtains total involvement of an emotional kind.

This leads me to believe that one can create in the new drama strong and meaningful montage, wild horses running under the taut rains of narrative, interesting the viewer to the point where he becomes emotionally involved and where his built-in resistance is released by a leap of faith and he flies with the director into a world where total meaning is not within the objects pictured but in the space between them.

Here, at any rate, is the beginning of the use of objectivity to overcome the 'one step removed' feeling that persists in 'nat' plays. If it can be developed and a real breach made in the barriers, then the new drama should be through and into the open where it can run freely.[3]

Despite the fact that he avoids the term, Troy Kennedy Martin's 'new drama' has all the hallmarks of a modernist drama. Significantly, as I have suggested in Chapter 4, its reference points are Eisenstein and Resnais in the cinema; it sets as its objective the freeing of time and space from the straitjacket in which naturalistic drama places them; and its method is montage. Epistemologically, it is not concerned with the realist apprehension of a world already endowed with meaning, but with setting a world in motion where 'total meaning is not within the objects pictured but in the space between them'. At the same time, the 'new drama' is to be a popular drama, specific to television and using its specific technology to excite and involve the viewer, shifting his responses 'into a different key': a popular modernism for a mass medium.

It will come as no surprise, of course, that modernism is every bit as complex a term as realism or naturalism, with its own history

---

3 Troy Kennedy Martin, 'Nats go home: first statement of a new drama for television', *Encore*, no. 48 (March/April 1964), 31.

of debates, its own instabilities, and its own uncertain boundaries. In one account, the whole of cinema is already part of a modernist culture—the age of mechanical reproduction; and, often in the same account, television, in the age of electronic transmission, has already tipped over into a new culture which must be postmodern. In another account, the whole notion of a popular modernism within capitalist culture is a contradiction in terms, popular culture compromised by commodification to the point at which it can only be an extension of capitalist rationality rather than a negation of it. And in yet another account, modernism is simply a repertory of techniques. It is worth spending a little time, then, sorting out some of the things which one might mean by insisting on a tradition of modernism within television drama.

At one level, modernism is simply a modernization. In his classic account of realism, Roman Jakobson shows the ways in which verisimilitude evolves historically, constantly revitalizing itself in order to retain the truth of the 'reality effect':

> Everyday language uses a number of euphemisms, including polite formulas, circumlocutions, allusions, and stock phrases. However, when we want our speech to be candid, natural, and expressive, we discard the usual polite etiquette and call things by their real names. They have a fresh ring, and we feel that they are 'the right words'. But as soon as the name has merged with the object it designates, we must, conversely, resort to metaphor, allusion or allegory if we wish a more expressive term. It will sound more impressive, it will be more *striking*. To put it in another way, when searching for a word which will revitalize an object, we pick a farfetched word, unusual at least in its given application, a word which is forced into service.[4]

While Jakobson is talking about the revitalizing of the conventions of verisimilitude, a similar process can be traced on the world-historical level in the development of twentieth-century modernism. Most sharply, the new forms of Soviet revolutionary art, including cinema, responded to the perception that the Revolution had remade the world, and if art was to engage with that world and reflect the new reality, it must remake itself. The forms which expressed a bourgeois reality could not express the reality of the proletarian state. Since the proletarian state was still in the process of being constructed, the only art which could reflect that reality was a constructivist art. More generally, modernity itself—the 'constant revolutionizing of production, uninterrupted disturbance of all social conditions, everlasting

4 Roman Jakobson, 'On realism in art', in Ladislav Matejka and Krystyna Pomorska (eds.), *Reading in Russian Poetics: Formalist and Structuralist Views* (Ann Arbor: Michigan Slavic Publications, 1978), 40.

uncertainty and agitation' of which Marx and Engels speak in *The Communist Manifesto* (1848)—seemed itself to be remaking the world: 'All fixed, fast-frozen relations, with their train of ancient and venerable prejudices and opinions are swept away, all new-formed ones become antiquated before they can ossify. All that is solid melts into air . . . '.[5] To be modern was to feel the shock of the new which unfixed us from the conventions of the past. If art too was to be modern, it would have to modernize its means of representation to engage with the new experience of speed, fragmentation, alienation, and dissonance.

This process of modernization, however, worked against another social process, traced by Jürgen Habermas in his essay 'Modernity— an incomplete project',[6] in which art, in post-Enlightenment rationality, was more and more separated from everyday practice or the 'life-world', and became the province of the expert. Following Max Weber, Habermas traces a narrative in which the three areas of 'substantive reason'—science, morality, and art—no longer formed an organic, unified whole, but drifted apart, each claiming its own form of rationality and understanding—'cognitive-instrumental', 'moral-practical', and 'aesthetic-expressive'—and each requiring its own 'specialists who seem more adept at being logical in these particular ways than other people are'.

> As a result, the distance grows between the culture of the experts and that of the larger public. What accrues to culture through specialized treatment and reflection does not immediately and necessarily become the property of everyday practice. With cultural rationalization of this sort, the threat increases that the life-world, whose traditional substance has already been devalued, will become more and more impoverished.[7]

On the one hand, art seeks out new forms in which to capture the modern age and to shock the public out of the grip of the past; on the other hand, the public, seeking consolation in art for the alienation of industrial society, is content with the familiar, rejects the difficulty of the new, and modern art becomes the territory of an educated elite.

In this analysis, the process is intensified by the increasing commodification of culture, a cultural economy which in order to secure a mass market, substitutes diversion and entertainment for

---

5 Karl Marx and Frederick Engels, 'Manifesto of the Communist Party', in *The Communist Manifesto: A Modern Edition* [with introduction by Eric Hobsbawn] (London: Verso, 1998), 38.

6 Jürgen Habermas, 'Modernity—an incomplete project', trans. Seyla Ben-Habib, in Hal Foster (ed.), *Postmodern Culture* (London/Sydney: Pluto Press, 1985).

7 Ibid. 8–9.

'authentic' or 'genuine' art, putting in its place what the Marxist art critic Clement Greenberg, in 1939, called Kitsch:

> To fill the demand of the new market, a new commodity was devised: ersatz culture, kitsch, destined for those who, insensible to the values of genuine culture, are hungry nevertheless for the diversion that only culture of some sort can provide.
>
> Kitsch, using for raw material the debased and academicized simulacra of genuine culture, welcomes and cultivates this insensibility. It is the source of its profits. Kitsch is mechanical and operates by formulas. Kitsch is vicarious experience and faked sensations. Kitsch changes according to style, but remains always the same. Kitsch is the epitome of all that is spurious in the life of our times. Kitsch pretends to demand nothing of its customers except their money—not even their time.[8]

Faced with a culture of experts, modernity, according to the Habermasian analysis, separates culture off from the life-world and institutes the division between 'art' and 'entertainment', 'high' culture and 'low' culture, with modernism not only as a modernization of art but as its refuge from the debasement of low culture. Faced with advanced commodification, according to Greenberg, modernism is pushed more and more towards an avant garde which separates itself from the public's desire for an art which represents reality and pre-occupies itself with the very matter of representation itself:

> the true and most important function of the avant garde was not to 'experiment', but to find a path along which it would be possible to keep culture *moving* in the midst of ideological confusion and violence. Retiring from the public altogether, the avant-garde poet or artist sought to maintain the high level of his art by both narrowing and raising it to the expression of an absolute in which all relativities and contradictions would be either resolved or beside the point. 'Art for art's sake' and 'pure poetry' appear, and subject matter or content becomes something to be avoided like the plague.
>
> It has been in search of the absolute that the avant garde has arrived at 'abstract' or 'nonobjective' art—and poetry too. The

---

8 Clement Greenberg, 'Avant Garde and Kitsch', in *Art and Culture: Critical Essays* (Boston: Beacon Press, 1981), 10. It is worth noting, when we come to consider Dennis Potter's use of popular song, that Greenberg's list of the debased objects which fall into the category of Kitsch ends with 'Tin Pan Alley music, tap dancing, Hollywood movies, etc., etc.'. It is also worth noting, for Potter, the term which T. J. Clarke applies to Greenberg's mixture of elitism and socialism: 'Eliotic Trotskyism' combining T. S. Eliot's yearning for an elite tradition with Trotsky's yearning for the permanent revolution. See T. J. Clark, 'Clement Greenberg's theory of art', in Francis Frascina (ed.), *Pollock and After: the Critical Debate* (London: Harper & Row, 1985), 47–65.

avant-garde poet or artist tries in effect to imitate God by creating something valid solely on its own terms, in the way nature itself is valid, in the way a landscape—not its picture—is aesthetically valid; something *given*, increate, independent of meanings, similars or originals. Content is to be dissolved so completely into form that the work of art or literature cannot be reduced in whole or in part to anything not itself.[9]

All of this may seem a long way from television drama. What it suggests, however, is a logic of modernism, a kind of centrifugal spin in which art is pushed to the outer edges in order to preserve its 'authenticity'. Within this logic, television drama operates with its own sets of discourses, and its own limits and pressures. It is precisely the ways in which television drama finds its place between 'art' and 'the popular', negotiating between the demands of the different and the new which make it 'authentic' as art and the demands of the familiar which make it accessible within the 'popular', which make it important within aesthetic and cultural debate.

The discourse of modernization, of a technology which can revitalize dramatic forms, is pervasive from the earliest days of television transmission. There was wide recognition of the new intensification which the close-up could give to theatrical action, or the excitement of a liveness and immediacy which cinema could not offer, and this recognition becomes the central thrust within Kennedy Martin's call for a 'new drama' which will stretch directors and will use the technology of film and television to the outer edges of its potential.

It is to be hoped that the great demands this kind of drama makes will stir some kind of response—and that [directors'] basic television thinking, which is reminiscent of Victor Sylvester's fox-trots being danced in the world of the Beatles, will be fragmented into something a little closer to the modern scene.[10]

The objection to 'naturalism' which Kennedy Martin shares with many writers and directors of the 1960s and 1970s is not simply that it is theatrical, but that it belongs to the theatre of a more sedate culture. If television drama is to address 'the modern scene'—post-1956 politics, the New Waves of cinema and theatre, the 'swinging sixties', the events of May 1968—it will have to modernize. And this means more than simply introducing new contents; it means capturing for television the 'striking' new forms of theatre and cinema which have been developed in modernism: from theatre, the 'distanciation effects' of Brecht; and from cinema, the montage of Eisenstein and the temporal and spatial disjunctions of the French *nouvelle vague*.

9 Greenberg, 'Avant garde and Kitsch', 5–6.
10 Martin, 'Nats go home', 32.

More fundamentally still, modernism meant a new kind of apprehension of the real which was defined by a scepticism about representation and the absolute truth of beauty. The function of art was no longer simply to reveal a truth which already existed by condensing the real in representation, but rather, by exposing the material processes of construction, condensation, and representation, art exposed truth to relativity, contingency, and contradiction. The montage of modernist art had the capacity not only to represent contingency and contradiction, but to activate it for the reader or viewer, inviting her to make sense of the social or the personal rather than to consume a meaning which had already been fixed. The new drama in television, then, was not simply to engage with new contents, but to give us new ways of seeing and thinking, showing 'the frame in the picture when most television is busy showing the picture in the frame', owning up to construction in order to remind the viewer that what is on the screen is not the real but 'a play. A Play. A *Play*.'

At the same time, if modernism is most commonly associated with new ways of seeing and thinking, it is important not to lose sight of the fact that it also gave us new things to think about. Automatic writing, stream of consciousness, even Greenberg's abstract expressionism were not simply self-reflexive strategies, laying bare the means of production of meaning, they were also intricate webs for catching the unconscious unawares. Since the early days of live studio drama, it had seemed that the television camera could approach inner realities in a particularly intimate way. The television close-up seemed to evoke the possibility of inner speech with an intensity denied to theatre and an intimacy and immediacy which the cinema could not achieve. The development of editing techniques and the fluidity of the filmed image seemed to promise ways of engaging the viewer in the instabilities and disorientations of dream states, fantasies and the surreal, and of making the unconscious material. Modernism, then, does not begin and end with the distanciating, non-naturalistic, self-reflexive devices of Potter, but is strongly marked in the subjective dramas of the unconscious found in the work of David Mercer. What seems central to all forms of modernism, however, is that they reveal, and are addressed to a subjectivity which is conceived to be in process, not yet fixed, available to change, engaged by the pleasures of thinking and material existence as much as by the sensuous pleasures of the beautiful illusion.

Television, it has to be said, does not provide an entirely comfortable space for a modernism whose natural home seemed to be in the gallery or at least in a gallery culture, separated, as everyone from the surrealists to Habermas complained, from the life of the street. The modernism of television drama is in constant tension with the everyday space of television itself; the desire for critical detachment is qualified by the vision of a viewer who 'lurches with a growl towards the off-button'; and the boundaries between the modernist techniques of distanciation and montage and the modernizing techniques of 'jazzing-up' are very thin indeed. In this respect, the modernism of television drama can be placed within historical boundaries, situating it in a territory bounded on the one side by the avant garde of which Greenberg speaks and on the other by postmodernism.

The boundary with the avant garde is perhaps easiest to describe, though the term is often used quite loosely when people are excited by the new and experimental. At its most sharply defined, the 'historic avant garde' is associated by Peter Bürger with those movements in the early part of this century whose aim was not simply to add something new to the repertory of artistic forms but was to attack the very status of art in bourgeois society.

> The European avant-garde movements can be defined as an attack on the status of art in bourgeois society. What is negated is not an earlier form of art (a style) but art as an institution that is unassociated with the life praxis of men. When the avant-gardistes demand that art become practical once again, they do not mean that the contents of works of art should be socially significant. The demand is not raised at the level of the contents of individual works. Rather, it directs itself to the way art functions in society, a process that does as much to determine the effect that works have as does the particular content.
>
> ... In bourgeois society, art has a contradictory role: it projects the image of a better order and to that extent protests against the bad order that prevails. But by realizing the image of a better order in fiction, which is semblance (*Schein*) only, it relieves the existing order of the pressure of those forces that make for change. They are assigned to confinement in an ideal sphere. Where art accomplishes this, it is 'affirmative' in Marcuse's sense of the term.[11]

As Jochen Schulte-Sasse says in his foreword to Bürger's book, even modernist art in bourgeois society 'can both protest and protect the status quo',[12] offering the satisfactions of acceptable difference. In these circumstances, the avant garde aspires to transgress the boundaries of the acceptable, and to call into question the authority and the dignity which is accorded to art by an elitist culture. By a fatal paradox, however, the provocations of the historic avant garde, which were intended to reintegrate art with everyday life and to bring it onto

11 Peter Bürger, *Theory of the Avant Garde* [1974]; trans. Michael Shaw (Minneapolis: Minneapolis University Press, 1984), 49–50.

12 Jochen Schulte-Sasse, 'Foreword', ibid., p. xxxv.

the streets, in fact drove art deeper into the gallery, a gallery presided over by the expert. A similar logic is apparent in Greenberg's more formalist account of the avant garde, or in Adorno's insistence on authentic art as a negation of the administrative rationality of capitalism. In its retreat from the commodification which constantly threatens to absorb it, art becomes more and more difficult, interrogating itself rather than its referent and seeking new forms of shock and difference which will hold back for a little longer the tide of accommodation.

Understood in this way, an avant-garde practice in broadcast television seems beyond the bounds of contemplation. Not because it is impossible at the level of form, but because it seems mildly absurd within the institution of television and its mode of circulation. As Bürger shows, the project of the historic avant garde itself was condemned to failure by its blindness to the adaptability of the institution Art; why then would a similar project be any more likely to succeed in television? While television may offer a strategic site in which the productions of an avant garde may be relayed from elsewhere—the early films of Derek Jarman, the art videos of Bill Viola—the idea of an institutionalized avant garde produced by television seems like an inescapable contradiction in terms. The use of 'avant-garde' as a descriptive term seems to circulate only in its weakest and most formalistic sense, meaning 'experimental', 'innovative', 'a bit weird', or, I suppose, 'non-naturalistic'. This is not to say, however, that there is not an avant-garde sensibility or an avant-garde aspiration in television drama which dreams of revolutionizing the relationship between art and everyday life, but it takes forms which are much more negotiated and accommodating than the heroic and agonistic avant garde of early twentieth-century art forms.

If there are fairly sharp boundaries to be drawn between the possible modernisms of television drama and the avant garde, the boundaries between modernism and postmodernism are open to much more debate—some invigorating and some wearying—which have occupied several books of their own. In television studies, there seems to be a creeping sense that television is so thoroughly a technology of postmodernity—perhaps even the defining technology which makes the decisive break with the 'modern age' and reshapes everyday life as postmodern—that all its forms must be *ipso facto* postmodernist. If television is viewed in its generality it is hard not to feel some sympathy for this position. If we are to make sense of the particular, however—in this instance, the particularity of television drama—it still seems necessary to be able to make some discriminations and to identify boundaries, however permeable these boundaries may be and however much they may be crossed and criss-crossed. To do this briefly, I want to return to the question of irony which was discussed in the last chapter, and to bring to it a provisional description of modes of irony developed by Alan Wilde in his book, *Horizons of Assent: Modernism, Postmodernism and the Ironic Imagination.*[13]

Wilde distinguishes, very provisionally—'an ad hoc shorthand', he calls it, 'deliberately "inadequate"'—three divisions of what he calls the 'ironic imagination': 'mediate irony', 'disjunctive irony', and 'suspensive irony'. Mediate irony is the mode of satire; essentially, Wilde argues, a premodernist mode. It 'imagines a world lapsed from a recoverable norm'.[14] Disjunctive irony is the form of irony which Wilde associates with the heroic attempts of the high modernists to fashion meaning out of the fragments in a world in which 'the centre cannot hold'. 'The ironist confronts a world that appears inherently disconnected and fragmented. . . . Disjunctive irony both recognizes the disconnections and seems to control them.'[15] Suspensive irony Wilde identifies with postmodernism.

> Suspensive irony . . . with its yet more radical vision of multiplicity, randomness, contingency and even absurdity, abandons the quest for paradise altogether—the world in all its disorder is simply (or not so simply) accepted. . . . Ambiguity and paradox give way to quandary, to a low-keyed engagement with a world of perplexities and uncertainties, in which one can hope, at best, to achieve what Forster calls 'the smaller pleasures of life', and Stanley Ilkin, its 'small satisfactions'.[16]

Wilde is careful to insist that he is not constructing a teleology or even a rigid critical taxonomy, but that each of the ironic modes may be present in any text or any author in particular but shifting configurations and hierarchies. The classifications are intended to enjoy, he says, 'a strictly performative function as discriminating and temporary instruments . . . a truly empirical sounding of the movements and sinuosities within the concrete appearances of single or grouped phenomena'.[17]

At one level, Wilde's 'empirical sounding' is simply that: an instrument which allows us to draw boundaries between, say, the modernist disjunctive ironies of Mercer or Potter for whom disjunction matters in quite passionate and painful ways, and the postmodernist, suspensive, and fundamentally playful ironies of American series like *Moonlighting* (1985–9) or, more recently, *Ally McBeal* (1997–).

13 Alan Wilde, *Horizons of Assent: Modernism, Postmodernism and the Ironic Imagination* (Baltimore: Johns Hopkins University Press, 1981).

14 Ibid. 9–10.

15 Ibid. 10.

16 Ibid.

17 Ibid. 9.

If nothing else, the 'sounding of movements and sinuosities' may prevent us from lumping them all together because they share 'non-naturalistic' formal strategies, homogenizing them under the headings either of a unified 'non-naturalism' or a unified 'postmodernism'. But much more significantly, Wilde does not rely solely on the formal properties of the ironies to make his discriminations but identifies these properties with an ironic imagination which is grounded in the historical formations of premodernism, modernism, and postmodernism. *Moonlighting* may have some of the same distanciating formal devices as *Moonlight on the Highway* (Potter, 1969), but it belongs to a radically different historical consciousness and it is in this historical consciousness that the boundaries between modernism and postmodernism lie.

In this respect, Wilde echoes the historical emphasis which characterizes Peter Brooks's highly influential study of the 'melodramatic imagination',[18] and points towards an insistence on modernism—like melodrama—as, firstly, a historical sensibility and experience, and only secondly a formal movement. We find this same insistence in Raymond Williams's discussion in *The Politics of Modernism*.[19] Williams stresses the diversity of the modern sensibility.

> Although Modernism can be clearly identified as a distinctive movement in its deliberate distance from and challenge to more traditional forms of art and thought, it is also strongly characterized by its internal diversity of methods and emphases: a restless and often directly competitive sequence of innovations and experiments, always more immediately recognized by what they are breaking from than by what, in any simple way, they are breaking towards. Even the range of basic cultural positions within Modernism stretches from an eager embrace of modernity, either in its technical and mechanical forms or in the equally significant attachments to ideas of social and political revolution, to conscious options for past or exotic cultures as sources or at least fragments *against* the modern world, from the Futurist affirmation of the city to Eliot's pessimistic recoil.[20]

This diversity he attributes to 'the specific cultures and situations within which different kinds of work and position were to be developed',[21] resisting the notion that the various movements were simply voluntaristic decisions of the artists. What gives the 'defining

---

18 Peter Brooks, *The Melodramatic Imagination: Balzac, Henry James, Melodrama and the Mode of Excess* (New Haven, Conn.: Yale University Press, 1976).

19 Raymond Williams, *The Politics of Modernism: Against the New Conformists* (London: Verso, 1989).

20 Ibid. 43.

21 Ibid.

sense'[22] to the 'modern' in the art of the twentieth century, however, is the feeling shared by all the movements that they had to make a break within the wider sensibility of the modern age, and that that break had to be made tangible at the level of form.

Modernism, of course, is not the first movement to call for a break from the shackles of the past, and it is inherent in the romance of capitalism that it is energized by crises and little revolutions. The modern age stretches back deep into the nineteenth century, and many of the anxieties of the twentieth century—urbanism, rootlessness, acceleration, the debasement of language by the speed of communications—can already be found in Wordsworth's 1801 Preface to the *Lyrical Ballads*:

> For a multitude of causes, unknown to former times, are now
> acting with a combined force to blunt the discriminating powers
> of the mind, and, unfitting it for all voluntary exertion, to reduce
> it to a state of almost savage torpor. The most effective of these
> causes are the great national events which are daily taking place,
> and the increasing accumulation of men in cities, where the
> uniformity of their occupations produces a craving for
> extraordinary incident, which the rapid communication
> of intelligence hourly gratifies.[23]

Just as Wordsworth's response to his historical situation was to call for a revolution in poetic diction, so the modernists, from their historical situation within what Williams calls 'the changing milieu of the metropolis', called for a break in the language of art—even for a revolution in the status of art itself. And just as Wordsworth found in nature and common language a break from a classical vocabulary that was no longer adequate to the daily lives of men and women, so, in their turn, the movements of modernism sought a break from a nature and a natural order which had been thoroughly commandeered by a bourgeois and capitalist common sense which no longer made sense of experience. From the perspective of a historical analysis such as this, montage and the breaking free of narrative from natural time and space were not simply formal options within a repertory of techniques but offered a way of expressing the disjunctions of the late modern age, whether these were experienced as the joy of speed in the age of machine or as the pains of alienation and dislocation in a godless world.

What seems clear is that the 'seriousness' of television drama within the peculiarly British context of a broadcasting system still

22 Williams, *The Politics of Modernism*, 43.

23 William Wordsworth, 'Poetry and poetic diction', in E. Jones (ed.) *English Critical Essays: Nineteenth Century* (London: Oxford University Press, 1947), 6.

wedded to notions of public service and social responsibility and still marked by notions of the commitment and engagement inherited from the post-1956 generation, could not be explained easily by the playfulness of postmodernism or even the suspensiveness of its irony. The current of ethical seriousness associated with modernism runs deep in British television drama.

The two writers who can most closely be identified with modernism in television drama are David Mercer and Dennis Potter. Neither is uniform in the forms of modernism which he adopts, and within the work of each there is considerable formal diversity. Much of the early work of Mercer—*A Suitable Case for Treatment* (1962), *The Parachute* (1968), *On the Eve of Publication* (1968)—shows some influence in the complex interplay of interior and exterior realities both of the French *nouvelle vague* cinema of Resnais and the French *nouveau roman* of Robbe-Grillet, while the later plays—*The Cellar and the Almond Tree* (1970) or *Shooting the Chandelier* (1977)—have a realist surface laid over a disorienting and surreal historical situation. Potter's work shifts between the vaguely Brechtian use of distanciation devices in fairly conventional biographical narrative—the Nigel Barton plays (1965)—through the everyday and naturalistic treatment of the supernatural in *Brimstone and Treacle* (1976, first transmitted 1987), to the fable form interrupted by 'non-naturalistic' songs in *Pennies from Heaven* (1978), the more fully modernist montage structure of *The Singing Detective* (1986), and the ironic play with the musical and science fiction genres in *Lipstick on your Collar* (1993), *Cold Lazarus* (1996), and *Karaoke* (1996). What is common to each, however, running as a thread of modernism through all the work, is a concern with the means of representation, symptomatic of a loss of faith in the capacity of the conventions of narrative dramatic realism—whether critical or naturalistic—to express complex realities. Faithful to modernism, the complex reality is one in which the subjective and the objective compete for validity, in which memory and history, fantasy and reality, dream and everyday life, the natural and the supernatural each claim their own materiality. At its worst, mainly in the work of Potter, non-naturalistic devices are formalistic and tricksy, a way of backing off from seriousness. At its best, however, modernist form is a way of dissolving hierarchies, resisting the unifying order of plots and subplots, identification and resolution, catching the viewer instead in the dialectic of competing realities which refuse to cohere into the plenitude of an organically unified world.

The fact that Mercer was never awarded the celebrity status of Potter is symptomatic of a difference in their work and their contexts. Most obviously, Mercer died quite privately and prematurely in 1980 at the age of 54 without having achieved public fame or notoriety, while Potter, having attracted more than his fair share of both obloquy and celebration, died very publicly indeed at the age of 61 in 1994. Glen Creeber quotes Jenny Diski: 'the death of Potter may have been authored by God, but it was adapted for television by Dennis Potter'.[24] While seven books have been published on Potter since 1993, the critical literature on Mercer is very thin.[25]

This difference in their status as celebrities also seems to me to reflect a significant difference in the way their personal histories and authorship function in the work. While there is a consistency of concerns in Mercer's work, and a fineness of writing and intelligence which can be attributed to his authorship, the biographical David Mercer who has a life independent of the writing is absent. Potter, on the other hand, is everywhere present in the work, obsessively wrestling with very personal demons. The scandal which followed him was not simply because the works themselves were scandalous, but because there was always the suspicion, confirmed by later biographies, that these were lived nightmares. However much the orthodoxy may inveigh against biographical criticism, there is a very strong sense in which the biography of Potter is itself a form of criticism which, more than any other, makes the work complex, unique, and uniquely painful. It is perhaps Potter's greatest achievement as a modernist that, at one and the same time, he used his own pain and guilt as the subject matter of his work and simultaneously laid intricate traps for those who confused fiction with reality. Creeber recounts that Potter's mother successfully sued Mary Whitehouse for publicly assuming that the fictional adultery *in flagrante* depicted in *The Singing Detective* was derived from a biographical truth which lay behind the real Dennis Potter's sexual depravity—but Mrs Whitehouse is only the most obvious victim of Potter's duplicity.[26] Authorship is one of the things *The Singing Detective* is about, and its vertiginous effect is the result of an uncertainty about who is writing whom, an uncertainty which is extended outwards by a deliberate confusion between the known reality of Dennis Potter in the world and the fictional reality of Philip Marlow in the play. Although Potter may seem obsessively present within his work, and sometimes wearyingly so, the presence of actual biography (Potter and Marlow

24 Glen Creeber, *Dennis Potter: Between Two Worlds* (London: Macmillan, 1998), 14. Jenny Diski was writing in the *London Review of Books*.

25 Apart from Glen Creeber, cited above, these are: Peter Stead, *Dennis Potter* (Bridgend: Seren Books, 1993); Dennis Potter and Graham Fuller, *Potter on Potter* (London: Faber & Faber, 1993); John Cook, *Dennis Potter: A Life on Screen* (Manchester: Manchester University Press, 1995); W. Stephen Gilbert, *Fight and Kick and Bite: the Life and Work of Dennis Potter* (London: Hodder & Stoughton, 1995); Humphrey Carpenter, *Dennis Potter: The Authorised Biography* (London: Faber & Faber, 1998).

26 Ibid. 11–12.

both have psoriasis and both come from the Forest of Dean) is no guarantee that this play is not a game (as Mrs Whitehouse learned to her cost). It is this play of duplicity, the traps of a *mise en abîme*, which makes the drama a work of modernist art rather than a more or less non-naturalist fiction concealing a more or less true autobiography. (The game has a double edge, of course: while Mrs Whitehouse is a worthy dupe and attracts little sympathy for thinking that fiction is reality, there is a nasty feeling when one's mind wanders to the real people in Potter's life—his mother, for example—who discover that their reality has been taken away from them to make the material of Potter's fiction.)

Mercer and Potter seem to me to offer a consistent level of investment in some of the great modernist themes—sexuality, the individual in history, the irrepressible unconscious, class and power, the role of the creative artist, god and godlessness—which make their work exemplary. Within television drama, they also seem to pose quite different contexts and strategies of negotiation between modernism and the popular. Since I am more interested in exemplifying modernism than in interpreting a body of work or assessing an author, I am going to concentrate quite briefly on two plays—*The Parachute* and *The Singing Detective*—as illustrative of possibilities rather than definitive of a form.

The Parachute, produced by Tony Garnett for The Wednesday Play, and directed by Anthony Page, was transmitted as a BBC Play of the Month on 21 January 1968. It interweaves history, memory, and fantasy, but unlike Potter's drama, it is not Mercer's history and memory which is at stake, but Europe's. Mercer is perhaps the most European of television dramatists of the pre-1982 period; his themes return to European history, particularly to the period at the end of the second European war of this century, and the formal and stylistic influences of European cinema are apparent in the film sequences of *The Parachute*. Most strikingly, the film sequence towards the end of the play in which young Werner is married in the gardens of Laugstein to his cousin Anna, who may also be his father's mistress, Fräulein Bechner, echoes quite resonantly Alain Resnais's *L'Année dernière à Marienbad/Last Year at Marienbad* (1961) in both *mise en scène*—the formal gardens and stately camera movement—and in theme—the indeterminacy of memory and time.

The present time of the drama, shot as a mixture of film and studio recording, begins during the war, with Werner von Reger (John Osborne), son and heir of one of the leading families in the German aristocracy, in a training camp for paratroopers, having elected to be an ordinary soldier in the German army despite his father's offer to smuggle him out to Switzerland or to get him a commission. The play ends with Russian paratroopers parachuting into the gardens of the von Regers' country home, Laugstein. Despite his father's assertion that the von Regers are 'strong enough to piss on history', by the end of the war Werner is in a wheelchair having broken his back in a training jump, his mother (Isabel Dean) is mad, his father, Baron von Reger (Alan Badel), has been killed in an air raid on Berlin, and his cousin Anna (Jill Bennett) has probably died in a concentration camp. The present time narrative is intercut with flashbacks to the period before the war, to Werner's childhood and his early manhood under the Nazi regime. The past time of the narrative is shot entirely in the studio, and, in many ways, forms the core of the drama. It is from this perspective that we understand the significance of what is yet to come in a narrative of little dramas—stories of off-screen events which point to the decadence of aristocratic society, the on-screen drama of Anna's communist commitment which leads to an assassination attempt, capture, and interrogation, and dialogues which play out social, political, familial, and paternal power. It is in this past time that the interior reality of dream and fantasy is rooted: a world which breaks free from historical reality into a magical reality in which Werner dreams of childhood and romance. This magical reality is shot entirely on film.

If *The Parachute* is a history play, however, it is not a history play like Hare's *Licking Hitler* or *Dreams of Leaving* or Trevor Griffiths's *Country*. It is, if you like, a psychic history, overlaying a narrative situated within a historical period with a psychic reality of power and class which transcends that period. Alan Badel's Baron von Reger is a wonderful display of both the power and fascination of a detached, aristocratic, and narcissistic fascism which is absorbed with itself to the exclusion of all social responsibility. Young Werner, held in awe of his father's ironic detachment, repeats the duties of the aristocrat which he has clearly learned by rote:

'The aristocrat owes allegiance to nothing and to no one. The true aristocrat has a duty to insulate himself against all forms of vulgarity. He transcends nationality, race, religion. His purpose is to accomplish only himself. His role in society is one of detachment, of vigilant irony.'

Werner's physical paralysis at the end of the play is the exterior sign of a moral and emotional paralysis inflicted on him by the power of the father, an inability to break through irony into the political commitment which Anna, his cousin and intended bride, displays in her assassination attempt on Schecht: a political act which, she tells Werner, was intended to show him what is to be done. Beyond its particular history, then, the drama is one of detachment and commitment, and the psychic seduction of an ironic authority which cannot be touched, even by the agents responsible for the day-to-day running of fascism: 'I have a servile temperament,' says the SS officer (played, ironically, by Lindsay Anderson). 'And like all servile people I have a masochistic admiration for those who humiliate me.' The historical reality of paternal, class, and state power is underpinned by Werner's dreams and idealized memories of his father, on horseback and dressed as a Teutonic knight, killing wolves with his lance and instructing him on the nature of nobility. Mercer seems to be interested not simply in the reality of Europe's past, but in the formation of the European imaginary: a complex of realities in which one reality informs and collides with the other.

Like *The Singing Detective*, then, *The Parachute* is made up of a montage of times and realities. In both, identities slip: Anna, Werner's intended bride, becomes Bechner, the Baron's mistress in something of the same way that the actress (Alison Steadman) who plays Marlow's mother in one narrative strand of *The Singing Detective* also plays the whore/spy in another. In both, there are rhyming motifs which link the realities: most distinctly, there seems to be a rhyme in *The Parachute* between the parasol tip which Bechner reputedly puts into the nostril of one of her lovers, the tip of von Reger's lance with which he slays the wolf, and the tip of the machine gun which the SS interrogators put into Anna's vagina—a complex system of imagery which links the imaginary and the real, political power and sexual power. If I were to distinguish the two writers in their modernism, I would point to a complex allusiveness (and elusiveness) in Mercer's play which is uncharacteristic of the literalness of much of Potter's. In *The Singing Detective*, for example, while Alison Steadman plays both mother and whore, there is no narrative confusion between them, and the device points to the woman/whore conflation which is familiar in much of Potter's work. In *The Parachute*, on the other hand, just at the point in the fantasy sequence at which Werner is about to marry Anna, his parents begin to address her as Fräulein Bechner, his father's mistress: at one and the same time she is both Anna and Bechner, the kind of slippage of identity which belongs only to the logic of dream and the Oedipal fantasy. There is the sense that if you pick up all the clues in *The Singing Detective* you will solve its conundrums. But if *The Singing Detective* offers conundrums, *The Parachute* offers resonant enigmas. Mercer seems to resist a reductive interpretation, putting metaphors and images, real time and imaginary time into play rather than tying them down to a referent: the image of the parachute (like the image of the piano in Jane Campion's film) which forms the title and is frozen in the final image is significant without being reducible to a literal meaning.

While Mercer's stylistic references are to the European art cinema, it is instructive to note the particular form which television in the 1960s imposes on the modernism of *The Parachute*. The complex levels of reality are not simply made up of a montage of past and present or history and memory; they are also made up of film and television. While the memory/dream sequence filmed in the gardens of Laugstein has all the ethereal beauty and classical formality of a landscape which is not quite real—like the gardens in Marienbad—the prewar sequences are shot in the very material real time of the studio. The image is a scanned image, the transitions are mixed, faces move in and out of shadow, and the camera movements are full of little reframings. Stylistically, *The Parachute* is much more dated than the smooth transitions between location and studio in *The Singing Detective*, and this may make it much less impressive to an audience at the end of the 1990s. The *mise en scène* of the studio makes the continuity from the art cinema of Resnais more difficult to see. Nevertheless, it seems to me to be precisely this insistence of the televisual, the possibilities and limitations of a disjunction between technologies of the real, which makes *The Parachute* an exemplary text for an understanding of the conditions and constraints of modernism in television drama. The technology of the studio creates a literal space which stands in stark contrast to the imaginary space created by film in the Laugstein gardens.

Turning to *The Singing Detective*, it may already be apparent to the reader that I have never felt particular sympathy towards Potter's work, and my reaction to what seems to me to be an overvaluation of his very uneven career may have hardened into prejudice. I find it hard to avoid the suspicion that the BBC needed Dennis Potter as a testimony to its boldness, and, more than any other writer, Potter was given the right to fail. While I admire Potter for sticking to drama—even when he failed—while everyone else was making films, I wish I could like the drama better. For what it is worth, my own estimation is that much of his work is marred by a certain cleverness; that he has a facility for pain which at its worst tends towards cynical manipulation and is often, precisely, facile; and that his constant revisiting of his demons and recycling of his work represents not so much a deepening of his vision as a failure of his imagination. While a reading of Humphrey Carpenter's excellent biography[27] reveals the complex and painful aetiology of his misogyny and sexual fears and loathings which adds immensely to my understanding of the man, it does not make me love the work.

Having said that, however, *The Singing Detective*, after repeated viewings, seems to me to be one of the major works of postwar British

27 Carpenter, *Dennis Potter: The Authorised Biography.*

culture, and since I am not alone in considering it Potter's masterpiece, it may be instructive to speculate for a moment on why this
work might be so distinctive. I would attribute it to two factors
which have to do with authorship: Jon Amiel and Michael Gambon.
Carpenter's biography makes it strikingly clear how quickly many of
Potter's dramas were written and how quickly they went into production and then onto the screen. The process within BBC drama before
the days of the internal market and producer choice may indeed have
been fertile ground for creative freedom, but they may also have
lacked the creative discipline which Potter's work needed in order to
fully externalize his vision and sharpen his metaphors. A more disciplined regime might have noticed that there were simply too many
songs in *Pennies from Heaven*, and that a device which was intended
to extend the significance of the drama was in fact distracting from
it and becoming cute. From all the accounts, including his own,
Jon Amiel played an important part in restructuring *The Singing
Detective* and in saving Potter from some of his own *coups de théâtre*:
for example, the planned tricksy ending in which the whole drama is
revealed to have been imagined by Noddy, the senile old gent in the
hospital ward who has been a bit part throughout the play. *The
Singing Detective* seems to me to have benefited from that creative
tension between director and script which the respect for the writer in
television drama often replaces with a service (and servile) ethic.

The other key factor in *The Singing Detective* is in casting: particularly the casting of Michael Gambon as Philip Marlow, but also in
giving him an actress with the strength of Janet Suzman to stand
against him as a wife; a wife who, almost uniquely in Potter, turns out
not to be a whore in anything but Marlow's fiction. Gambon's performance gives a depth and a vulnerability to the pain of Marlow which
prevents it slipping off the hook with the ironic and protective twist
which Potter often gives to his scripts. Imagine *The Singing Detective*
with Denholm Elliott, or Bob Hoskins, or even Nicol Williamson
who was originally intended for the part. Carpenter quotes Jon Amiel
on Williamson: 'he had the rage, cynicism, irony and eloquence, but
he would never make you cry'.[28] It is precisely the ability to make you
cry in Gambon's performance that makes the play of realities matter,
registering the experiences of young Philip on his disfigured face and
failing to turn them into melodramatic fiction. It is this which gives
the modernist structure of the narrative its dialectical edge.

That *The Singing Detective* cannot adequately be described by a
term like 'non-naturalism' seems self-evident. It is a modernist
drama, and at its core is the characteristically modernist figure of the
creative artist who tries *and fails* to use art to sublimate pain and order

28 Ibid. 452.

a disordered reality. Processes of writing and reading form the central narrative strand. Reginald (Gerard Horan) reads Marlow's novel, *The Singing Detective*, absorbed by the clues in the fiction without knowing that the author is along the ward; Gibbon, the cruelly named psychotherapist played by Bill Paterson, reads the novel to find clues to the enigma of Marlow's disease; Marlow, in his head, writes a fiction in which his wife/whore, Nicola (Janet Suzman), and Finney (Patrick Malahide), the emanation of his childhood victim, Mark Binnie, steal his script and propose to sell it to Hollywood. Increasingly, Nicola and Finney speak Marlow's script:

FINNEY: Nicola, I know this sounds crazy; but I feel as if he's made it all up. . . . I have this awful, dash, he stops himself, comma, and all but shudders, full stop.

NICOLA: Darling, dash, question mark.

The resolution comes when Marlow relinquishes the control which fiction gives him and begins to trust reality.

Potter uses the expansiveness of the six-part serial—a form which has its own place in modernism—to adapt to his own ends the segmented narrative structure and multiple plot lines which are familiar from the continuous serials of popular television. Not only does he interweave narrative strands, but he cuts between time and genre.

- There is a hospital situation comedy set in present time.
- There are interludes from the musical which interrupt historical time with fantasy. (The interruption by lipsynch songs is less frequent and more versatile than in *Pennies from Heaven*.)
- There is a *film noir* set in the postwar 1940s, the heyday of *film noir*, in which Finney (Patrick Malahide) is involved in the death of a beautiful Russian spy and contracts the singing detective to get him out of trouble. This is the pulp novel by Philip Marlow which Reginald is reading.
- There is a crime story about the theft of Marlow's script, involving Nicola, Marlow's wife, and Finney, which seems to be evolving in Marlow's head, and is set in an uncertain present time.
- And there is a biographical narrative set mainly in the Forest of Dean, and briefly in London, which involves his mother's adultery, his separation from his father, and his return after her suicide. This narrative also involves his own little betrayal when he successfully fingers young Mark Binnie, son of his mother's adulterous lover, for the classroom defecation which he committed. (This scene is almost identical to one in Potter's very early play, *Stand Up, Nigel Barton* [1965]. The same actress, Janet Henfrey, plays the teacher in both dramas, and so it functions as a kind of memory within Potter's creative history.)

- Underlying all of these, and to some extent unifying them, is a narrative of illness and recovery, a process of self-discovery through psychoanalysis which climaxes in an acknowledgement of guilt. This is the redemption narrative which gives the drama its moral, and possibly spiritual, core.

These narrative strands are continually punctuated by recurrent motifs, represented in brief shots or sequences:

- The body of a naked dead woman being lifted from the river below Hammersmith Bridge. She is sometimes Philip's mother who committed suicide from the bridge, and sometimes the Russian spy/whore.
- Young Philip in the tree which represents both his freedom, and the place from which he watches his mother making loving with Raymond Binnie.
- A London subway station in which Philip runs away from his mother, a flight associated with his feelings of guilt for his mother's suicide.
- The image of a scarecrow which he first sees from the train on his way to London, and which mutates in his mind first into Hitler and then the teacher from the classroom scene.

Potter had used the technique of actors lip-synching to 1930s music before—in *Moonlight on the Highway* (1969) and most notably in *Pennies from Heaven*—to suggest the ability of popular music to reach a level of affective sentiment which lies on the border between real feeling and maudlin sentimentality. In *The Singing Detective* the popular songs are part of a wider discourse of the popular and the authentic which includes popular film and television genres (*film noir*, musical, and hospital melodrama) as well as popular music. Here, the affective core is caught between fiction and experience, between conventional narratives of betrayal and detection and a personal narrative (Bakhtin's biographical narrative) of guilt and redemption. In this context, the dialectical tension between cheap emotion and real pain may be ironic, but it is irony with a savage edge. (It is no accident that Marlow takes his name both from a fictional detective and from one of the cruellest of the Elizabethan tragedians.) The scene in which Marlow makes his real and painful breakthrough in psychoanalysis with an acknowledgement of his shame and pity may end with Gambon and Paterson lip-synching to a cheap song, but the joke is affirmative, and even life-enhancing, precisely because it does not obliterate the pain.

In his *Theory of the Avant Garde*, Peter Bürger places considerable emphasis on the non-organic work as definitive for a modernist avant garde. What he calls 'the classicist' ('without', he adds, 'meaning to introduce a specific concept of what the classical work may be'), produces work with the intent of giving a living picture of the totality. And the classicist pursues this intention even while limiting the represented reality to the rendition of an ephemeral mood. The avant-gardiste, on the other hand, joins fragments with the intent of positing meaning (where the meaning may well be the message that meaning has ceased to exist). The work is no longer created as an organic whole but put together from fragments . . .[29]

And while the organic work of art seeks to conceal 'the fact that it has been made', the avant-garde work 'proclaims itself an artificial construct, an artifact'. It is in this process of proclaiming itself a construct that 'montage may be considered the fundamental principle of avant-gardiste art'.[30]

Potter fits into this in complicated ways. On the one hand, it is quite clear that *The Singing Detective* is an artifact, brimming over with self-reflexive devices and constructed as a montage of narrative strands, genre pastiche and recurrent motifs. On the other hand, the fragments are unified by the central consciousness of Marlow, in whose fevered and diseased imagination all of the elements of the montage form a whole. If it is not a contradiction in terms, then, Potter's modernism is of the 'classicist' mode rather than the avant-gardiste. The narrative montage of *The Singing Detective* is not inorganic: the fragments and fractures are organically unified in the consciousness of the surrogate author who seeks meaning and redemption through self-discovery and creativity.

While Mercer belongs in the context of a wider European modernism, Potter seems to be that slightly odd thing, an English modernist. English almost to the point of parochialism (he took his first trip abroad in 1972 when he was 37), he seems isolated from the intellectual forces which shaped modernism and prides himself instead on a very English kind of anti-intellectualism. In his peculiar and obsessive mixture of guilt and redemption, repression and excess, sexual fear and sexual aggression, he seems at least psychically related to that other great English artist with his roots in modernism: Alfred Hitchcock. What is most striking and valuable about him, whatever my lack of sympathy or my prejudice, is that he remained with television, expanding the boundaries of the possible in television drama and taking the audience where it had not been before. Humphrey Carpenter quotes John Naughton's review of *Blackeyes* in the *Observer*: 'He is the only writer I know who *writes television*. Others merely write *for* television.'[31] While the term 'non-naturalism',

29 Bürger, *Theory of the Avant Garde*, 70.

30 Ibid. 72.

31 John Naughton, *Observer Magazine*, 10 March 1990; quoted in Carpenter, *Dennis Potter: The Authorised Biography*, 502.

in its formalism and generality, may be adequate to some of his plays, it seems important to insist that *The Singing Detective* is a key work of British modernism, and (*pace* Jameson) one of the monumental works of modernism in television drama.

The 'Yosser's Story' episode of Alan Bleasdale's *Boys from the Blackstuff*, directed by Philip Saville for BBC2 in 1982, opens with a dream sequence in which the unemployed Yosser (Bernard Hill), whose mind seems permanently to be on a very dangerous edge, leads his children into a pond in the park and loses them one by one. Situated right at the beginning of the episode without any lead-in, the scene, which lasts about five minutes, carries none of the markers which separate dream from reality in film and television, and places the viewer on that same dangerous edge, familiar to the Surrealists and, here, the unemployed, where dreaming has as much logic as reality.

Later in the same episode, Yosser visits the confessional. He is unemployed, his wife has left him, Social Services want to take away his children, and all the identity that is left to him is the continual assertion of his name—'I'm Yosser Hughes'—to anyone who can hear him, from a tramp to Graham Souness, the then actual manager of Liverpool Football Club. Yosser is desperate. The priest is only aware of his presence by his inarticulate sobbing, and tries to make the usual encouraging platitudes: 'The guardians of the spirit, my son, some kind of help in a time of need . . .' The scene is filmed in the confines of the confessional box, mainly in the priest's cubicle, with Yosser sobbing on the other side of the curtain.

> YOSSER [*struggling to control his sobs*]: I'm Yosser Hughes.
> I'm desperate, Father.
> PRIEST: It can be a desperate world at times, Mr Hughes.
> YOSSER: Yosser Hughes.
> PRIEST: It can be a desperate world at times, Yosser Hughes.
> [*Sounds of sobbing on the other side of the curtain*]. Tell me, would it make any difference if. . . . [*More sobbing*] A trouble shared in a place of peace, my son. A haven. . . . I'm Father Thomas. 'Doubting' for short. [*He draws back the curtain to see if Yosser has got the joke. Yosser's face, immobile, appears through the grate.*] Doubting Thomas. [*No response*] Daniel Thomas. . . . I'm here to help you, Yosser Hughes. Daniel. Don't worry about the 'Father'.
> YOSSER: I'm desperate, Father.
> PRIEST: Call me Dan . . . [*With emphasis.*] Dan.
> YOSSER: I'm desperate, Dan.
> [*The camera cuts to Yosser's side of the screen in a very high shot. Yosser, realizing what he has said, head butts the wall and the crucifix falls off its nail. End of scene.*]

The effect of this joke is to work one of the many lurches in perspective and response with which *Boys from the Blackstuff* is peppered. Yosser's desperation is serious, his grip on immediate reality is becoming desperately fragile. When the pathos of the situation ends up in the absurdity of the joke (Desperate Dan) the effect is like the cheap laugh on the way up meeting the tears on the way down: it is exact that the viewer does not know whether to laugh or cry. It is in the best traditions of the scene at the end of *Waiting for Godot* (1948–9) when the tramp, at the end of his tether in a meaningless world, whips off his belt to hang himself from the tree—and his trousers fall down.

Boys from the Blackstuff is a realist drama about the effects of unemployment, shown in five episodes each of which includes the same cast of characters but in relatively autonomous narratives. I am introducing it briefly and abruptly at the end of this chapter to act as a kind of epilogue to television drama's modernism, showing the adaptability of realism and the very thin line which sometimes separates it from surrealism. To the extent that modernism is not simply about formal strategies but about putting the subjectivity of the viewer into play and undermining the securities by which he knows the world, *Boys from the Blackstuff* promises the security of realism and a familiar reality, only to undermine it with something else. As a popular drama, it does not offer the avant-garde surrealism of the inorganic text, but rather a kind of reflectionist surrealism in which only the logic of the surrealist joke can express the absurdity and meaninglessness of a system which requires permanent unemployment. If it seems realist in its apparent form, the lurches of subjectivity, of not knowing how to read it, whether to laugh or cry, follow the spirit of the modernist absurd.

While *Boys from the Blackstuff*—like Bleasdale's later play, *GBH* (1991)—fits uneasily into the kind of aesthetic we conventionally associate with modernism or the surrealist avant garde, it also fits uneasily into realism. It is precisely this unease—this 'in-betweenness' —which makes television drama such interesting territory for a consideration of the aesthetics of modernism and realism. The conditions of television offer particular forms of relationship between the author and the audience, between art and the popular, between different technologies of the real, and out of these relationships come particular and specific aesthetics—modalities of modernism or realism, lurches between the everyday and the surreal, between literal and imaginary space, new alignments of naturalist immediacy and modernist montage. It seems to me important to insist on the place of television drama within the wider cultural and aesthetic movements of the latter part of the century. But it is also important to understand the particular articulations and transformations of these movements which take place within television drama.

7

Television Drama and the Art Film: The Logic of Convergence

IN his application for the post of first Chief Executive of Channel Four in 1980, Jeremy Isaacs, aware of the role which television had played in stimulating film production in Germany and Italy, expressed his desire 'to make, or help make, films of feature length for television here, for the cinema abroad'.[1]

John Hill explains that although Jeremy Isaacs had recognized the potential in overseas markets he had not originally anticipated theatrical release for Channel Four films in the domestic market. Union agreements made films aimed only at television transmission cheaper to produce, and the 'barring policy' then operated by the Cinema Exhibitors Association (CEA) meant that films given a cinema release could only be transmitted on television three years after their initial cinema exhibition. Nevertheless, films destined for Channel Four's Film on Four strand were being completed before the Channel went on air in November 1982, and the filmmakers were keen to get them into cinemas as soon as possible. With the Channel's blessing, Colin Gregg's *Remembrance* and Neil Jordan's *Angel* (both 1982) were given a limited theatrical release before their Channel Four screening. 'As a result', says Hill,

> 'Films on Four' began to appear in cinemas on a selective basis and the channel was able to achieve some flexibility with the CEA regarding their early television transmission. This resulted in a formal agreement, in 1986, when the CEA agreed that the bar would not apply to films costing under £1.25 million, a figure then increased to £4 million in 1988.[2]

In 1981, the year before Channel Four went on air, David Rose was appointed as first Senior Commissioning Editor for Fiction, and was

---

1 Quoted in John Hill, 'British television and film: the making of a relationship', in John Hill and Martin McLoone (eds.), *Big Picture, Small Screen: The Relations between Film and Television* (Luton: John Libbey Media/Luton University Press, 1996), 156.

2 Ibid. 156–7.

put in charge of Channel Four's film programme strand, Film on Four. He was given a budget of £6 million to commission around twenty films of feature length a year. Rose, who had worked in BBC drama since 1951 and had been the first producer of *Z Cars* in 1961, came to Channel Four from his post as Head of Drama at BBC Pebble Mill, the Birmingham regional centre which had become the base for many of the most significant dramas in the Play for Today strand in the 1970s. It was Rose who had encouraged David Hare to direct his dramas *Licking Hitler* and *Dreams of Leaving* on film. In 1988, Rose's title at Channel Four was changed to Head of Drama.

In 1990, Rose was succeeded as Head of Drama by David Aukin, who came not from television or film but (somewhat to the surprise of the industry) from the National Theatre in London, where he had been Executive Director. At Channel Four, he was given a budget of around £12 million, twice as large as Rose had received nine years earlier, but a budget which was generally spent on fewer films (twelve films in 1993, fifteen in 1994). In 1997, Aukin's title was changed from Head of Drama to Head of Film, and in 1998 he left Channel Four to form his own company, HAL, which will develop film projects for the American company, Miramax.

At a seminar organized by students at Glasgow University in 1998, Aukin remarked that when he was being offered the post, Michael Grade, Jeremy Isaacs's successor as Chief Executive of Channel Four, gave him the option, since the British film industry seemed to be beyond real recovery, of taking the Channel out of feature film production altogether and returning to television drama. Aukin elected to stick with film for a trial period, and the success of the films which he backed—*The Crying Game* (1992), *Four Weddings and a Funeral* (1994), *Trainspotting* (1996), for example—formed the basis for a recovery in British film which has proved to be more real than most.

In the free preview magazine for the 1995 Edinburgh Film Festival, there was a half-page Channel Four advertisement which announced:

CHANNEL FOUR FILMS
AT THE FOREFRONT
OF BRITISH FILM MAKING

It then lists the films in whose success Channel Four 'is proud to have been involved', together with the awards which indicate their international distinction. The list includes: *The Crying Game* (Neil Jordan, 1992), *Howard's End* (Merchant/Ivory, 1991), *Naked* (Mike Leigh, 1993), *Backbeat* (Iain Softley, 1993), *Raining Stones* (Ken Loach, 1993), *Three Colours Red, White and Blue* (Kieslowski, 1993–4), *Four Weddings and a Funeral* (Mike Newell, 1994), *Ladybird, Ladybird* (Ken Loach, 1993), *Shallow Grave* (Boyle/Macdonald/Hodge, 1994), *The Madness of King George* (Nicholas Hytner, 1994). In a full-page advertisement in the same magazine, the BBC lists fifteen new films to be shown at the Festival—including Ken Loach's *Land and Freedom* (1995), screened as the opening gala—which trail fewer clouds of glory but nevertheless constitute 'an unprecedented number of films' from the BBC to be given a film festival screening. This advertisement bears the logos of both BBC Television and BBC Films.

Channel Four's funding models varied considerably between full funding, co-investment, and the pre-purchase of television rights. Full funding was relatively rare in the period between 1982 and 1991. John Pym, in his survey of Film on Four in this period,[3] lists 136 films commissioned by the Channel of which only fourteen were fully funded. One of these, however, was *My Beautiful Laundrette* (1985), scripted by Hanif Kureishi and directed by Stephen Frears, which, as John Hill, says, 'initially looked quite uncommercial but subsequently proved to be one of the Channel's biggest successes of the 1980s and virtually became identified as the "archetypal" Film on Four'.[4] In the 1990s, *Riff-Raff* (1990), *Raining Stones, Ladybird, Ladybird, Bhaji on the Beach* (1993), and *Trainspotting* were all fully funded. Below full funding, the Channel's participation varies from 6 per cent of the total budget (£325k for *Hope and Glory* [1987]) to 95 per cent (£955k for *She'll Be Wearing Pink Pyjamas* [1984]). Through Film on Four, the Channel has also invested in a number of international films, particularly European art films, as a way of securing first transmission rights: Wim Wender's *Paris, Texas* (1984) may be the best-known example, but the list also includes Agnes Varda's *Vagabonde* (1986), Tarkovsky's *The Sacrifice* (1986), Kieslowski's *Three Colours* trilogy (1993–4), and Gregory Nava's *El Norte* (1983), an American independent feature developed through the Sundance Institute with a Channel Four contribution of only £25,000.

Importantly, Channel Four's involvement is editorial as well as financial. Michael Grade, who succeeded Jeremy Isaacs as Chief Executive in 1988, suggests the significance which even minority participation may give to Film on Four as script editors rather than simply as bankers or investors:

> Even where we are a minority partner, our involvement can be crucial financially and also artistically. There are many occasions where, without our investment, films simply wouldn't get off the ground—or the page. And artistically, our editorial input can be considerable: for instance with *Four Weddings*. We invested only a third of the budget, but it is no disparagement of Richard Curtis—one of the funniest and nicest writers in Britain today—to emphasize the role of David Aukin and his team in helping to

---

3 John Pym, *Film on Four: A Survey, 1982–1991* (London: BFI Publishing, 1992).

4 Hill, 'British television and film', 158.

focus Richard Curtis's comic genius to its ultimate effect through all the script revisions.[5]

The initial breakthrough in the convergence of television drama and the film industry came with the recognition on the part of television that, contrary to the previous orthodoxy, a cinema release might provide a shop-window for television transmission, attracting critical and popular attention which would build an audience for the television transmission; and the recognition on the part of the film industry that without television's participation the British film industry was liable to sink without trace. The crisis of the mid-1980s, when both film production and cinema exhibition reached their lowest point ever, like the prospect of a hanging, focused minds wonderfully, and both the trade unions and the cinema exhibitors sought a more flexible accommodation with Channel Four.

These are some of the sign-posts which point British television drama down the road towards British film and the British art cinema—and which, simultaneously, point the British cinema back towards a new dependency on British television. The Senior Commissioning Editor for Fiction becomes the Head of Drama, and the Head of Drama subsequently becomes the Head of Film. The £6 million budget to produce twenty films a year becomes a £12 million budget to produce around fifteen. Costs go up and volume comes down; the need to fill a programming strand is replaced by the need to ensure that each product has the quality which will enable it to find its place in the market. To find its place in the international market, British cinema is increasingly dependent on funding from national television. The boundaries between cinema and television become indistinct, and lines of development and aspiration converge. What is significant is that this process of convergence seems to follow a logic which few people were aware of at the time: neither Jeremy Isaacs nor David Rose anticipated that Channel Four films would have a determining impact on British cinema, and, as recently as 1990, neither Michael Grade nor David Aukin were confident that the future lay in film for theatrical release rather than in drama for television. The logic does not seem to be dependent on policy, but is driven by histories of British film and television which surface at various points in this book—histories of independence and public service; of commodification; of a *télévision d'auteurs*; of technologies of immediacy and technologies of film; and, in particular, histories which trace a complex movement between television as national culture and television in the international market. The complexity of the movement produces surprises—from *My Beautiful Laundrette* to

---

5 Michael Grade, 'Getting the right approach: Channel Four and the British film industry', in Hill and McLoone (eds.), *Big Picture, Small Screen*, 179–80.

Trainspotting—but the underlying logic seems to draw television drama away from the rough edges and awkward shapes of the single play towards the more rounded landscape of quality control and the late twentieth-century art film. In this chapter, I want to tease out some of the strands which make up the logic of convergence.

Channel Four, then, whether by accident or design, transformed the British audiovisual space, bringing the film and television industries into a new relationship of interdependence in which it became difficult to fix the boundaries between a dramatic film and a filmed drama. Whereas previously the label 'Made for Television' attached to a movie denoted the routine, the cheap, and the anonymous, after Channel Four, the label 'Film on Four' came to mean quality and, increasingly, an art cinema which was almost incidentally shown on television. *The Crying Game* and *Trainspotting* carry their affiliation with television very lightly indeed. The fact that Channel Four came into being in an economic and political context—'Thatcherism'—in which large, monolithic institutions and restrictive practices were being attacked under the name of 'liberalization' gave it an influence within broadcasting disproportionate to its size and maturity. Channel Four, as a decentralized, flexible business, sensitive to the market, became the model for the various re-regulations of broadcasting in the 1980s and 1990s, creating uncertainties not only about what television drama was, but about what public service broadcasting was in the new market economy. Although in its ethos it was the child of the 'new social forces' of 1968 radicalism, in its structure it was the somewhat unruly child of Thatcherite economic liberalism, its occasional misdemeanours overlooked as long as its success in the broadcasting market could be used as a stick with which to beat the 'big broadcasters' and the restrictive practices of the broadcasting trade unions.

It is important to stress the enormous difference which Channel Four made to the way in which British television functioned. For my generation, it seems almost as difficult to remember what television was like before Channel Four as it is to remember what television was like before recording, and for a generation which has grown up with Channel Four as part of the natural order of things it seems important to point out that it was not always thus. The 'moment' of Channel Four—the period in the early to mid-1980s when the old stabilities of British broadcasting were being shaken loose—seems like a structural shift in film and television culture, and in the culture at large, of immense significance. Indeed, it may turn out to have been the last structural shift in a broadcasting system conceived as a central component of a national culture or of the British public sphere. Subsequent shifts towards the proliferation of channels expand the private sphere of leisure choice but at the expense of the public sphere: the public sphere becomes virtual. The Peacock Committee's advocacy in 1986 of 'consumer sovereignty' in the 'full broadcasting market' appeals to a pragmatic sensibility in a way which makes the Pilkington Committee's insistence on social responsibility seem very old-fashioned, but it does so by addressing the individual as private consumer rather than as public citizen.[6] Channel Four in 1982, whatever the charges of cultural elitism, still seemed motivated by a desire to extend and expand what could be conceived in Britain in the 1980s as the citizenry. Whatever the dilutions which government made to the original proposals for a fourth channel, the concept of a more open broadcasting arrangement was retained at least as a principle, and was translated in practice into a diversification of access and dissemination. For producers and aspiring producers, the diversity may have had limits—it was easier to stay in than to get in—but it was nevertheless unprecedented in British audiovisual media. And for the public, there was an access to forms of cinema and filmmaking previously restricted to colleges, film schools, and universities and to a few independent film exhibitors in London.

The Annan Committee, like the Pilkington Committee before it, was established by Government to review broadcasting at the end of the 1970s, and, on the basis of that review, to make recommendations on the allocation of a fourth—and possibly final—terrestrial television channel with universal coverage. Its title, 'The Committee on the Future of Broadcasting', gives a sense of the significance of its ambitious range. Like the Pilkington Committee, it was not a committee concerned simply with technical decisions but was invited to take the pulse of the nation and to contemplate the cultural role of broadcasting in the last decades of the century. Just as the Pilkington Committee in 1962—with its emphasis on the 'burdens of responsibility' in broadcasting and its exorcism of the sins of triviality—can be read as a translation into official discourse of a post-1956 sensibility of engagement and social purpose, similarly the Report of the Annan Committee in 1979 addresses quite explicitly a post-1968 sensibility abroad in the culture which challenged centralized and paternalistic authority.

the most striking change in broadcasting was brought about by the change during this period in the culture of our country. The ideals of middle class culture, so felicitously expressed by Matthew Arnold a century ago, which had created a continuum of taste and opinion, always susceptible to change and able to

---

6 See *Report of the Committee on Financing the BBC* [Cmnd. 9824] (London: HMSO, 1986). The Committee, commonly known as the Peacock Committee, was chaired by Professor Alan Peacock.

absorb the *avant-garde* within its own urbane, liberal, flexible principles, found it ever more difficult to accommodate the new expressions of life in the sixties. The new vision of life reflected divisions within society, divisions between classes, the generations and the sexes, between north and south, between the provinces and London, between pragmatists and ideologues. Sometimes the divisions existed but were given new publicity: sometimes they were postulated and then were brought about. At once inflationary in the expectations of what political power could achieve and deflationary towards those in power who failed to give effect to those expectations, the new mood expressed itself in a rhetoric of self-conscious unrest, in exploration rather than explanation, in the politics of perpetual crisis and strain, in innovation rather than adjustment, in the potentialities rather than in the probabilities of the future. It was a rhetoric of anxiety and indignation simultaneously utopian and sardonic. It was often hostile to authority as such; not merely authority as expressed in the traditional organs of State but towards those in any institution who were charged with its governance. People working in an organisation demanded that management shared with them the power of taking decisions which affected their lives.[7]

A radical shift in the culture requires a radical reconsideration of how broadcasting is to be reviewed and brought back in tune with the climate of the nation.

It has been put to us that broadcasting should be 'opened up'. At present, so it is argued, the broadcasters have become an overmighty subject, an unelected elite, more interested in preserving their own organisation intact than in enriching the nation's culture. Dedicated to the outworn concepts of balance and impartiality, how can the broadcasters reflect the multitude of opinions in our pluralist society? Their obsession with obtaining as large a mass audience as possible, so the argument runs, contorts the scheduling of programmes and constricts the creativity of the producers. Perhaps the only way, therefore, to break up the mass audience is to break up the broadcasting organisations. These contentions emerged from some important submissions which have come to us, and uppermost in them have been demands that we should re-examine the whole structure of broadcasting and the political assumptions on which the British system rests. Fifteen years ago people would have found this astonishing. Just as the ground of the debate about broadcasting

---

7 *Report of the Committee on the Future of Broadcasting* [Cmnd. 6753] (London: HMSO, 1977), 14.

has shifted, so have the demands which people make of the broadcasters changed.[8]

Just as the Pilkington Committee had established a discourse about the place of broadcasting which can be identified by certain key terms—'seriousness of purpose', 'the sins of trivialization', 'challenging'—so the Annan Committee seemed to initiate a new discourse which had as its central terms 'openness', 'plurality', 'diversity'.

If the intellectual tone of the Pilkington Committee is resonant with the voice of Richard Hoggart in its disdain for triviality and trash, the liberal tone of the Annan Committee can be associated with the Chairman himself, Lord Annan, a Labour peer, an academic historian, and an intellectual, and with Anthony Smith, who gave very substantial written and oral arguments to the Committee. Smith, who subsequently became Director of the British Film Institute in the 1980s before being appointed President of Magdalen College, Oxford, had published on international broadcasting[9] and was a passionate and highly articulate defender of the liberal principles of broadcasting as an extension of the democratic state. A liberal intellectual, Smith was associated with the Social Democratic Party (SDP) formed in the early 1980s as a breakaway from the Labour Party by the 'Gang of Four' (David Owen, Roy Jenkins, William Rodgers, and Shirley Williams) who were disaffected by the growing power of the Left in the Parliamentary Labour Party. High on the agenda of the SDP was a new kind of politics, based on proportional representation, which would seek coalition rather than the traditional titanic confrontation between the monolithic polarities of Right and Left. It may help to situate the particular liberal complexion of the Annan Report in its desire to break the straitjacket of the broadcasting duopoly if it is seen in the same historical context as the SDP which set out to break the mould of British politics.

The Pilkington Committee had been established to judge between the BBC and ITV as the most worthy custodians of a new channel, and their report was a declaration of faith in public service broadcasting. The result was not only a second channel for the BBC, but, from the perspective of television drama, the report provided a framework within which new ground could—and should—be broken. The Annan Committee was also established to make recommendations on a new channel, but whereas the thinking in the Pilkington Committee was framed by the existing duopoly of one public service broadcaster and one commercial broadcaster, the Annan Committee resisted the

---

8 *Report of the Committee on the Future of Broadcasting*, 16.

9 See Anthony Smith, *The Shadow and the Cave: A Study of the Relationship between the Broadcaster, his Audience, and the State* (London: Allen & Unwin, 1977); Anthony Smith, *Books to Bytes: Knowledge and Information in the Postmodern Age* (London: BFI Publishing, 1993).

temptation to think in terms of a restored equilibrium in which an ITV1 and an ITV2 would balance BBC1 and BBC2. Anthony Smith is quoted in the report:

> if the fourth channel is placed in the hands of the IBA [independent Broadcasting Authority] and the companies it will complete the symmetrical straight-jacket of broadcasting in Britain and continue it for ever: two public institutions would each supervise two channels and they would compete, two by two, for parallel audiences in perpetuity. In other words awarding a new channel or even a substantial part of it to the IBA and the companies would damage broadcasting irreparably. Better not to award it at all than to place it in these particular wrong hands.[10]

Instead the Committee sought to open out the structure of broadcasting and to break out of the kind of equilibrium which could only be maintained by one large institution competing with another for the audience. Rather than allocating the new channel within the duopoly, they recommended a new authority to be named, appropriately if tendentiously, the Open Broadcasting Authority.

> We recommend that an Open Broadcasting Authority (OBA) should be established. . . . We do not consider that the Open Broadcasting Authority should be required to schedule a balanced evening's viewing in which sport, light entertainment, education, news, current affairs and all the other types of programming are shown. Nor should the OBA be required to take responsibility for the content of its programmes in the same way as the BBC and the IBA do. The OBA should operate as a publisher and its obligations should be limited to those placed upon any other publisher. Like any publisher the Authority would need to see to it that its programmes were not libellous, did not incite to crime, disorder, or racial hatred and were not obscene. Like any other Authority, the OBA would have to see that an overall balance was achieved in its programmes over a period of time, but we should like to see this done in new and less interventionist ways. . . . In general, we recommend the Authority should have the maximum freedom which Parliament is prepared to allow. The Authority would therefore itself be an experiment in new ways of exercising responsibility for broadcasting and we see this as anticipating and exploring the consequences of the greater freedom which should be possible when many more channels are available to cable.[11]

This is heady stuff. The new authority was to oversee a new kind of broadcaster: a 'publisher-broadcaster'. Instead of producing

---

10 *Report of the Committee on the Future of Broadcasting*, 231.

11 Ibid. 236.

programmes, the fourth channel was to commission programmes from independent producers or to buy them from other broadcasters both at home and overseas. Under the duopoly, virtually all domestic television was produced by the BBC or the ITV companies, and there were quite rigid union rules, designed to protect the livelihoods of the union membership, which governed crewing and technical standards. These rules made it extremely difficult, if not impossible, for new producers to gain access to television. In the 1970s there was a small but active independent sector in the film industry clustered around the Independent Filmmakers' Association (IFA) and the Association for Independent Producers (AIP) who made a precarious living by producing films either through cultural subsidy or through commercial sponsorship. They were in many senses the descendants of the Documentary Movement and Free Cinema, but they were considerably more marginalized because, with the decline of the 'short' in the pattern of exhibition, they had limited access to cinema, and no access at all to television—and it was television which had replaced cinema as the public 'pulpit' through which Grierson had addressed the democratic citizenry. The intention of the new arrangement of broadcasting recommended by the Annan Committee, for which both IFA and AIP had lobbied hard, was that the independent sector would play an increasingly significant role in production (the aim was 25 per cent of the new channel's broadcast time), and that this would open out broadcasting by making it possible for new voices to be heard and new kinds of programming to be seen on television.

> Above all, there will be programmes from a variety of independent producers. We attach particular importance to this . . . category as a force for diversity and new ideas. These programmes could vary from a major theatrical production or sporting event to programmes made by a small group of people with an idea for a programme such as the existing channels do not today accept. We would expect the OBA, by commissioning from independent producers, to guarantee a place where new ideas for programming can flourish.[12]

It is worth noting that the Annan Committee considered, but rejected, a number of proposals for a formal relationship between the new channel and the film industry which were designed to bolster British film. This seemed to be a dream too far. Nevertheless, in its insistence on the importance of independent producers as a programming source it opened a bridgehead through which such a relationship might evolve.

---

12 *Report of the Committee on the Future of Broadcasting*, 237.

The Committee, which had been established by a Labour Government, reported just before the election of 1979. The Government of James Callaghan published a White Paper on broadcasting in its last year of office, but proceeded to lose the election, and the Annan Committee recommendations were left to the Conservative Government led by Margaret Thatcher to modify and implement. It is one of the glorious contradictions of British culture of this period: a report which translates the radicalism of 1968 into the terms of liberal democracy and recommends openness and diversity comes face to face with the least liberal and most authoritarian government Britain has known this century. Some of the contradictions, of course, found their way into the new channel. The new Government, however, had not yet been purged of all its 'wets' (Thatcher's later name for 'moderate'—or even liberal—conservatives who had somehow found their way into her Cabinet), and fortunately it fell to one of the wetter and more liberal members of the Government, the first Home Secretary, Lord Whitelaw, to put the recommendations into practice.

The major modification which was made was that the idea of the Open Broadcasting Authority as a third, autonomous authority, was dropped, and the new channel was placed within the remit of the existing Independent Broadcasting Authority, the statutory body which regulated commercial television. This meant, in principle, that the duopoly was maintained with an equilibrium between a mass appeal and a minority channel in the public service system and a mass appeal and a minority channel in the commercial system. The justification for this very significant modification was that there were serious doubts that a new television channel would be financially viable, at least in the short term. By allowing the IBA to sell the advertising for both the ITV network and the new channel there was provision for cross-subsidy. Although there were fears at the time that this was a betrayal of the principle of openness, hindsight suggests that Channel Four might not have been as adventurous as it was in the early years if it had been thrown to the mercy of the market without the safety net of IBA funding. And to offset the loss of financial autonomy, the symbolic concession was offered that the new channel would not be identified as a second ITV channel (although many television sets had been sold with a button marked 'ITV2') but as Channel Four.

If this modification was thought to weaken the principles of the Annan Committee, William Whitelaw wrote into the Broadcasting Act of 1980 which brought the new channel into being injunctions on the Independent Broadcasting Authority which seemed, and still seem, astonishing for a Conservative Government.

(1) As regards the programmes (other than advertisements)
     broadcast on the Fourth Channel it shall be the duty of
     the Authority—

  (a) to ensure that the programmes contain a suitable
       proportion of matter calculated to appeal to tastes and
       interests not generally catered for by ITV;
  (b) . . . to ensure that a suitable proportion of the
       programmes are of an educational nature;
  (c) to encourage innovation and experiment in the
       form and content of programmes,

and generally to give the Fourth Channel a distinctive character
of its own.[13]

This injunction, which came to be known as 'the remit', acquired the
same status for Channel Four as the rather more general obligation
on the BBC to 'inform, educate and entertain', and operated for the
Channel as a licence to break the hidden rules of broadcasting in
a much more explicit way than the Pilkington Committee's implicit
advocacy of controversy and challenge as the mark of serious purpose.
The remit not only allowed the Channel to be different, but gave it a
statutory obligation to be so. It formed a protective cloak in which
Jeremy Isaacs could wrap himself when the unruly upstart over-
stepped the mark and brought down howls of fury from conservative
bodies such as the Viewers' and Listeners' Association, or its 'military
wing', the tabloid press. It was the remit which allowed Channel Four
to screen a Derek Jarman season which brought Jarman the recognition he deserved, or allowed them to mount a gay and lesbian current
affairs series. It was also the grounds on which producers could
appeal to the Channel when they were seeking support for something
which had never been done before, or which was eccentric, or scandalous, or for which the likely audience not previously catered for
could be numbered in the low thousands.

Channel Four, then, was established with a licence to rewrite the
orthodoxies of public broadcasting in Britain. It seemed strange in
the early 1980s when Thatcherism was taking shape that we had been
given such a Channel at such a time, when the moral and cultural
discourse of the Government was couched in terms of a return to
Victorian values and a rediscovery of middle, and little, England.
If Channel Four, however, often seemed to fly in the face of the moral
and cultural illiberalism of Thatcherism, within its economic liberalism it was wonderfully orthodox, and Thatcher was not above trading
ideological heresy for economic orthodoxy. Because, as a publisher-
broadcaster, the Channel commissioned rather than produced pro-

---

13 Broadcasting Act, 1980, chapter 64 (London: HMSO, 1980), paragraph 3, 3.

grammes, it required little fixed plant or contract staff and could 'travel light', making it much more responsive to the rise and fall of the market than the lumbering monolith of the BBC could ever be. The Channel was creating a new sector in television production, expanding employment at a number of different craft levels and decentralizing production away from the metropolis, and therefore it had the sympathy of the unions and was able to lever more flexible working practices. The restrictive practices of the broadcasting unions had been a prime target in the sights of Mrs Thatcher, and the new channel seemed to be at least a strange bedfellow if not an ally. Most wondrous of all, Channel Four was creating small businesses, the economic foundation of Thatcherism. In giving viability to the independent sector, Channel Four was taking filmmakers who had lived on subsidy, and sometimes dreamed of revolution, and was turning them into entrepreneurs, lean and hungry companies competing in the marketplace for their next commission, negotiating over producer fees, buy back arrangements, and intellectual property rights.

As it became apparent through the 1980s that the system of commissioning was to be the norm rather than the exception in the new age of broadcasting, and as the traditional broadcasters began to 'down-size' in response, more and more programme makers found their way, voluntarily or involuntarily, into the independent sector where job security was a thing of the past. In the independent sector, the producer was no longer a person like Sydney Newman, James McTaggart, or the David Rose of Pebble Mill days, who maintained a fatherly discipline over a creative team of young idealists and tried to curb their wilder excesses, but was the person who went out and got commissions and put the budget together. In the terms which Janet Staiger uses when describing Hollywood cinema,[14] British television was going through the same shift which Hollywood had gone through in the 1960s and 1970s from a 'producer-unit' system to the 'package-unit' system.

> The signal concept is that of the package. Rather than an individual company containing the source of the labour and materials, the entire industry becomes the pool for these. A producer organized a film project: he or she secured financing and combined the necessary labourers . . . and the means of production . . .
>
> The major differences between this system of production and the prior one, the producer-unit system, were the transitory

14 Janet Staiger, in David Bordwell, Janet Staiger, and Kristin Thompson, *The Classical Hollywood Cinema: Film Style and Mode of Production to 1960* (London: Routledge & Kegan Paul, 1985), 330–7.

nature of the combination and the disappearance of the self-contained studio. With the old producer-unit system, a producer had a commitment to make six to eight films a year with a fairly identifiable staff. The package-unit system, however, was a short-term film-by-film arrangement. Of course, often subordinate members of the labor hierarchy worked time and again with the same people because of skills and work habits; workers' employment was, none the less, based on a film not a firm. With the disappearance of the self-contained studio, the means of production was also a short-term combination. Instead of a filming unit owning its entire means of production for use in film after film, the unit leased or purchased the pieces for a particular project from an array of support firms. Costumes, cameras, special effects technology, lighting and recording equipment were specialities of various support companies, available for component packaging.[15]

The system when applied to television not only followed a film mode of production, but it also created an entire infrastructure of small and large companies, from facilities houses to caterers and prop makers, from makers of sound effects to rostrum camera operators: supply services, that is, which had previously only existed inside the BBC or the ITV companies.

In the extension of the package-unit system to television, the producer was the person who put the package together and sold it to Channel Four. After the 1990 Broadcasting Act, based on the unexpected success of Channel Four, the requirement that 25 per cent of broadcast time be commissioned out to independent producers was extended to all terrestrial broadcasters. Since the television companies do not always fully fund production—particularly film production—it was the producer who then went out and looked for investors or for subsidy to make up the shortfall. The language of production became increasingly entrepreneurial, with 'product' and 'markets' infiltrating an older language of 'programmes' and 'the audience'. Competition among producers for a finite number of commissions replaced the relative security of the 'studio' environment of, say, the BBC Drama Department, and the stability of staff contracts was replaced with a more or less casualized labour force whose short-term contracts lasted as long as a production. By the 1990s, market discipline was so enshrined in managerial thinking that the BBC invented an internal market where no real market existed. A system of Producer Choice was introduced which permitted BBC programme producers to go outside the BBC in pursuit of the most competitive tender for services. Reducing dependency on fixed labour on staff contracts, this acted as a purgative to speed up the

15 Staiger, in Bordwell, Staiger, and Thompson, *The Classical Hollywood Cinema*, 330.

process of 'natural wastage' and more and more services moved into the independent sector.

It is, of course, dangerously easy to be nostalgic when faced with the incursion of the market into the sphere of creativity, and the Golden Age of television drama is liable to become more golden in the memory when viewed from the perspective of down-sizing and internal markets. The image of young radicals plotting the downfall of capitalism and the subversion of Reithian broadcasting in the BBC canteen watched over by paternalistic and indulgent producers has sometimes acquired a legendary status, and like all legends probably requires a good dose of sceptical amnesia. By the late 1970s, the frustrations of BBC bureaucracy, the pressures of producing thirteen or twenty-six plays a year when only five or six offered a real challenge to the creative imagination, the rota system of crewing which meant that a camera operator or an editor moving between departments was treated as a technician rather than as part of a creative team, all made a persuasive case for independence, and, in both 'technical' and 'creative' grades, many were ready to take the leap into the new sector which was opening up. Predictably, it was often the most creative and innovative writers, directors, and producers who had the confidence and the reputation to break ties with the system which had nurtured them, and to step out from under the security blanket of the BBC studio system into the 'real world' of the competitive market. Increasingly, in television drama, there was the suspicion that not to be independent was a failure of nerve, and it was to the independent sector that one looked for creative boldness.

Even after the nostalgia has been stripped away, however, it is fairly clear that the success of Channel Four and the 'package-unit system' was double-edged. On the one hand, it marked a radical and refreshing shift in the culture of broadcasting and the public sphere, freeing up the centralization of the duopoly, opening television to new voices and introducing diversity at a number of levels. On the other hand, however, it introduced the beginnings of a competitive rationalization of broadcasting which very gradually through the 1980s and into the 1990s made it a little less likely that the eccentricities of creativity and the irrationalities of licensed subversion would be indulged, or that producers would animate the contradictory space in which a large public service institution satisfied the demand for seriousness of purpose with 'serious drama'. In the area of television drama, the sense of a collective identity which marked out both a series of programmes, the Wednesday Play or Play for Today, and the writers, directors, and producers who shaped them—and even the paternalistic and unwieldy institution which transmitted them—was important in carving out a place for drama in the national consciousness and in establishing the conditions of possibility in which boundaries might be tested and values interrogated. Very often, of course, values were not interrogated and plays played safe; but perhaps the boundaries were tested just often enough to give the series the sense of a project, and controversy was 'talked up' by producers in a way which made it seem like a responsibility. The moment of Troy Kennedy Martin's manifesto in 'Nats go home', or the controversy which surrounded the drama documentaries of Loach and Garnett, or the ironic subversion of Trevor Griffiths, seemed to depend on a certain commonality of concern and collective engagement in television drama. With the arrival of Film on Four, there were enormous leaps in production values, and the *mise en scène* and narrative possibilities of film laid the memories of studio television to rest once and for all. The films, however, were emphatically 'one-offs', each with its own production unit; and producers and directors—sometimes even the same producers and directors—who before had fought their battles inside the BBC as part of a more or less common project to make television drama serious, now fought their individual battles to win commissions and to secure their company's future in a highly competitive arena. Undoubtedly, as Thatcherism told us it would, competition led to quality, but it also dissipated that sense, however tenuous, of a common identity and a cultural project which had made the Wednesday Play a central component of the national culture.

A number of competing logics were coming into play which had a transformative impact on television drama. There are the final stages of a technological logic which transforms television from live transmission to recorded tape or film: the transformation whose beginnings we noted in early television which gave television drama a commodity form. Increasingly, with the extension of the global market in television, drama was one of the commodities which could enter the global market most successfully as a tradable good. The economic context in which this technological logic takes shape is one in which the increasing costs of television drama make it more and more essential for the broadcaster or the independent producer to recoup costs through overseas sales. The logic of independence is that drama is produced as one-off films and distributed to reach as many markets as it can, the ultimate measure of success being the international market and the combination of a global television market and the cinema box-office. As Film on Four began to break through into cinema success with surprises like *My Beautiful Laundrette* and began to reap in awards and nominations in international film festivals, television drama has been more and more defined by its aspiration to be cinema. Film on Four became Film on Four International.

In the meantime, in the 1980s, there is another technological logic at work: the rise of domestic video. Television, television drama particularly, and, most particularly, films on or for television no longer circulate as single events within a national schedule. The audience no longer 'comes together' on a Wednesday night around the Wednesday Play, but may choose to time-shift in dispersed domestic groupings. A programme can be watched when it is convenient rather than when it is scheduled. This change in the mode of reception has been noted to the point of banality, and there is very little reliable empirical evidence on the nature of time-shifting and audience dispersal. It would be dangerous, however, to underestimate the difference which individual, privatized choice introduces into reception for an understanding of the historical process by which television drama is absorbed into a new and more generalized audiovisual space. The technological capacity to choose when to view (and, ultimately perhaps, to pay per view) seems to erode that earlier specificity of television drama as a cultural form which circulated as an event within a national space and time.

All of these logics work together, then, to produce that difficult space where the local and the global, public service and the market grate against each other and reshape their boundaries. Again, it is never a question of one pole simply replacing the other, but of a readjustment of the 'pressures and limits', a realignment of emergent forces and residual forces. Nationally, single plays shot on film continue to be produced, but they circulate as one-offs in a different climate and a different audiovisual space. Even if the dramas themselves had not changed, everything else has. Viewers use television differently, and come to it with different demands. A play no longer has the allure which a film has, and drama no longer compensates with a sense of danger. At the international level, somewhere in the entrepreneurial process there is likely to be some glint of an international sale which might be made easier by conceding something to international taste: a softening of regional accents, a recognizable actor, a human rather than a political problem. This is slippery ground, and producers tirelessly refute accusations from observers that the market determines the kinds of film which are made, and that films increasingly circulate images which will confirm rather than challenge the national image in the international imaginary.

It is, indeed, possible to exaggerate the processes of the global market, and to render the local helpless against the depredations of the major players in the international market. There is an issue at stake here which it is important to make clear since it is often missed in the generalized paranoia about globalization. It is not that the global market has no place for nationally specific representations: the international success of films like *The Snapper* (1993), *Gregory's Girl* (1981), *My Beautiful Laundrette*, *Ladybird, Ladybird*, or *Trainspotting* demonstrates that there will always be an audience for precise observation, however localized it may be—even for a film whose accents are sometimes impenetrable to anyone except the most immediately local. The point, I think, is that what the international market values in national specificities are precisely those qualities which transcend the local and make it universal: humanity, character, and in particular, character in adversity. It is more difficult to sell on the international market the material social conditions which produce the adversity. Characters coping with their social situations are universal and therefore marketable, but the political conditions which produce the situations can be very, very local and, hence, more difficult to sell. This is not meant as an appeal for a return to an exclusive diet of social responsibility and socialist realism, but simply to suggest the limits of the international market for a national television. There is a very genuine excitement about the development of a British art cinema and it should be celebrated, but it seems worth reminding ourselves of the gaps which begin to appear in its wake in representations of the local and the national. It is never that anything is impossible—market conditions make everything contingent (Ken Loach or Stephen Frears carry reputations which are themselves marketable) —but some things gradually become less possible than others.

To establish some continuity in my argument, let me single out Ken Loach and, in particular, *Cathy Come Home* and *Ladybird, Ladybird*. The comparison may be a little obvious: twenty-eight years after *Cathy Come Home* (BBC, 1966)—and seventeen years after *The Spongers* (BBC, 1977)—Loach returns again in 1994 to the theme of a mother trying to hold her family together against a social service system which seems intent on driving them apart. Scripted by Rona Munro, the narrative this time has an international dimension: Maggie (Chrissie Rock) is a survivor of childhood abuse who lives on a very short fuse and has already had three children taken away by the Social Work Department on the basis of evidence that she is dangerously irresponsible and an unsuitable mother. She forms a relationship with a Paraguayan political refugee, Jorge (Vladimir Vega), who is gentle, caring, and a poet. They have a child, but because Jorge is a foreign national whose visa is uncertain, the home is not accepted as a stable environment and social workers place this child too in care. Unlike *Cathy*, this film is given a qualified happy ending in final captions which tell us that Maggie and Jorge have finally been accepted as good and caring parents and their children have been restored to them.

Much of the territory is familiar, and Chrissie Rock's astonishing performance retains some of the raw authenticity of *Cathy*. Where the key difference lies, it seems to me, is in the absence of the social document, the 'report on which law should be based'. In *Cathy* the montage of voices, however critical they may be individually of uncaring social services, add up collectively to a complex context in which one voice plays against another and the individual drama is located in material social conditions. In *Ladybird, Ladybird* the individual drama drowns out other voices. This gives it an intensity and a unity which is extremely moving, but, in a way which *Cathy* does not, it substitutes emotional impact for social analysis. The result is that the instability of Maggie is 'explained' by the narrative of her childhood abuse, but the brutality of the social services is unexplained, and social workers seem to become simply the agents of an uncaring state. The narrative is underpinned by the politics of betrayal which sorts out the discourses into a hierarchy of sympathetic and unsympathetic characters in which individuals and agencies occupy their familiar places: characters who are struggling versus the 'meddlers' of the system. It is precisely a drama of character in adversity, the kind of universal drama which is at home in the international art cinema.

Interestingly, a similar point has been echoed recently in some comments by Peter Mullan, the Scottish actor and director who received a Best Actor award at Cannes in 1998 for his role in Ken Loach's *My Name is Joe* (1998). In an interview in *Sight and Sound* about his own film *Orphans* (1999)—which won four awards at the 1998 Venice Film Festival—Mullan is asked if he was aiming for magical realism. 'Absolutely,' he says:

> I wanted the film to upset visually as well as verbally. The problem with the social realists is that they want to have their cake and eat it. They maintain that their films are in a social-realist style and therefore credible, but they're not. Almost all social-realist films revert to melodrama if and when it suits them. Take *My Name is Joe*: a young lad throws himself out of a window with a rope around his neck, thus all sins are absolved and Joe might get together with the woman. Absurd, it's absurd. It achieves nothing except moving an audience to tears. It gives us no insight into other options he might have taken. The tradition I come from is experimental and very un-British. I like expressionist cinema, Spanish surreal cinema and silent cinema.[16]

It is hard not to find some significance in the fact that Channel Four, having contributed 50 per cent of the film's budget, refused to distribute *Orphans* after it was not accepted for the Berlin Film Festival—because, Mullan says, 'After *Trainspotting*, the attitude was money, money, money, and they thought *Orphans* would be too hard to sell.'[17]

16 'Tearing the roof off: Liese Spencer talks to Peter Mullan about *Orphans*', *Sight and Sound*, vol. 9, issue 4 (1999), 14.

17 Ibid. 13.

So what is my anxiety? At its simplest, it is a doubt that the full cultural remit of a national broadcasting system can be sustained within the economic logic of an international market in images and representations. More abstractly, it is a suspicion that the prestige of an art cinema and a quality television which wants to be film may begin to dissolve the local specificities and diversities and small recognitions of a complexly national television. Most concretely, it is a sense that a very fundamental shift has occurred between *Cathy Come Home* and *Ladybird, Ladybird*, and that the gain of a British art cinema may be at the expense of something quite valuable and immediate in a national television system. This is not a nostalgia for a lost golden age, and it is certainly not a criticism of the power of Loach's recent work. It is, rather, a sense that, whatever the intentions, the social anger of *Ladybird, Ladybird* circulates within an aesthetic and a cultural sphere which is given prestige (and economic viability) by international critics' awards, whereas *Cathy Come Home* circulated as a national event and functioned as documentary evidence within the political sphere.

Returning to John Hill's characterization of *My Beautiful Laundrette* as a film which 'initially looked quite uncommercial but subsequently proved to be one of the Channel's biggest successes of the 1980s and virtually became identified as the "archetypal" Film on Four', it is instructive to ask if such a film would be made in such a way in the late 1990s. My suspicion is that it would not. It is too untidy in its shape, too uncertain in its narrative focus, too many themes are pursued and too few conclusions are reached. It is about race *and* sexuality *and* gender *and* exile *and* Asian entrepreneurialism *and* the Asian domestic sphere *and* Thatcher's Britain. In 1985, Daniel Day-Lewis was not yet a star who could carry a film, Hanif Kureishi was not yet an established writer, and only Stephen Frears could lend weight to the package. And most of all, the film inhabits a complex politics of race, immigration, and enterprise, in which good guys and bad guys shade into each other: white Johnny (who has marched with the neo-Nazis) evicts an Afro-Caribbean Rastafarian poet at the behest of the Pakistani businessman, Nasser (Saeed Jaffrey)—'I'm a professional businessman,' says Nasser, 'not a professional Pakistani; and there's no question of race in the new enterprise culture.' 'We'll drink to Thatcher', says Nasser, 'and your beautiful laundrette.' 'Do they go together?', asks Johnny. 'Like dal and chapatis.' The gay sexual relationship between Johnny and Omar (Gordon Warnecke) is not a plot motivation, heterosexual relationships lead nowhere, and Tania's (Rita Wolf) escape from the increasingly surreal confines of the family is not a life-affirming conclusion. It is a mosaic of issues and situations rather than a well-made narrative. Like *Up the Junction* twenty years earlier, *My Beautiful Laundrette* still seems to belong to a tradition of drama which is interested in a social and historical environment rather than 'in the ingenuity of a well-invented story, developed according to certain rules' (Zola).[18] It belongs to a tradition of description rather than narration, though any attempt to ascribe it to naturalism would immediately bump up against the comic, the surreal, and the tradition of magic realism associated with postcolonial literatures.

My suspicion—and it has to be speculative and generalized—is that what makes *My Beautiful Laundrette* an 'archetypal' Film on Four in the 1980s would have made it 'too hard to sell' in the 1990s. The unexpected success of *My Beautiful Laundrette* in the international market of the 1980s seems to have been replaced by an expectation of success in the 1990s, an expectation which has been confirmed over and over again by the films which Channel Four celebrates in its Edinburgh Film Festival advertisement. To secure this success requires precisely that artistic participation which Michael Grade quite rightly sees as one of Film on Four's virtues. That artistic participation, however, increasingly points to a shift in dominance in the creative process away from the untidiness of writers and directors towards the more surgical skills of producers and script editors; away from the difficult territory of art towards the more predictable and marketable characteristics of 'quality' and 'production values'. This is not to deny the achievements of many of the films of Channel Four in the 1990s, but to trace the slow process by which the tradition of the single play, still found in many of the films of the 1980s, becomes attenuated to breaking point by the increasing acceptance in the 1990s that success finds its measure in the international cinema.

This points finally to a general unease about the logic of convergence. While the convergence of film and television may have gained us the beginnings of an internationally prestigious British art cinema it may also have restricted some of the possibilities of a national television drama which gave television a particular edge within the British public sphere. At another level, within the independent film sector there are forces of convergence which may have lost us some of the diversity which was introduced into film and television in the early 1980s by Channel Four. In the 1970s, the Independent Filmmakers' Association (IFA) argued for a cinema which was oppositional and autonomous from the mainstream—radically different rather than merely pluralistic. By the beginning of the 1980s arguments were beginning to be made against hand-to-mouth casualization and for the development of a more professionalized infrastructure, with union recognition, script development funding, and training schemes from entry-level to in-service. These arguments

18 See above, Chapter 4.

fed into the development of the Workshop Movement, a system of regionally and socially based production units which opened broadcasting, in quite radical ways, to new voices. The Workshop Movement could only have existed through the support of Channel Four, the British Film Institute, the Regional Arts Association, and the Association of Cinematograph and Television Technicians (the ACTT, the main union in film and broadcasting production). It was given substance by a Workshop Agreement which gave union recognition to a limited number of franchised workshops whose work could be produced for television with a lower than union minimum level of staffing and salary in recognition of the collective and community nature of their work. As a condition of the agreement, they were essentially non-profit-making and they were to be regionally based or they were to represent specific social groupings which had not previously been represented in television production. Workshops were established in places like Newcastle, Birmingham, Cardiff, Edinburgh; there were gay workshops, black workshops, and women's workshops. They received initial capital funding from Channel Four, and could expect revenue funding in the form of commissions from its Department of Independent Film and Video. The productions were shown mainly on the Eleventh Hour, a minority strand which went out at 11p.m. on Mondays. More than simply production companies, the workshops provided entry-level training and had a commitment to film culture in their region. While much of their work was in documentary, the workshops also produced fiction and drama documentary, and provided perhaps the most tangible evidence of the Channel's commitment to real diversity. Precisely the excitement of the early days of Channel Four was that there was an attention to new voices, a space in which the local could be heard without the pressures of the international market, and the potential for new kinds of drama.

There was always something conditional, however, in the support for Workshops. For Channel Four, the Workshops satisfied the remit which demanded diversity, and for the unions it expanded employment both geographically and economically, introducing new entry points and new training facilities at a time when the large institutions were being forced to 'down-size' and cut back their training schemes. The Workshop sector was still different, but it was now institutionalized within the industry rather than apart from it or in opposition to it, and increasingly the viability of a workshop was measured by the same standards as the viability of any other company. Caught within an increasingly entrepreneurial logic as Channel Four moved towards autonomy in the market and faced the prospect of a reliance on its own ability to sell advertising, the Workshops became a charitable anachronism in a market economy. When Channel Four withdrew revenue funding the Workshops became so many small businesses, dependent for their commissions, like all the other small businesses in the independent sector, on the increasingly product-hungry broadcasters.

There is no malice or oppression in this logic; no voracious capitalists gobbling up the last remaining vestiges of integrity; no 'big broadcasters' stamping out the economic untidiness of low-budget production. Increasingly, the 'big broadcasters' recognize the need for a diversity of entry points to the industry and the urgency of replacing the training facilities which they themselves have lost. Again, interdependency is the name of the game. BBC Scotland, for example, in collaboration with the Scottish Film Production Fund and the Glasgow Development Agency, has been creative in developing series strands like 'Tartan Shorts' and 'First Reels' as a way of introducing entry points for young and/or first-time film-makers. It seems ungracious to do anything but celebrate this, and, within the prevailing logic, it is indeed to be celebrated. But the logic of this convergence of interests and dependencies, like the logic of convergence of film and television, is pragmatic rather than principled. It assumes a unified industry within a unified culture, and the principle which is at stake is diversity and difference. For television drama and film, what Channel Four seemed to offer for a brief period in the 1980s was the possibility of alternative forms of television, the space for a kind of avant garde which would never have mass appeal or international success, but which would be precisely a workshop in which ideas could be tested and new ways of making drama could be tried. The loss of this space is yet another sign-post pointing towards the absorption of both film and television into that new space: the audiovisual landscape.

The 1980s produced a diversity in British cinema and television, the public profile of which can be captured in the names of Ken Loach, Mike Leigh, Derek Jarman, Sally Potter, Peter Greenaway, Hanif Kureishi, Terence Davies, Isaac Julien, Black Audio Film Collective, Gurinder Chadha, but whose roots went down into the infrastructure of Channel Four, the unions, IPPA (Independent Programme Producers' Association), PACT (Producers' Alliance for Cinema and Television), and the Workshop Movement. That diversity was embodied as a principle in the establishment of Channel Four: a principle which was enshrined in an Act of Parliament as the culmination of arguments which circulated in the Annan Committee Report and debates which were being conducted in the independent film sector in both its mainstream and its oppositional manifestations. It is difficult to see where, in the convergence of tributaries and mainstreams and in the economics of film and television, such principles—particularly the pragmatically uncomfortable ones—are still to be defended.

The principle seems to me to circulate around what it is we want to celebrate in the notion of a national cinema or a national television. Is it a national cinema or television as *representation* of the nation, capturing the images around which the complexity of the nation can identify itself as a unity, representing itself to the outside and securing its continuity in the global market? Or is it a national cinema or television as *representative* of the nation, offering channels for different voices, capturing its diversity and reflecting the fault lines which disunite the culture into differences and complexities rather than imposing on it the imaginary and marketable identity often implicit in the desire for a unified national culture or a national cinema or a national television? If the terms of the opposition are rather obviously loaded, it is not because I seriously believe that one can exist without the other, but rather because I think that there is a danger that the celebration of a kind of art cinema—a cinema alive and well in television—may obscure what is local, awkward, and complex within the nation, and that the logic of convergence may lose sight of the specific and divergent possibilities of a national cinema and a national television.

It is important to return to television drama before the 'death' or 'dying' of television and the birth of the generalized audiovisual space because television drama for a time marked out a space where creativity was still rooted in the local and the particular, difference was still material, and viewing still mattered. In the 1990s, it seems increasingly difficult to separate out 'serious drama' from quality television and the art film, and the plays which gave, in a very specific way, the awkward shapes of immediacy to television, or the hard critical edges of modernism, begin to seem like distant memories.

8

Small Pleasures: Adaptation and the Past in the Classic Serial

THE account I am offering seems to have been one of deaths and disappearances, convergences and dissolutions, tracing the process by which, over the past fifty years, television drama has been eased into an audiovisual landscape—*le paysage audiovisuel*—whose features seem a little flatter and the ground a little less uneven: the landscape of the British art film and quality television. It is difficult to avoid the elegiac tones of a narrative of loss. But if loss creeps in, it is not the loss of an imaginary Golden Age in which every drama took us somewhere we had never been before and every author was an *auteur*, but the loss of certain forms of engagement and debate—both professional and critical—in which television drama seemed to matter politically and something quite important to the culture seemed to be at stake. Loss, however, can be read more productively as transformation and historical change, and the project of this book has been to try to recover some of these points of engagement and to map them as features which have left marks on the landscape.

At the level of programming the sense of loss is nowhere marked with more finality than in the death of the single play series: World Theatre, Armchair Theatre, the Wednesday Play, Play for Today. These series operated in a producer-unit mode of production, and they had established through weekly scheduling in seasonal blocks enough regularity to build an audience and enough identity to build an ethos. Perhaps most significantly they played to a *national* audience and seemed to be anchored in a national culture. They were, however, increasingly expensive, and the demands of finding twenty-six, or even thirteen plays every year which were fit and ready to be broadcast meant that, within the series, the quality of the plays could be very uneven. In an environment in which cost-efficiency was becoming more and more central to decision-making, the combination of rising costs and uneven quality was fatal, and, whatever the cultural value, the economic logic moved inexorably from the producer-unit to the package-unit, from in-house production to independent commissioning, and to the death of the single play series. Film on Four in the early to mid-1980s retained something of the ethos of the single play series in its low-budget films, but in an increasingly qualified way as it eased inexorably towards the logic of convergence.

There was, however, a wrinkle in the economic logic. While the drama series was becoming uneconomic, there was still an audience for 'serious' drama and an obligation within public service broadcasting to satisfy it, and the economics of serial scheduling were still very attractive. Domestically, the serial form had the advantage of economies of scale: the cost per hour of a serial was lower than the costs of a single play and made fewer demands on resources. It was also attractive because it carried its audience over from one week to the next in a way which a series of single plays could not. And ultimately, some serials were attractive because they could be marketed in an economy more and more dependent on overseas sales. Much of the best, and most 'serious', drama of the 1980s and 1990s appeared in serial or series form: not only *The Singing Detective* (1986) and all the late work of Dennis Potter, but *Boys from the Blackstuff* (1982), *Edge of Darkness* (1985), *The Monocled Mutineer* (1986), *The Life and Loves of a She-Devil* (1986), *Tutti Frutti* (1987), *Oranges Are Not the Only Fruit* (1990), *GBH* (1991), *Our Friends in the North* (1997). The list is representative rather than exhaustive. These became the 'public events' of the 1980s and 1990s, albeit in a more attenuated way than the 'classics' of the Wednesday Play and Play for Today when the concept of a national audience was still untouched by time-shifting, multi-channel broadcasting, and niche audience targeting. After the re-regulation of terrestrial broadcasting in the 1990 Broadcasting Act, the requirement that 25 per cent of all production be commissioned from independent producers was extended to the BBC and the ITV companies. As the one-off film was increasingly produced out of house, the BBC, in particular, was able to concentrate its in-house production on a scale of drama which only an institution of its size, resources, and tradable reputation could afford.

In the last chapter, I was concerned with the conditions in which the increasing convergence of film and television transformed the single play into the art, or 'quality' film. There is, however, a parallel transformation: the transformation of the single play into the multi-part serial. What we encounter in the 1980s and 1990s in television drama is not so much a cul-de-sac as a fork in the path: one path leads drama towards film and cinema; the other path, however, leads drama back towards the serial narrative form which has a long history in popular fiction and a particular history in popular television. What is perhaps most significant is that both paths lead television drama further and further away from its historical affiliation with theatre and its allegiance to theatrical form.

If there is a classical form of television narrative, it may be the dramatic serial. While the television film emulates, to a greater or lesser extent, the form of the cinema feature film, and the single play derives its form from the theatre play, the drama serial, having failed to establish itself as a continuing tradition in cinema, now seems specific to television and radio. The particular patterns of regularity which scheduling offers, and the domestic accessibility of broadcasting provide the conditions in which serial narrative becomes the staple diet of broadcasting fiction. Well-trained by soap operas, crime series, and other forms of serial or series narrative to sustain plots and characters over time, the audience develops an aptitude for interrupted and interruptable narrative. More than that, lacking the concentrated forms of identification which the articulation of point of view invites in the cinema, television drama substitutes familiarity for identification, a familiarity which depends on recognition, repetition, and the extension of time. If the space of the look is foundational for our engagement in cinematic forms of narrative, the extension of interrupted time gives us forms of engagement, involvement, and subjectivity specific to television.

There is, of course, a quite separate book to be written about the historical development of serial narrative in television which would follow the development of the different traditions, tracing the precise lines of connection between soap opera and *This Life* (1996–7), say, or between the early crime series such as *Z Cars* (1962–78) and *Softly, Softly* (1966–76) and serial forms such as *Prime Suspect* (1991, 1992, 1993) and *Between the Lines* (1992–4).[1] In the line which I would identify with the single play tradition, there seems to have evolved in the 1980s and 1990s a significant, almost generic development of what might be called 'paranoid narrative' in which the extension of time allows the slow erosion of order and the invasion of everyday normality by irrationality and unreason. *Edge of Darkness, The Life and Loves of a She-Devil, The Monocled Mutineer, Tutti Frutti*, and *GBH* all seem to trace, over their six or so episodes, the gradual, sometimes almost imperceptible intrusion of madness—of individuals and institutions—and the transformation of realism into the surreal. This echoes the mixing of social reality and the surreal madness of unemployment in each episode of *Boys from the Blackstuff*, which, I have suggested, characterizes the adaptability of the realist tradition and its ability to subvert its own rationality from within.

Whatever generic form it takes, the extension in time of an interrupted dramatic narrative seems to me to be one of television's specific contributions to the long history of the novelistic. Bakhtin's

---

1 For an important contribution to the study of British crime fiction, see Charlotte Brunsdon, 'Structure of anxiety: recent British television crime fiction', *Screen*, vol. 39, no. 3 (1998), 223–43.

biographical narrative in which characters are taken on a spiritual or intellectual journey through time and space—whether it be through the historical environment of *Our Friends in the North* or the paranoid environment of *Edge of Darkness*—reaches a particularly developed form in the television dramatic serial.

Somewhat perversely, I want to turn in this chapter to a serial form which has been treated with much less respect by academic criticism despite its immense popularity with international audiences: the classic serial adapted from the nineteenth- and early twentieth-century novel, a form of drama which has been bundled with 1980s and 1990s British cinema into a genre known as 'Heritage', and consigned to the depths of nostalgia and the marketing of the past. While the paranoid narratives or the generational histories mentioned above might sit more comfortably in the argument which runs through this book, I want to give priority to the classic serial in this final chapter because it seems to me to raise some significant questions both about the place of television drama in the late 1990s and about television criticism.

Very obviously, the reinvention of the past has become one of the most significant operations in British culture over the past decade or so, and it is a process in which television drama participates as a primary agent. Masterpiece Theatre has become a key component in establishing British television's hegemony in a certain area of international broadcasting, it has placed England in a particular light in the international imaginary, and it is a significant element in the economy of British television. In this sense, it completes the process anticipated by Hugh Carleton Greene in the article mentioned earlier in this book, 'Television transcription: the economic possibilities':

> In television transcription this country has a potential means
> of enormous power for spreading knowledge of its way of life
> through the most intimate and immediate of all the senses,
> through the eyes of the viewers in all parts of the world.[2]

The process which begins in the late 1940s and early 1950s with the development of recording comes to its full flowering in the 1990s with the television art film and the classic serial. Historically, then, the classic serial, with the art film, seems to complete that narrative which begins with the transience of immediacy and liveness and ends with the solidity of a fully achieved commodity form, a narrative which is paralleled by the movement from the necessity of the national to the demands of the international. This in itself seems to give a certain

2 Hugh Carleton Greene, 'Television transcription: the economic possibilities', *BBC Quarterly*, vol. 7, no. 4 (1952–3), 217. See above, Chapter 2.

centrality to the classic serial in understanding the development of television drama.

What is surprising, then, is that academic television criticism—inclined by habit towards the analysis of popular culture, more comfortable with the obviously 'progressive' than with the 'retrospective', and always suspicious of the 'elitist' pretension of adaptation and the literary tradition—has treated the classic serial with a certain disdain.[3] Quite apart from its centrality to the development of television drama, I am interested in addressing the classic serial in this chapter—albeit in a way hedged round by ambivalence—because it allows me to open up three critical questions. First, I think it is time to break down some of the resistances to literature and adaptation which many of us inherit from the split from 'lit crit', and to reopen some of the questions of language and discourse at which literary study is particularly adept. Second, I am interested in trying to say something about acting, a function of drama which seems central to the allure and pleasure of the classic serial, and about which the criticism of television drama—and indeed of film—seems particularly tongue-tied. And third, I have a suspicion that behind the disdain for the classic serial, literary adaptation, and the costume drama lurks a resistance to the feminine, a masculine dominant in the critical vocabulary which has been most marked in the criticism of television drama.

The adaptation of classic literature, or more precisely the construction of certain literary works as classic—the classic serial—has been a characteristic of British television almost since television began. Certainly, since television resumed its normal service in 1946, the novels of Jane Austen, the Brontë sisters, Conrad, Dickens, Hardy, and Henry James, have been adapted and sometimes readapted.[4] In the mid-1990s, adaptations of *Pride and Prejudice* (1995), *Middlemarch* (1994), and *Martin Chuzzlewit* (1994) not only reaffirmed the status of the BBC as the cornerstone of national broadcasting, but also confirmed its cultural prestige overseas. It also, of course, secured it a healthy slice of the substantial international market in 'quality television'. In the 1980s, endless adaptations of E. M. Forster, suffused with the charms of manners and costume and basking in the warm glow of the past, have made adaptation central to the mythology of Britain in international cinema, helping to shape the perception of

---

3 I should point here to the work of Julianne Pidduck as an exception to this disdain. See her articles, 'Travels with Sally Potter's *Orlando*: gender, narrative, movement', *Screen*, vol. 38, no. 2 (1997), 172–89, and 'Of windows and country walks: frames of space and movement in 1990s Austen adaptations', *Screen*, vol. 39, no. 4 (Winter 1998), 381–400.

4 For the record, the adaptation history of some recent classic serials is as follows: *Pride and Prejudice* (1952, 1958, 1967, 1980, 1995), *Jane Eyre* (1956, 1963, 1973, 1983, 1997), *Great Expectations* (1959, 1967, 1981, 1991, 1999), *Vanity Fair* (1956, 1967, 1987, 1998), *Middlemarch* (1968, 1994), *Martin Chuzzlewit* (1966, 1994).

Britishness—or at least of Englishness—as a quality whose real meaning can be found in the past, and whose commodity value can be found in the heritage industry.

There are, of course, material reasons for this which mean that it cannot simply be attributed to something which is happening in the national psyche. One of the virtues of the study of film and television in an academic context is the extent to which such obviously commercial forms force a new dialogue between industry and art, commerce and creativity. Some dialogue between these terms, which idealist versions of cultural criticism have seen as mutually exclusive since at least the middle of the nineteenth century, seems necessary if we are to prevent consideration of identity and culture from slipping off into national, or nationalistic, essentialisms. Cultural identities happen under certain conditions, and they are shaped not simply by the private insights and expressions of individual artists but by the public determinations of law, economy, and money. This is not to say that private insight, passion, and imagination are terms to be extirpated from critical discourse by a ruthless materialism (though we in Film Studies came dangerously close to such an 'intellectual cleansing' in the enthusiasm for scientific analysis and remorselessly rationalist discourse out of which our discipline was formed after 1968). Rather, the terms of creativity and imagination exist in particular relations with the material conditions which form, transform, and sometimes deform them. Film and television—at least at the international level—are tradable goods, and what they ultimately and increasingly deal in are marketable images. As the terms of public service are more and more diluted by the terms of the market, even the BBC has to trade on its reputation overseas in order to make the kinds of drama which maintain its domestic standing.

At a time when Britain struggled to sell much else on the international market, it became particularly adept at selling the past. The BBC was able to co-produce, or, better still, co-finance drama productions with the United States and occasionally with Australia, which it could not have afforded to produce if it relied entirely on the licence fee. The attraction was that this allowed it a scale of ambition in terms of production values which few public service broadcasters could emulate. The price it paid was that the American end of 'the deal' had to be assured that what was produced would be what the American producers believed American audiences wanted to see from Britain. While in the 1980s and 1990s an important strand developed in the dramatic serial which attempted to reflect the changing complexities of our lives to ourselves, in co-production or co-financing serials are expected to project the kinds of images of our lives which others have come to expect of us. For Britain, this has very often meant the representations of a classic literature in which irony and wit are rendered as English quaintness, and the national past is captured like a butterfly on a pin in a museum of gleaming spires, tennis on the lawn, and the faded memory of empire. This is where the relationship between national cultures and markets begins to become clear, and where we can see most sharply the dangers of reading a national identity out of images which function both as cultural representations *and* as tradable goods.

These developments were given a particular edge by a minor 'scandal' in 1984 when the BBC scheduled a bought-in serialization of *The Thorn Birds*, a somewhat breathless adaptation of a block-buster novel starring Richard Chamberlain, against Granada's wonderfully tasteful and prestigious adaptation of Paul Scott's quartet of the Raj, *The Jewel in the Crown*. Since this followed Granada's equally tasteful and prestigious adaptation of Evelyn Waugh's *Brideshead Revisited* in 1981, a trend was identified: it seemed to many that the prestige of British broadcasting was no longer the monopoly of the BBC, and that the BBC was losing its way. Not only this, but Denis Forman, the Chairman of Granada, was able to demonstrate that *The Jewel in the Crown* was a highly cost-effective way of making television since it had recouped all its production costs in advance overseas sales before shooting started. In the face of the re-regulation of broadcasting in a new multi-channel environment, the battle in British television was not so much for ratings, as for 'quality'.

This term, 'quality', needs some brief description since it has acquired a significance in Britain which is perhaps unique. In British cinema, the notion of a quality film is associated with critics like Dilys Powell, C. A. Lejeune, and Graham Greene writing in the 1940s and 1950s in the midst of the postwar cultural reconstruction which covered all the arts.[5] For the cinema this attempt to found a British tradition of quality hinged on the distinction of the best of British cinema, and it was expressed as a conscious desire for a national cinema distinct from the mere entertainment of Hollywood. The guarantee of that distinction was frequently adaptation either from texts which were already prestigious in theatre or literature, and it is associated with theatrical adaptations like *The Importance of Being Earnest* (1952), Olivier's *Henry V* (1945) or *Hamlet* (1948), literary adaptations like *Brighton Rock* (1947) and *Odd Man Out* (1947), and perhaps most characteristically, with David Lean's adaptations of Dickens in *Great Expectations* (1946) and *Oliver Twist* (1948).

---

5 See Christopher Cook (ed.), *The Dilys Powell Film Reader* (Manchester: Carcanet Press, 1995); Anthony Lejeune (ed.), *The C. A. Lejeune Film Reader* (Manchester: Carcanet Press, 1995); David Parkinson (ed.), *The Graham Greene Film Reader: Mornings in the Dark* (Manchester: Carcanet Press, 1993). See also John Ellis, 'The discourse of art cinema', *Screen*, vol. 19, no. 3 (1978), 9–50.

In the re-regulation of television in the late 1980s, the term 'quality' was given new life.[6] Fears of the complete destruction of the values of public service broadcasting if television were thrown completely to the market were addressed by introducing something called the 'quality threshold', a very loosely defined notion of quality which bidders had to satisfy if they were to be awarded a franchise to operate one of the regional commercial stations. Again, in the public debate which surrounded the introduction of new legislation for television, the shorthand for what was meant by quality in the public mind came to be defined with strong roots in adaptation: the titles which were wheeled out time after time as examples were *Brideshead Revisited* and *The Jewel in the Crown*. These two became the hallmark of quality, and it was their television success nationally and internationally, coming at the same time as such cinema successes as *Chariots of Fire* (1981), *Gandhi* (1982), and *Passage to India* (1985) which firmly established British quality cinema in a particular and peculiar relationship to the past, a relationship which, through the work of Merchant/Ivory, blossomed into an oddly obsessive love affair with the work of E. M. Forster. In television, also, 'quality' seems to return again and again to the adaptation of classic literature, with the international success of Andrew Davies's 1995 adaptation of *Pride and Prejudice* sealing the relationship.

'Quality', then, is a very loosely defined concept to identify a kind of consensual approval. It is a middle-brow term. While it is bounded very obviously on the one side by the trivial and the incompetent, it is also bounded on the other side—rather less obviously—by art. It seems to speak of pleasures without demands. In its use in the 1980s in debates about television, it came to represent the horizon of aspiration for a medium which increasingly suffered from a poverty of desire: with the single play which aspired to art more and more isolated, the advocates of 'quality' seemed to content themselves with production values and with making sure that the money appeared on the screen.

More particularly in her exploration of the values which seemed implicit in the identification of *Brideshead Revisited* and *The Jewel in the Crown* with 'quality television', Charlotte Brunsdon identifies four assets which seemed to assure quality: 'literary source', 'the best of British acting', 'money', and 'heritage export'.[7] The possession of all four of these, she says, allowed these two serials 'to function as *uncontroversial* indicators of quality. There is here no trouble with subjective factors, as there would be, for example, if *The Singing*

6 For a fuller account of this see Charlotte Brunsdon, 'Problems with quality', *Screen*, vol. 31, no. 1 (1990), 67–90.

7 Ibid. 85–6.

Detective, which had been one of the preferred tokens of those with more avant-garde tastes, had been used.'[8]

The notion of a 'quality television' seems to have come out of the 1980s inextricably linked to discourses of literary and cultural heritage. In the cinema of the 1980s, from *Chariots of Fire* (1981) to *Howards End* (1991), films continually returned not simply to the past but to a very particular past: to the period in the first few decades of this century before and after what in Britain is known as the 'Great War', the historical moment in which the land-owning aristocracy began to give up the reigns of power to the new urban bourgeoisie, and in which Britain began to detect the fault lines in its Imperial destiny. On television, drama cultivated the charms, the manners, and the costumes of the nineteenth-century novel. Charlotte Brunsdon quotes Raymond Williams: 'the past is all art and buildings, the present all people and confusion'.[9]

I want now to turn more directly to the classic serial, and to suggest some of the critical questions which it seems to me to raise. First of all, it seems impossible to talk about the representation of the past in images and narratives without acknowledging Fredric Jameson's magisterial warnings on the effacement of history by historicism, or without considering the place of this nostalgia mode within the wider nostalgia mode which Jameson locates as one of the characteristics of postmodernism—or, if you prefer, of the cultural logic of late capitalism. The nostalgia film, he says, 'was never a matter of some old-fashioned "representation" of historical content, but approached the "past" through stylistic connotation, conveying "pastness" by the glossy qualities of the image, and "1930s-ness" or "1950s-ness" by the attributes of fashion'.[10] The description clearly fits both television costume drama and the recreations of the world of Forster in the Merchant/Ivory series. The charge which Jameson lays against this 'mesmerizing new aesthetic mode'—'the waning of our historicity' —is that it denies us the 'lived possibility of experiencing history in some active way'.[11] History becomes the present in costume, showing us only human continuities and lingering generalities of tone and style—the seduction of the image—without the formal distance and the historical particularity which might enable us to experience difference and change.

8 Ibid. 86.

9 Ibid. The quotation comes from a 1971 article in Williams's collected essays on television: Alan O'Connor (ed.), *Raymond Williams on Television* (London/New York: Routledge, 1989), 135.

10 Fredric Jameson, *Postmodernism, or, The Cultural Logic of Late Capitalism* (London: Verso, 1991), 19.

11 Ibid. 21.

I have a great admiration, and even fondness, for Fredric Jameson's work, and I firmly believe that the most interesting postmodernists are the ones who are now or once were Marxists, but there is a constant danger that the cognitive mapping which Jameson proposes might end up as a tourist map, giving a certain security around the main points of orientation of postmodern culture, but without the difficult topographic detail which would allow us to distinguish between a precipice and a steep grassy slope. In particular, as I have argued elsewhere in this book, there is a danger that cognitive mapping, like postmodern criticism itself, at least in the hands of someone less passionate than Jameson, can end up only in the constant description and redescription of a kind of cultural phenomenology. As well as understanding the general relationship which postmodern culture has to the past, we need to be able to distinguish between *this* representation of the past and *that* representation of the past—to distinguish between *Chinatown* (1974), *The Conformist/Il conformista* (1970), and *Body Heat* (1981)—in a way which Jameson does not;[12] or between Fay Weldon's writerly and feminist adaptation of Jane Austen in 1980 and Andrew Davies's televisual and ahistoric adaptation in 1995; or even to distinguish between the historicism of Merchant/Ivory's costume drama adaptation of Forster in *Room with a View* (1985) and their more historical account of *Howards End*, which offers a more uneasy representation of class difference and change in England. The past and our relationship to it is not entirely stable nor is it lacking in its own contradictions and tensions, and it cannot simply be described by blanket terms like heritage or nostalgia. In Britain, there has been a tendency to ascribe heritage to Thatcherism and its (highly selective) appeal to the values of the Victorians (self-sufficiency and family, but not public works), and the association of anything with Thatcher seems to inhibit further thought.[13] While it is certainly true that Britain in the 1980s seemed to be saturated in images of the past, a critical understanding would have to afford to the heritage film and the representations of the national past in both film and television at least the same attention as we used to afford to the Western or the melodrama, discriminating between this Western and that Western, this melodrama and that melodrama, and finding in them, through critical analysis rather than description or cognitive mapping, the secret workings of values, ideologies, and subjectivities.

With this in mind, I want here to take a detour through Naomi Schor's discussion of detail in her book, *Reading in Detail: Aesthetics*

---

12 Jameson, *Postmodernism*, 19–20.

13 See, however, for an exception to this, John Corner and Sylvia Harvey (eds.), *Enterprise and Heritage: Crosscurrents of National Culture* (London/New York: Routledge, 1991).

and the Feminine.[14] I am interested generally in thinking about detail as part of a poetics which is specific to television, and here, particularly, in thinking about the ways in which analysis might approach representations of the past in both television and film. In the wider terms of the analysis of cultural history, it seems to me that Schor's discussion opens questions of the particular and the general which have been central to modernist and postmodernist debates in this century.

In her book, Naomi Schor traces the history of detail in aesthetics from the contempt in which it was held by Sir Joshua Reynolds and the Royal Academy in the eighteenth century to its new-found status in the dialectics of the particular and the general in modernism and in the historiography which derives from Foucault.

'The great style in painting', says William Hazlitt in the 1780s, 'consists in avoiding the details, and peculiarities of particular objects'; and 'Genius', according to Reynolds, 'consists principally in the comprehension of A WHOLE; in taking general idea only'. A 'nice discrimination', he says 'of minute circumstances, and a punctilious delineation of them, whatever excellence it may have (and I do not mean to detract from it) never did confer on the Artist the character of Genius'.[15] This privileging, as Schor demonstrates, is not gender neutral, for while the sublime (which is anti-detail) is 'manly, noble, dignified', Dutch painting is excluded by Reynolds from the Great Tradition because it is too much based on detailed observation of particularities: 'Flemish painting . . . will appeal to women, especially to the very old and the very young, also to monks and nuns and to certain noblemen who have no sense of true harmony'.[16]

In her introduction, Schor establishes some of the parameters of reading in detail and reading detail. To focus on the detail, she says:

> and more particularly on the *detail as negativity*, is to become aware, as I have discovered, of its participation in a larger semantic network, bounded on the one side by the *ornamental*, with its traditional connotations of effeminacy and decadence, and on the other, by the *everyday*, whose 'prosiness' is rooted in the domestic sphere of social life presided over by women. In other words, to focus on the place and function of the detail since the mid-eighteenth century is to become aware that the normative aesthetics elaborated and disseminated by the [Royal] Academy and its members is not sexually neutral; it is an axiology carrying into the field of representation the sexual hierarchies of the phallocentric cultural order. The detail does not occupy a

14 Naomi Schor, *Reading in Detail: Aesthetics and the Feminine* (London/New York: Routledge, 1989).

15 Ibid. 12.

16 Ibid. 20.

conceptual space beyond the laws of sexual difference: the detail is gendered and doubly gendered as feminine.[17]

The ornamental, the everyday, and the feminine: the resonances for television criticism are suggestive, and for the representation of the past in both cinema and television, from costume drama to classic adaptation, they are striking. Period detail and the particularities of manners rather than grand narratives and the Grand Style seem indeed to be central to the allure of the past.

Modernism's concerns, however, complicate the status of detail, throwing the detail into dialectical tension with the whole. 'The reconciliation of the general and the particular,' say Adorno and Horkheimer in their critique of the Culture Industry,

> of the rule and the specific demands of the subject matter, the achievement of which alone gives essential, meaningful content to style, is futile because there has ceased to be the slightest tension between opposite poles; these concordant extremes are dismally identical; the general can replace the particular, and vice versa.[18]

Without that tension, the detail is subsumed within the general, and becomes mere style. The detail loses its rebelliousness, its 'protest against organization', and 'is liquidated together with the idea' which it expressed.[19]

In the Arcades Project, Benjamin's ambition was to present the very consciousness of the nineteenth century through its material details. Starting from a citation from Goethe, 'everything factual is already theory',[20] Benjamin, according to Susan Buck-Morss,

> retained the notion that the Arcades project would present collective history as Proust had presented his own—not 'life as it was', nor even life remembered, but life as it has been 'forgotten'. Like dream images, urban objects, relics of the past century, were hieroglyphic clues to a forgotten past. Benjamin's goal was to interpret for his own generation these dream fetishes in which, in fossilized form, history's traces had survived.[21]

And as Benjamin himself says, 'As Proust begins his life story with awakening, so must every work of history begin with awakening;

---

17 Schor, *Reading in Detail*, 4.

18 Theodor Adorno and Max Horkheimer, 'The Culture Industry', in *Dialectic of Enlightenment* [1994] (London: Verso, 1979), 130.

19 Ibid. 125.

20 Susan Buck-Morss, *The Dialectics of Seeing: Walter Benjamin and the Arcades Project* (Cambridge, Mass.: MIT Press, 1991), 28.

21 Ibid. 39.

indeed, it actually must be concerned with nothing else. This work [the Arcades Project] is concerned with awakening from the nineteenth century.'[22]

The principle which Benjamin adopted was to be the presentation of what he called 'dialectical images' in montage: material details replete with history, a history which could be unlocked and allowed to speak for itself through the technique of montage. The principle of construction, says Buck-Morss,

> is that of montage, whereby the image's ideational elements remain unreconciled, rather than fusing into one 'harmonizing perspective'. For Benjamin, the technique of montage had 'special, even total rights' as a progressive form because it 'interrupts the context into which it is inserted' and thus 'counteracts illusion'.[23]

'Method of this work', notes Benjamin: 'literary montage. I have nothing to say, only to show.'[24]

How does this help us with television's encounter with the past in the classic adaptation? It seems to me it offers a way of approaching both the pleasures of classic period adaptation, and the disappointments. The pleasures are, indeed, pleasure in detail, our engagement held not by the drive of narrative but by the observation of everyday manners and the ornamental. In this context, it is interesting that the *Radio Times* published the cover photograph of the wedding of Elizabeth and Darcy in the 1995 adaptation of *Pride and Prejudice* (billing it 'The wedding of the year') the week before the wedding actually happened, anticipating wedded bliss while at that point in the sequence of the transmitted story the characters were still at loggerheads. The pleasure was not what will happen, but in how; the drama (or at least its publicity) was addressed to an audience which already knew the outcome.

The important point is that the pleasure in detail is a pleasure in profusion, and, for analysis, this pleasure has to be thought differently than a pleasure governed by the Law of the Father and driven by desire and lack. It is, if you like, a small pleasure, a pleasure of observation rather than of fantasy and identification, a pleasure in the ornamental and the everyday which the history of aesthetics has assigned to the feminine, a pleasure which the academy, and academic film and television theory, has not regarded as manly, noble, or dignified.

The disappointment, of course, is that the pleasure in period detail is not so much an awakening from the nineteenth century as a

22 Ibid.

23 Ibid. 67.

24 Ibid. 73.

slumbering in it: it does indeed, as Jameson claims, deny us the 'lived possibility of experiencing history in some active way'. History becomes the present in costume, showing us only human continuities and lingering generalities of tone and style—the seduction of the image—without the formal distance and the historical particularity —the rebellious detail or the materiality of Benjamin's 'dialectical image'—which might enable us to experience difference and change.

In this context we can begin to see where the boundary between 'quality' and 'art' might lie: quality television is an art television which has avoided its historical appointment either with modernism, with naturalism, or with critical realism. In the cinema, it is a similar evasion which sets the British art (or quality) cinema apart from the great modernist tradition of art cinema in Europe. 'Quality' is the art form of *le paysage audiovisuel*—the work of art in the age of the audiovisual landscape.

I want to suggest, then, that attention to detail offers a way of understanding both the pleasures and the disappointments of heritage film and classic serial, and provides a mode of approach which might allow us to account for those pleasures and disappointments in a more analytical way than blanket dismissals or denunciations of postmodern nostalgia permit. It might also raise questions about the gendering of taste. Let me suggest some of the questions that attention to detail might raise.

First, irony. It seems to me an irony in itself that British quality film and television adaptation is drawn, like a butterfly to a flame, to a literature which is itself deeply ironic, to texts whose central defining ironic trope resists easy translation into the visual. The nineteenth-century novels of Austen, Eliot, Dickens, the twentieth-century novels of E. M. Forster or Evelyn Waugh are sown through with an ironic discourse which continually nudges the reader into judgement, assigning to him or her an understanding of the social which the characters do not have. Consider Jane Austen's famous first line in *Pride and Prejudice* : 'It is a truth, universally acknowledged, that a single man possessed of a good fortune, must be in want of a wife.' In all recent adaptations, this line has been preserved and assigned to Elizabeth Bennet. What happens when it is transferred from the narrator's discourse to Lizzie's? It assigns to Lizzie a knowledge of her social and historical situation, a knowledge which in the novel is shared between author and reader over the heads of the characters. A Lizzie who has the wit to know escapes at least some of the ironies of prejudice. In adaptation, characters become knowing and textual irony, the discourse of the narrator, becomes Elizabeth Bennet's arch knowingness. The ironic trope of an embryonic modernism regresses historically into the wit of an earlier classicism.

As I have argued in Chapter 5, irony is not an impossible figure either for television or for cinema. It has been a commonplace of film theory, at least since Colin MacCabe's influential essay on realism in *Screen* in 1974,[25] that the metadiscourse, the discourse which is the discourse of knowledge and which allows us to place all the other discourses in a hierarchy of truth, is located in the realist film in the *mise en scène*. 'Don't trust what the characters say, trust what you see.' It is the *mise en scène* which gives to the spectator an understanding of the characters' situation which the characters themselves do not have. The detail of the *mise en scène* may stand in an ironic relation to the other discourses. But what happens when the space of irony, the *mise en scène*, is occupied by quality and the loving recreation of period? Quality cinema, the classic serial, sell a particular relation to the past, a relationship based on feel rather than on understanding, on slumbering rather than on awakening, on a profusion of detail rather than the dialectical image, on nostalgic longing rather than the 'lived possibility of experiencing history in some active way'. The money shots[26] fill the screen with connotations of pastness, a pastness which has become a thing in itself. The space of the ironic authorial discourse is taken up with shots which caress the past into living presence, the directness and complexity of Forster's ironic relationship to class and empire is suffused with warm light and lost in the lingering period detail which is the hall-mark—and the trademark—of the quality film. Or Jane Austen's gentle but precise irony, which put a pointed stick in the eye of the marriage trade and the disposal of women, is travestied as a romance in pretty frocks and heaving bosoms.

What has happened, of course, is precisely that 'reconciliation of the particular and the general' for which Adorno and Horkheimer reproached the Culture Industry. The detail which makes the past different from us has been absorbed and dissolved into a generality of style designed to give us the patina of pastness without its materiality: '1810s-ness' or '1890s-ness' communicated by the attributes of fashion. This, however, need not always be the case. In the BBC's 1996 serialization of *The Tenant of Wildfell Hall* detail stands out, thrown into relief by a photographic style which very clearly frames its shots. A highly composed and beautifully lit shot of three women seated on a chaise longue, dressed in evening gowns of contrasting colour and vivid texture, sipping tea, is held static for long enough for its pastness to register as something different. The exquisitely composed framings of the Brontë landscape recall Victorian landscape painting in a way

25 Colin MacCabe, 'Realism and cinema: notes on some Brechtian theses', *Screen*, vol. 15, no. 2 (1974).

26 'Money shots' are the shots in which the film proclaims that it is expensive—and therefore 'quality'.

which situates the drama in a time, an ethos and a way of seeing. This precise location in time makes all the more shocking the theme of sexual and physical domestic abuse, giving us the same sense of horror which the novel gave to the Victorians, and, at the same time, historicizing domestic violence. The fact that *The Tenant of Wildfell Hall* was the first post-*Piano* classic serial suggests that television drama may have discovered a different way of revisiting the past.

Charlotte Brunsdon identifies the 'best of British acting' as one of the trade marks of quality television,[27] and I want to insert some general discussion of acting here because it is in what the actor does that detail may be most sharply observed. Acting seems to be one of the things which gives the classic serial its most particular pleasure, and the perennial attraction of the nineteenth-century novel for television is not simply the visual pleasure of pretty costumes and expensive sets, but is the pleasure of watching a gallery of characters being performed by stellar display of actors: think of John Mills's aged and wandered Mr Chuffy in the 1994 *Martin Chuzzlewit* constantly haunted by memories of the same actor as young Pip in David Lean's 1946 film adaptation of *Great Expectations*; or Olivier in *Brideshead Revisited* or Peggy Ashcroft in *The Jewel in the Crown*. *Martin Chuzzlewit*, in particular, with Paul Scofield, Tom Wilkinson, Elizabeth Spriggs, and Keith Allen playing alongside John Mills, seemed to offer an opportunity to show off, precisely, 'the best of British acting', exploiting the eccentrics, villains, and grotesques who populate Dickens's novels to construct not so much a narrative as a performance of characters and cameos.

Given the centrality of acting to the classic serial, to quality television, and to television drama in general (think of Michael Gambon in *The Singing Detective*) the absence of theoretically informed critical writing about acting is surprising. There is a considerable body of writing about film stardom, and some about television personalities —which are the constructs that we make out of actors—but there is very little about what actors actually do when they act. In a tradition of criticism which uses the vocabulary of cineliteracy and teleliteracy, and of reading the screen, there is very little attention to reading the actor. Acting is, of course, very difficult to nail down analytically in a way which goes beyond the impressionistic vocabulary of honesty and truth to life, and while we have a vocabulary that describes and understands the effect of a cut or a close-up, we lack a critical language to describe and understand an expression that flits across a face or a hesitation in the voice. Acting, like landscape, poses the problem of endless description: at what point could you stop?

27 Brunsdon, 'Problems with quality', 85–6.

For the critical tradition which has grown up around film and television since the late 1960s, discussion of acting is doubly doomed. In the first place, acting is the ineradicable link between film and television on the one hand, and theatre on the other hand; and the theatrical, the stagy, has been a term of abuse—formally, culturally, and politically—at least since the 1920s in cinema and since the late 1950s in television. Secondly, and I think more significantly, the actor acting is a messily humanist component of the specific signifying practices of film and television, a kind of impressionistic marshland without shape or solidity for a discipline which gained its firm academic footing through the quasi-scientific language of its analytic procedures. The result has been yet another point of division between one school of criticism which was content to use the humanist and often moralistic vocabulary of honesty, truth, and courage to describe acting, and another more rigorously academic school which tried to explain and analyse acting by a vocabulary which squeezed the life out of it and replaced it with a semiotics of gesture and movement in which the actor becomes part of a system of signs and signifiers.

What lies behind this division is a more fundamental division for theory between formalist, materialist, and constructivist notions of representation on the one hand, and realist, reflectionist, and revelatory notions of representation on the other. For Eisenstein or Brecht the point is not to discover a truth in the world which is always already there, but to construct a meaning which will change the world. In their films or stagings they break up the world and force us to look at it in a new way *as if* for the first time. The film-maker's technique, his or her formal strategies—montage, the techniques of distanciation—are ways of breaking up the world and constructing a meaning which does not pre-exist the representation. For André Bazin, on the other hand—realist, catholic, and socialist—the world was already meaningful, it had a truth, and it was the responsibility of the filmmaker to look at it honestly and directly in order that that truth will be condensed on the screen. Von Stroheim, he tells us, looks at the world, and keeps on looking until the truth comes out. 'Take a close look at the world, keep on doing so, and in the end it will lay bare for you all its cruelty and ugliness.'[28] The film-maker's technique—looking directly but not directing the look—is a way of uncovering a meaning which was there waiting to be uncovered. For Eisenstein, the spectator's look is to be directed, her view of the world shaped and changed; for Bazin, the spectator, in an act of imaginative identification, discovers the meaning of the world which was previously concealed in noise and distraction.

28 André Bazin, 'The evolution of the language of cinema', in *What is Cinema?*, selected and translated by Hugh Gray (Berkeley and Los Angeles: University of California Press, 1971), 27.

What interests me about acting is the way it participates in, and confuses, both systems, blurring the edges of the division between constructed meaning and revealed meaning, and creating an area of fuzzy logic. Certainly, there are techniques of expressiveness, repertories of gesture and expression which signify feeling and construct meaning. Actors pretend to be people that they are not and to have experiences that they have not had. That is what they are paid for, and that is why they are banished from Plato's Republic. In order to pretend, they learn through practice and observation a vocabulary of recognizable and individuated signs which are reproducible at will. But actors also en-act and em-body feelings *as if* they were real, in a way which makes them real for them and *for us*, and that is why Aristotle brought them back into the city to play out pity and terror on our behalf. In order to embody feeling, actors learn techniques of physical relaxation and they play games of risk-taking and trust to minimize the barriers between a feeling and its expression: the expression of a truth that is held—somewhat miraculously, despite all pretence—to be always already there within the actor. It is the processes of emotional identification with the role which animate the techniques and devices, allowing the meaning to emerge, and confronting academic formalist criticism with the messiness of truth, honesty, feeling, and sometimes courage.

At one constructivist extreme there are the nineteenth-century actors' manuals—Delsarte is the most famous, and, at least in the United States, was probably the most widely used[29]—which teach the actors precise gestures and facial expression to portray grief, anger, or moral outrage at a woman's disgrace; at the other revelationist extreme, is the practice of someone like Grotowski for whom the actor's technique is a *via negativa*, a stripping away of all the resistances until there is only pure affect left.[30]

In the philosophical or theological debates between representation as construction of meaning and representation as reflection, the appeal of constructivism was not simply that it was felt to be more materialist but that it was also found to be more teachable. You could *show* the point of view shot which constructed your subjectivity. It is precisely the fuzziness of acting, its participation—sometimes simultaneously—in both the forms of expression and the content of expression, the construction of pretence and the revelation of feeling, that makes it difficult ground for an academic discourse which is founded on formalist textual analysis. But it is also this fuzziness

---

29 See François Delsarte, *Delsarte System of Oratory: All the Literary Remains of François Delsarte*, trans. Abby L. Alger (New York: Edgar S. Werner, 1893). For other sources, see Toby Cole and Helen Chinoy (eds.), *Actors on Acting* (New York: Crown Publishers, 1970).

30 See Jerzy Grotowski, *Towards a Poor Theatre* (London: Methuen, 1969).

which makes it extremely interesting as a way of addressing questions of affect and identification. The production of subjectivities—of ways of seeing—are crucial components of film and television theory, but we may have bought in too readily to the belief that identification is an almost mechanical process produced through the manipulation of the look of the camera. Identification is also, occasionally but importantly, a recognition of and identification with the revealed truth of the actor—with emotions and glimpses of feeling honestly and sometimes courageously revealed. While the identification with the camera explains how we are held within the narrative, identification with what the actor is doing when she acts may sometimes explain the lump in the throat or the hollowness in the stomach which suggests that we are having an experience.

In her book, *Eloquent Gestures*, on acting in the silent cinema, Roberta Pearson quotes from one of Henry James's essays in 'The Art of Fiction':

> What is character [James says] but the determination of incident? What is incident but the illustration of character? What is either a picture or a novel that is *not* of character? . . . It is an incident for a woman to stand up with her hand resting on a table and look at you in a certain way. . . . At the same time it is an expression of character.[31]

At the risk of generalization, British television drama—the drama which goes under the shorthand of 'serious drama'—seems to me to have evolved as a drama of incident and character rather than of what David Bordwell defines as goal-oriented narrative. It is situation which holds the attention rather than the suspense of resolution, and it is recognition of characters in situations which forms the characteristic pleasure (not the universal pleasure) of television drama, rather than the fantasy of identification with ideal egos. This gives a particular significance to acting in television drama, since it is a drama in which a woman standing up with her hand resting on a table and looking at you in a certain way is an incident. It is, in other words, a drama in which detail plays a very particular part.

In the terms of the eighteenth-century discourses in the Royal Academy which Naomi Schor traces, my argument is that the classic serial belongs to the tradition of the detail rather than the tradition of the sublime, the tradition, that is, which Schor associates with the domestic, the everyday, and the ornamental—characteristics which are associated historically with the feminine. In the terms of the critique which Adorno and Horkheimer make of the aesthetics of the culture

---

31 Henry James, 'The art of fiction', quoted in Roberta E. Pearson, *Eloquent Gestures: The Transformation of Performance Style in the Griffith Biograph Films* (Berkeley and Los Angeles: University of California Press, 1992), 31.

industries that the detail is simply subsumed in the general, losing its rebellious nature, acting seems to me to retain the possibility of a small rebellion, of a drama in which the regularities of increasingly commodified production values are animated, made material, and sometimes made strange by the precise and disconcerting moment of an actor's revealed truth—or more precisely, by the perceived truth of her pretence.

There is a remarkable sequence in *The Jewel in the Crown* in which Peggy Ashcroft as Barbie comes with her employer Mabel Layton (Fabia Drake), the matriarch of the regiment, to a show of presents in the officers' mess, and fails to see displayed the set of apostle spoons which she had given as a wedding gift. Barbie, who has been a mission teacher, is now in genteel service as a companion, and her various encounters in the mess, with her employer's nieces, with the padre and his wife, play out with understated glances, hesitations, and shifts of tone the intricate layering of class in a tribal society. While I recognize that any discussion of acting comes up immediately against the difficulty of quotation and description—a difficulty which cannot be resolved by the close textual analysis of a shot breakdown, there are nevertheless one or two things I want to say about this scene as a way of approaching the question of acting.

In the first place, there is no point at which I do not know that I am watching Peggy Ashcroft—Peggy Ashcroft, that is, pretending to be Barbie in a virtuoso display of acting.[32] That is to say, Brecht notwithstanding, that the actor's identification with her role does not mean that I am lost in an identification with an illusory real. My response to the scene is a complex one, in which I am aware both of the interiorized social inferiority of the character, Barbie, which is signified in every move and gesture she makes, and of the superior status and authority of the star, Ashcroft. At one and the same time, I can watch the display of skill and detail *and* be moved by the character's awkwardness *and* be angered by the ritual humiliations of class. Rather than the simplicities of identification *or* distanciation, watching acting on television seems to raise the possibility of a complex simultaneity.

This is a particularly important point to make about television because it is a medium in which familiarity is one of the conditions of existence. Repetition—the fact that television is there, week in, week out, and actors appear repeatedly in different roles and with different functions—means that the television actor is more likely to carry a

32 I first presented this analysis at the conference on television drama, 'On the Boundary', organized by the Wednesday Play Research Project at Reading University in April 1998. I am grateful to my fellow panel member, the actor Timothy West, who pointed out that Ashcroft was perfectly aware of her own star status in the serial, and played with and against it.

history with him. Bill Paterson, for example, moves in a single week between the impersonation of dramatic acting and the authority of documentary voice-over. Or the celebrity actor who moves between commercials, game shows, and drama. Or Anita Dobson and Leslie Grantham who will always carry the memory of an earlier life in *EastEnders*. Television acting is layered with little histories which give no purchase to the theoretical divisions of identification and distance, and make watching the actor acting a complex and diverse process.

There are also different economies of acting within the scene in *The Jewel in the Crown*. The padre and his wife are played with an economy based on impersonation and believability, a well-judged economy that is precise in its service to the role. They are function-aries within the demands of the narrative. Barbie is profligate with detail—hesitations and glances—which serve the feeling of the character but which in some sense exceed the economic requirements of the narrative and of the impersonation of a former mission teacher. These details are engrained with a whole history of social injury. This economy can be referred back to the distinction which Lukács makes when he distinguishes between realism and naturalism, narration and description in the essay 'To narrate or to describe' which is discussed in Chapter 4.[33] To recall the distinction briefly, it is based on horse-race scenes in Zola's *Nana* and in Tolstoy's *Anna Karenina*. In *Nana*, he argues, detail is superfluous, merely (in his terms) situat-ing the scene in its social context. In *Anna Karenina* detail is cut to the measure of the narrative, everything contributing to the developing crisis in the relationship between Vronsky and Anna. It seems to me that this distinction, which implies an economy of detail, gives us a way into thinking about an economy of acting: a continuum opens up between acting which is cut to the measure of narrative and acting which goes beyond, offering an excess of detail at the service of the intricacy and complexity of character. Lukács notwithstanding, it seems to me that the detail of Peggy Ashcroft's performance material-izes and historicizes a social caste system: a form of critique based on affect rather than intellect.

An analysis based on the formal properties of the scene can reveal certain explicit meanings. The cut to a 'native' servant's feet foregrounds the issue of race. It proclaims: 'Look at this! This is significant! This is race!' It is from Barbie's point of view that we see it. The reactions of the other characters to Barbie proclaim class, the subtle gradations of a colonial class system. Such an analysis, which has formed the basis of film and television studies, is helpful

---

and it is teachable. But the meaning of class—the helplessness and awkwardness of class inferiority—is also read out of the way Peggy Ashcroft holds her sherry glass and the expression of a face which carries that history of subtle social injury in a way which is much more difficult to describe with the confidence of an established vocabulary. Interpretation slides into response. The cutaways and reactions say 'Look at this'. But Ashcroft's hesitations and demeanour invite a process of reading in detail and reading detail for which critical language has a much more tentative vocabulary.

When it decided that film was narrative, film theory seems to have forgotten that it was also the performance of a narrative, actors pretending to be people they were not. However much the classic serial may lovingly recreate the past with a profusion of detail, the body of the actor is stubborn: the furniture may be authentic nineteenth-century, but the body of the actor and its gestures are our contemporary. When Jennifer Ehle as Elizabeth Bennet runs down the hill in the opening scene of the 1994 *Pride and Prejudice*, her costume is early nineteenth-century but her run *feels* like the present. It is these complex readings which make acting so fascinating and so difficult. The pleasure in the classic serial seems quite crucially to be a pleasure in watching performance rather than the more seductive pleasure of losing oneself in the fantasy of identification: a pleasure in the observation of the details of gesture and inflection, in watching skill with the relaxed detachment and critical judgement which Brecht associates with the aficionado of boxing, or which Benjamin associates with the loss or aura: a small pleasure in ornament and the everyday rather than the overwhelming seduction of the Sublime and the Grand Style.

To suggest finally where the profusion of detail and the rebellious detail might meet, and to think about how otherwise the past might be represented, I want to refer to Andreas Huyssen's recent book, *Twilight Memories: Marking Time in a Culture of Amnesia*.[34] Huyssen is intrigued by 'the paradox that novelty in our culture is ever more associated with memory and the past rather than with future expectation.'[35] Rather than express this purely in the terms of loss which Jameson employs, however, he sees in it something of 'society's need for temporal anchoring when in the wake of the information revolution, the relationship between past, present, and future is being transformed.'[36] Rather than simply dismissing the new relationship to

34 Andreas Huyssen, *Twilight Memories: Marking Time in a Culture of Amnesia* (New York/London: Routledge, 1995).

35 Ibid. 6.

36 Ibid. 7.

the past as a mixture of nostalgia, heritage and enterprise, he sees in the museum a chance to 'reclaim a sense of non-synchronicity and of the past'.[37] But it is a past reconceived as something different. He proposes in the figure which forms the title of his book, twilight memories, an image which might make the past strange again. Twilight, he says,

> is that moment of the day that foreshadows the night of forgetting, but that seems to slow time itself, an in-between state in which the last light of the day may still play out its ultimate marvels. It is memory's privileged time.[38]

I would add to that that twilight is also the time when detail stands out and begins to break its organic relationship with the general: the 'floating detail' which Naomi Schor sees as both authenticating memory and making it strange, or the rebellious detail which Adorno and Horkheimer see as a point of resistance to the generality of administrative rationality. This seems to me to evoke a different relationship to the past and to adaptation which can be sensed in the in-betweenness of Sally Potter's *Orlando* (1993), or in the floating detail of Jane Campion's *The Piano* (1993), or in the queerness of Jarman's *Edward II* (1991), or in the 'composedness' of detail and landscape in *The Tenant of Wildfell Hall*. The object, then, is not to lose the connection to the past which adaptation and the classic serial offer us, but to discover it, yet again, as another and a different country.

37 Ibid. 34.

38 Ibid. 3.

9

Epilogue: The Return of Value

WHAT I have tried to do in this book is, I think, twofold: on the one hand, I have tried to insert television drama into a central place in the mainstream of postwar British culture; on the other, I have tried to bring to television drama a critical vocabulary which is adequate to its cultural centrality and aesthetic complexity. For some of the reasons I suggested in the introductory chapter, this seems to place the arguments of the book somewhere outside the orthodoxies which have developed in the academic study of television. In the now somewhat dubious division which was foundational for much cultural studies, I am identifying television drama with a vocabulary which is more familiar to art criticism and 'high culture' than it is to the commodified 'low culture' of the Culture Industry.

Running through the book, sometimes implicitly, sometimes explicitly, is an argument about value and values: aesthetic, cultural, and political. In this epilogue, drawing on an article on popular television genres which I published in *Screen* in 1990, I want to make that argument a little more explicit and a little more general. The article was called 'Adorno's reproach',[1] and the short extract I am introducing here is intended to return to the question of values I signalled in the introductory chapter. Its proposition is that critical theory still offers a sticking-point against the accommodation and commodification of values in an advanced capitalist culture—a sticking point which still has to be negotiated.

With or without Horkheimer, with or without the Frankfurt School, the name of Adorno has come to stand in cultural criticism for an immediately knowable, instantly impeachable thought-crime: 'cultural pessimism'. His denunciations of the 'stylized barbarity' of the Culture Industry, most notably in *Dialectic of Enlightenment* written with Max Horkheimer in 1944,[2] have provided an effective

---

1 John Caughie, 'Adorno's reproach: repetition, difference and television genre', *Screen*, vol. 32, no. 2 (1991), 127–53.

2 Theodor Adorno and Max Horkheimer, *The Dialectic of Enlightenment* (London: Verso, 1979; first published as *Dialektik der Aufklärung*, 1944), particularly the essay, 'The Culture Industry: Enlightenment as mass deception'. The phrase 'stylized barbarity' (p. 128) is quoted from Nietzsche.

springboard from which to launch counter-proposals for an approach —to television particularly—more user-friendly to the complexities of address and response in popular or 'mass' culture. With irresistible irony, Adorno and Horkheimer's brilliant critique of the re-mythologization of the Enlightenment has itself, in precisely their own terms ('using the devices of familiarity and straightforward dismissal to avoid the labour of conceptualization'[3]), been turned into myth. While it may not now be possible fully to recover their critique of mass culture from the totalizing force of its own negative rhetoric, it is at least possible to regret the ease with which it has been adopted as the convenient apostasy of a new rhetoric, operating as a kind of semaphore, signalling correct positions across great distances with a simplified and purely functional code. Here, briefly, I want to take their critique seriously as a way of identifying the issue of value, of resisting the more celebratory aspects of an accommodation to the logic of commodification and consumption, and of recovering some of the ground lost or forfeited by critique.[4]

In *Late Marxism: Adorno, or, The Persistence of the Dialectic* Fredric Jameson finds in Adorno's cultural critique

> one crucial thematic differentiation between 'genuine art' and that offered by the Culture Industry: both raise the issue and the possibility of happiness in their very being, as it were, and neither provides it; but where the one keeps faith with it by negation and suffering, the other assures us it is taking place.[5]

Negation—the refusal of the administrative rationality of the bourgeois Enlightenment—lies at the heart of Adorno's project, and at the heart of the whole notion of critique and critical theory. The immediate historical provocation for their critique of conformity, indifference, and the apparent predisposition to barbarity is clearly, for Adorno and Horkheimer, the rise of fascism; but what is more generally at issue is the intrusion of Enlightenment rationality, capitalist common-sense and the logic of commodification into the very core of the cultural field and the aesthetic. In Adorno's aesthetics, the value of the cultural and the aesthetic lies in difference and negation and it is this which is threatened by the commodification of culture.

Developing since the Enlightenment of the eighteenth century, accelerating in the nineteenth century in step with the acceleration of capitalist industry, the process of intrusion increasingly separated

---

3 Ibid., p. xiv.

4 I am grateful to Patrice Petro, and the students on her 1988 graduate seminar on 'Critical Theory and the Frankfurt School' at the Center for Twentieth Century Studies, University of Wisconsin-Milwaukee, for arguing me out of blinkered Brechtianism towards a more sympathetic reading of Adorno.

5 Fredric Jameson, *Late Marxism: Adorno, or, The Persistence of the Dialectic* (London: Verso, 1990), 147.

culture out into the familiar contours of 'high' and 'low', isolating what it could not assimilate. By the middle of the twentieth century, Adorno found himself confronted with a cultural field in which the squeezed and narrowing pinnacle of aesthetic difference and negation had all but detached itself completely from the squat, commodified mass of capitalist 'affirmative' culture. For Adorno (as, at around the same time, for Clement Greenberg), the 'genuine' avant garde, represented most emblematically in his writing by his teacher, Schoenberg, was the last vestige of 'authentic art' whose difficulty and inaccessibility were the marks of its unassimilable difference, and its negation of bourgeois rationality, capitalist purposiveness, and what Peter Sloterdijk would later call 'cynical reason'.[6] The planned and formulaic rationality of the Enlightenment, according to the critique, is increasingly marked by the familiar, the conventional and by 'sameness': a sameness which need not exclude difference, but contains it within the rational, functional, and acceptable forms of its own choosing. Acceptable difference, rather than weakening the force and the confidence of normative rationality, tightens its grip and extends its appeal.

> It is characteristic of the sickness that even the best-intentioned reformer who uses an impoverished and debased language to recommend renewal, by his adoption of the insidious mode of categorization and the bad philosophy it conceals, strengthens the very power of the established order he is trying to break. False clarity is only another name for myth; and myth has always been obscure and enlightening at one and the same time: always using the devices of familiarity and straightforward dismissal to avoid the labour of conceptualization.[7]

Adorno's critique, therefore, and in particular the critique of the 'Culture Industry', is mounted from the increasingly beleaguered and restricted field of an avant-garde sensibility, and it is this, in part, which wins it the current disapproval of the more enthusiastically affirmative, apparently democratic, or outright populist approaches to popular culture.

Undoubtedly, the failure or unwillingness of Adorno and Horkheimer to find difference in the cultural field which they survey in the 'Culture Industry' essay—American popular culture of the 1930s—is damaging. The particular avant-garde perspective of their critique (as of Greenberg's) makes it difficult to avoid first impressions of a conflation in their work of 'genuine art' with 'elite art'. It is, however, worth noting some symptomatic cracks in the uniformity of their scorn for the products of the 'Culture Industry'. The suggestive

---

6 Peter Sloterdijk, *Critique of Cynical Reason* (Minneapolis: University of Minnesota Press, 1987).

7 Adorno and Horkheimer, *Dialectic of Enlightenment*, p. xiv.

outlines of a hierarchy of disdain can be traced: the 'tragic Garbo' is preferred to Mickey Rooney, Betty Boop to Donald Duck.[8] Their most acerbic denunciations are reserved not for 'amusement' or 'light' art in themselves, but for the attempt by the culture industry to absorb 'light' into 'serious' art, accommodating difference to the familiar— 'Benny Goodman appears with the Budapest string quartet',[9] or, in the context of this book, the more middle-brow versions of the classic serial. Entertainment seems historically rather than essentially debased, and what emerges is a recognition of the historical *possibility* of popular entertainment as an autonomous art which might turn on its head the seriousness of official, rational discourse. Adorno and Horkheimer, the apostates, may not be so far away from Bakhtin, the new prophet, as some critical celebrants of carnival might admit: 'The eccentricity of the circus, peepshow, and brothel is as embarrassing to [the Culture Industry] as that of Schoenberg or Karl Kraus.'[10]

Like Bakhtin, Adorno and Horkheimer recognize the capacity of physical art and non-sense to negate oppressive reason, though they shut off (only more explicitly than Bakhtin) the possibility of this capacity being realized in contemporary culture: 'In some revue films, and especially in the grotesque and the funnies, the possibility of . . . negation does glimmer for a few moments. But of course it cannot happen.'[11] It cannot happen not because the forms of negation are mindless, but precisely because they are too mindful of meaning and significance, constantly reminded of rationality and purposive thought:

> The culture industry is corrupt; not because it is a sinful Babylon but because it is a cathedral dedicated to elevated pleasure. . . .
> The culture industry does retain a trace of something better in those features which bring it close to the circus, in the self-justifying and nonsensical skill of riders, acrobats and clowns, in the 'defense and justification of physical as against intellectual art' (Wedekind). But the refuges of a mindless artistry which represents what is human as opposed to the social mechanism are being relentlessly hunted down by a schematic reason which compels everything to prove its significance and effect. The consequence is that the nonsensical at the bottom disappears as utterly as the sense in works of art at the top.
> The fusion of culture and entertainment that is taking place today leads not only to a depravation of culture, but inevitably to an intellectualization of amusement.[12]

8 Ibid. 134.
9 Ibid. 136.
10 Ibid.
11 Ibid. 142.
12 Ibid. 143.

Like Bakhtin, again, Adorno and Horkheimer maintain that mass or popular entertainment finds the condition of its existence and its significance in its relationship to 'official discourse' and the culture industry. Bakhtin continually recognizes that the parodic force of popular-festive forms could not survive unqualified after the force of the sacred word which they parodied had itself been qualified by the dawning administrative rationality of the Renaissance: the dawning of exactly that rationality which provides the pre-history of Adorno and Horkheimer's critique.[13] Similarly, though from a different historical perspective, Adorno and Horkheimer, confronting the massive extension and technical development of that rationality, acknowledge the possibility, and even the residue, of difference and negation in the nonsense of eccentric entertainment—a residual refusal of official meaning—but can place no faith in its capacity to survive as anything more than fun, as anything other than acceptable difference within the logic of capitalist culture and the totality of the culture industry.

Where Adorno and Horkheimer differ from Bakhtin, and where their 'pessimism' emerges most clearly, is in the absence of his sense of the dialogic: of 'serious' and 'light', 'authentic culture' and 'entertainment', in dialogue with each other, each working on the other, each qualifying and transforming the other, sometimes in unpredictable ways. However rhetorically brilliant, the critique which Adorno and Horkheimer in *Dialectic of Enlightenment* offer is ultimately a totalizing discourse in which the dialectic struggles and twists against itself, serving only to tighten the knot which binds it. It is in the myth of Odysseus that they most poignantly figure out the tragic paralysis of the dialectic, and, by extension, the quandary of cultural critique: to steer past the temptations of the Sirens whose fatal song cannot be resisted, Odysseus stuffs his men's ears with wax so that they will not be distracted from their rowing, and binds himself to the mast with orders that he must not be released. He, 'the seigneur', hears the ravishing beauty of the song, but cannot act and is not free; they labour and act in a practical fashion, but do not hear.

> What Odysseus hears is without consequence for him; he is able only to nod his head as a sign to be set free from his bonds; but it is too late; his men, who do not listen, know only the song's danger but nothing of its beauty, and leave him at the mast to save him and themselves.[14]

The sense of tragic beauty which characterizes their recasting of the myth of Odysseus permeates much of the critique. Its metaphors of inevitability and its intricate dialectical traps construct a myth of

---

13 See 'From the prehistory of novelistic discourse', in M. M. Bakhtin, *The Dialogic Imagination: Four Essays*, ed. Michael Holquist, trans. Emerson and Holquist (Austin: University of Texas Press, 1981), particularly p. 71, quoted below.

14 Adorno and Horkheimer, *Dialectic of Enlightenment*, 34.

Enlightenment which has emotional as much as analytic power. At the same time, it builds a prison-house of rhetoric from which there may be no practical possibility of escape: as later with the writings of Baudrillard, their critique, in its totalizing embrace, always seems to have a neutralizing answer to suggestions of difference. It is not hard to see how attempts to value popular culture or television, or to legitimize their academic study, come up against Adorno and Horkheimer as a check which it may be easier to think around than to think through. Simply to dismiss their work as 'pessimistic', however, or to use it emblematically as a naive position which we now know better than to take seriously, seems to me hopelessly to devalue the currency of critique.

Television, in its regularity and its availability, seems regulated by repetition and modulated by acceptable difference. Somewhat perversely, however, what I want to retain from Adorno, and from his consistent reproach, is the centrality of difference as negation rather than as variation: a difference which is not 'indifferent', but in which something is at stake; and a difference, more difficultly, which is not solely dependent on what Raymond Williams somewhere calls 'the more negotiable process of consumption'. If this involves smuggling something of an avant-garde sensibility into the theorization of television, so be it.

The question of difference and singularity was always there for 'classical' film theory as an underpinning, whether acknowledged or not, for the valorization—and particularly for the legitimation as 'progressive'—of a popular culture which is produced as product and circulates as commodity. However anti-elitist and however defensive of a culturally democratic popular, within a modernist film criticism growing out of romanticism a canon emerges in which difference was (and is) identified with the author whose individual signature separates the text and the œuvre from the cynical indifference of mass production. Within a modernist film criticism inflected by structuralism or poststructuralism, generic production is valued as different by its inability to resolve the social contradictions which its repetitions and conventions are there to repress. In both, 'irrationality'—in the form of authorial personality, unconscious contradiction or excess—is discovered as negation at the heart of the commercial and purposeful rationality of capitalist production and bourgeois ideology. Adorno's critique, in fact, was never as far away from the motivations of cultural criticism as one would imagine from the myth.

Postmodernist criticism, however, slipping away from critique and negation with varying degrees of enthusiasm, seems to challenge the security of values. It seems to invert the hierarchy, apparently renouncing the modernist insistence on difference and originality, and seeking value instead in repetition in its various forms: recombination, refunctioning, pastiche. But it is worth noting that at least for the criticism of popular culture, and of television in particular, this apparently postmodern move may have less to do with a radical change in the terms of value than with a fundamental shift of attention—and of political faith—from the text to the audience. Rather than finally rejecting difference as the central term of critical value, this criticism instead relocates value onto the difference of consumers: it is in consumption rather than in the text that originality and creativity are to be found.

Clearly there is something very important going on in this move, and at one level it is indeed a necessary corrective to the textual isolationism of much modernist criticism. For television, in particular, where the text is itself both a theoretical problem (where does a television text begin and end?) and a banal critical object (in comparison with the things people do with it), it may be inevitable that attention fastens on an ethnography of consumption rather than on the objects of production. And there is empirical evidence in this ethnography for an understanding of the social subjectivity of viewers which is inescapable for theoretical work on television. Ethnography, however, is a disciplined pursuit, and it is worth stressing again David Morley's warning that the problem of the 'ethnography' of some recent writing is its lack of discipline, and its lack of an adequate sociology.[15] The warning is clearly important. Here, for my argument, I would extend it to say that, in the absence of an adequate sociology, such 'ethnography' comes dangerously close to confusing itself with aesthetics, confusing description with evaluation. Simply (or not so simply) to relocate value onto consumption not only misrecognizes ethnography, it also leaves behind it a problem in the aesthetics of production—a problem which has both critical and political dimensions. It gives criticism, and critical theory, no way of knowing what it is for: no way, that is, of arguing for one kind of production against another, or of valuing some forms over others. Critique is replaced by commentary, and by an act of faith in the capacity of consumers to do surprising and amazing things with what they daily receive.

The criticism of television's dramatic forms is inextricably bound up with questions of repetition and difference, and television raises these questions in quite specific ways. Adorno seems to me to situate the problem, without necessarily being the solution to it. While attentive to the spirit of his reproach, it is not enough to retreat into the security of a duality—even a dialectic duality—in which difference is always already valorized against the corrosiveness of repetition; but nor is it enough simply to reverse the poles and allow the current to run the other way. Fredric Jameson, in his article

---

15 David Morley, 'Where the global meets the local: notes from the sitting room', *Screen*, vol. 32, no. 1 (1991).

'Postmodernism and the video-text', comments that experimental video may provide a useful vantage point from which to think about commercial television:

> In that sense, thinking anything adequate about commercial television may well involve ignoring it and thinking about something else: in [this] instance, experimental video. . . . This is less a matter of mass versus élite culture than it is of controlled laboratory situations: what is so highly specialised as to seem aberrant and uncharacteristic in the [world] of daily life . . . can often yield crucial information about the properties of an object of study whose familiar everyday forms obscure it.[16]

While agreeing with the spirit of Jameson's suggestion that an avant-garde sensibility may displace and make strange the regularity of everyday television, it is not enough to appeal to an already formed avant garde—formed in another place or at another time and for another purpose—which can be hauled in and held up to television as a template of value. The notion of an avant-garde sensibility here functions simply as the 'other' of everyday, routine television (just as much of the most interesting experimental video refunctions existing television as *its* other), a point outside the discourse of actually existing television from which other possibilities can be thought, and from which we can argue about what it is that we actually want. Adorno seems to offer such a 'sticking-point', and for that reason it seems worth confronting his critique rather than burying it as myth.

Central to the arguments of this book is the argument that the criticism of television drama, 'serious drama', offers another sticking-point. The tradition which I have been tracing throws into question the homogeneity of an essentialized 'television itself', throws into question what we mean by television as 'popular culture', and reopens some old debates which still serve as sticking-points against the slide into accommodation. If I have been more concerned with the key theoretical and critical debates which have been formative for television drama than with a representative sample of the huge diversity of plays, films, and serials, writers, directors, and producers which its history contains, it is because, sympathetic to the avant-garde sensibility (a sensibility which also informs Troy Kennedy Martin's decisive polemic in 1964), I believe that theoretical and critical debate gives us a way of imagining a television and a television drama which still has the possibility of being other than it is.

---

16 Fredric Jameson, 'Postmodernism and the video-text', in Nigel Fabb *et al.* (eds.), *The Linguistics of Writing: Arguments between Language and Literature* (Manchester: Manchester University Press, 1987), 202. (The words in parentheses are corrections of what I take to be misprints in the published text.)

Bibliography

ADORNO, THEODOR and HORKHEIMER, MAX, *The Dialectic of Enlightenment* [1944] (London: Verso, 1979).

ALLEN, ROBERT C. (ed.), *Channels of Discourse, Reassembled: Television and Contemporary Criticism* (2nd edn.; London: Routledge, 1992).

AMIS, KINGSLEY, *Socialism and the Intellectuals*, Fabian Society pamphlet, 1957.

ANDERSON, LINDSAY, 'Stand Up! Stand Up!', *Sight & Sound*, 26:2 (Autumn 1956).

—— 'Get out and push', in Tom Maschler (ed.), *Declaration* (St Albans: MacGibbon & Kee, 1957).

ANDERSON, PERRY, 'Components of the national culture', *New Left Review*, no. 50 (1968), 3–57.

ANSORGE, PETER, *From Liverpool to Los Angeles: On Writing for Theatre, Film and Television* (London: Faber & Faber, 1997).

ARDEN, JOHN, 'The writer's view: writers and television—2' (interview with Alan Lovell), *Contrast* 2:2 (Winter 1962), 124–33.

BAKER, H. W. and KEMP, W. D. (BBC Engineering Division), 'The recording of television programmes', *BBC Quarterly*, 4:4 (1949–50), 236–48.

BAKHTIN, M. M., *The Dialogic Imagination: Four Essays*, ed. Michael Holquist, trans. Emerson and Holquist (Austin: University of Texas Press, 1981).

BARR, CHARLES (ed.), *All Our Yesterdays: Ninety Years of British Cinema* (London: BFI Publishing, 1986).

—— 'They think it's all over: the dramatic legacy of live television', in John Hill and Martin McLoone (eds.), *Big Picture, Small Screen: The Relations between Film and Television* (Luton: John Libbey Media/University of Luton [Academia Research Monograph 16], 1996), 47–75.

BARRY, MICHAEL, 'Problems of a producer', *BBC Quarterly*, 6:3 (1951), 167–70.

—— 'Shakespeare on television', *BBC Quarterly*, 9:3 (1954), 143–9.

BARTHES, ROLAND, *The Pleasure of the Text* (New York: Hill & Wang, 1975).

—— 'The death of the Author', in Stephen Heath (ed.), *Image-Music-Text* (London: Fontana, 1977), 142–8.

BASKIN, ELLEN, *Serials on British Television, 1950–1994* (Aldershot: Scolar Press, 1996).

BAZIN, ANDRÉ, *What is Cinema?*, vols. 1 & 2, trans. Hugh Gray (Berkeley and Los Angeles: University of California Press, 1971, 1972).

BBC GOVERNORS, 'Television and the film industry', Draft paper for the BBC Board of Governors, 11 July 1948.

BELLOUR, RAYMOND with BANDY, MARY LEA (eds.), *Jean-Luc Godard: Son + Image, 1974–1991* (New York: Museum of Modern Art, 1992), 159–68.

BENJAMIN, WALTER, 'The work of art in the age of mechanical reproduction', in *Illuminations*, trans. Harry Zohn; edited and with introduction by Hannah Arendt (London: Harper Collins, 1982), 219–53.

BENNETT, TONY *et al.* (eds.), *Popular Television and Film: A Reader* (London: Open University/BFI, 1981).

BIRD, LIZ and ELIOT, JO, '*The Life and Loves of a She-Devil*', in G. W. Brandt (ed.), *British Television Drama in the 1980s* (Cambridge: Cambridge University Press, 1993), 214–33.

BIRKINSHAW, D. C. (Superintendent Engineer, Television), 'The television studio', *BBC Quarterly*, 4:2 (1949), 105–17.

BLACK, PETER, 'A fair price', *Contrast*, 3:2 (Winter 1963), 84–7.

BODDY, WILLIAM, *Fifties Television: The Industry and its Critics* (Urbana/Chicago: University of Illinois Press, 1990).

BORDWELL, DAVID, STAIGER, JANET, and THOMPSON, KRISTIN, *The Classical Hollywood Cinema: Film Style and Mode of Production to 1960* (London: Routledge & Kegan Paul, 1985).

BOURDIEU, PIERRE, *Distinction: A Social Critique of the Judgement of Taste* (Cambridge, Mass.: Harvard University Press, 1984).

BOWEN, JOHN, 'The worm in the bud', *Contrast*, 1:2 (Winter 1961), 78–88.

BOYLE, ANDREW, *Only the Wind Will Listen: Reith of the BBC* (London: Hutchinson, 1972).

BRANDT, GEORGE W. (ed.), *British Television Drama* (Cambridge, Cambridge University Press, 1981).

—— (ed.), *British Television Drama in the 1980s* (Cambridge: Cambridge University Press, 1993).

—— '*The Jewel in the Crown*', in G. W. Brandt (ed.), *British Television Drama in the 1980s* (Cambridge: Cambridge University Press, 1993), 196–213.

BRAUN, EDWARD, 'Trevor Griffiths', in G. W. Brandt (ed.), *British Television Drama* (Cambridge: Cambridge University Press, 1981), 56–81.

BRIGGS, ASA, *Sound and Vision: History of Broadcasting in the United Kingdom, Volume 4* (Oxford: Oxford University Press, 1979).

Broadcasting Act, chapter 64 (London: HMSD, 1980).

BROOKS, PETER, *The Melodramatic Imagination: Balzac, Henry James, Melodrama and the Mode of Excess* (New Haven, Conn.: Yale University Press, 1976).

BROWN, IVOR, 'In search of the critic', *BBC Quarterly*, 1:2 (1946), 42–6.

—— 'Television in the Englishman's castle', *BBC Yearbook 1951*, 17.

BRUNSDON, CHARLOTTE, 'Problems with quality', *Screen*, 31:1 (1990), 67–90.

—— 'Structure of anxiety: recent British television crime fiction', *Screen*, 39:3 (1998), 223–43.

BUCK-MORSS, SUSAN, *The Dialectics of Seeing: Walter Benjamin and the Arcades Project* (Cambridge, Mass.: MIT Press, 1991).

BURCH, NOËL, *Correction Please; or, How We Got Into Pictures* (London: Arts Council, undated).

—— 'Porter, or, ambivalence', *Screen*, 19:4 (1978/9), 91–105.

BÜRGER, PETER, *Theory of the Avant Garde*, trans. Michael Shaw (Minneapolis: University of Minnesota Press, 1984).

BUSCOMBE, EDWARD, 'Creativity in television', *Screen Education*, 35 (Summer 1980), 5–17.

BUSSELL, JAN, *The Art of Television* (London: Faber & Faber, 1952).

CARDIFF, DAVID, 'The serious and the popular', *Media, Culture and Society*, 2:1 (January 1980), 29–48.

CARPENTER, HUMPHREY, *Dennis Potter: The Authorised Biography* (London: Faber & Faber, 1998).

CAUGHIE, JOHN, 'Progressive television and documentary drama', *Screen*, 21:3 (1980), 9–35. Reprinted in T. Bennett *et al.* (eds.), *Popular Television and Film: A Reader* (Milton Keynes: Open University Press, 1981).

—— 'Rhetoric, pleasure and "art television"—*Dreams of Leaving* ', *Screen*, 22:4 (1981), 9–31.

—— 'Television criticism: a discourse in search of an object', *Screen*, 25:4/5 (1984), 109–20.

—— 'Broadcasting and cinema (1): converging histories', in Charles Barr (ed.), *All Our Yesterdays: Ninety Years of British Cinema* (London: BFI Publishing, 1986).

—— 'Before the Golden Age: early television drama', in J. Corner (ed.), *Popular Television in Britain: Studies in Cultural History* (London: BFI Publishing, 1991), 22–41.

—— 'Adorno's reproach: repetition, difference and television genre', *Screen*, 32:2 (1991), 127–53.

—— 'The logic of convergence', in J. Hill and M. McLoone (eds.), *Big Picture, Small Screen: The Relations between Film and Television*, Academia Research Monograph 16 (Luton: John Libbey Media/University of Luton, 1996), 215–23.

—— 'Small pleasures: adaptation and the past in British film and television', *Ilha do Desterro: A Journal of English Language, Literatures in English and Cultural Studies*, 32 (Editora Universidade Federal de Santa Catarina, 1997), 27–50.

CLARK, KATERINA and HOLQUIST, MICHAEL, *Mikhail Bakhtin* (Cambridge, Mass./London: Harvard University Press, 1984).

COLE, TOBY and CHINOY, HELEN (eds.), *Actors on Acting* (New York: Crown Publishers, 1970).

COLLINS, NORMAN, 'Television and the future', *BBC Quarterly*, 4:1 (1949), 26–31.

Contrast editorial, 'Partialities', *Contrast*, 1:2 (Winter 1961), 128–9.

COOK, CHRISTOPHER (ed.), *The Dilys Powell Film Reader* (Manchester: Carcanet Press, 1995).

COOK, JOHN, *Dennis Potter: A Life on Screen* (Manchester: Manchester University Press, 1995).

CORNER, JOHN (ed.), *Popular Television in Britain: Studies in Cultural Criticism* (London: BFI Publishing, 1991).

—— and HARVEY, SYLVIA (eds.), *Enterprise and Heritage: Crosscurrents of National Culture* (London/New York: Routledge, 1991).

CORRIGAN, TIMOTHY, 'Music from heaven, bodies in hell: *The Singing Detective*', in Corrigan, *A Cinema without Walls: Movies and Culture after Vietnam* (London: Routledge, 1991), 179–93.

Cosgrove, Stuart, 'Refusing consent: the *Oi for England* project', *Screen*, 24:1 (1983), 92–6.

Coward, Rosalind, 'Dennis Potter and the question of the television author', *Critical Quarterly*, 29:4 (1987), 79–87.

Creeber, Glen, *Dennis Potter: Between Two Worlds* (London: Macmillan, 1998).

Daney, Serge, '*La Remise en scène*', in *La Rampe: Cahiers critique, 1970–1982* (Paris: Éditions Gallimard, 1983), 54–63.

—— and Godard, Jean-Luc, 'Godard makes (hi)stories: interview with Serge Daney', in Raymond Bellour with Mary Lea Bandy (eds.), *Jean-Luc Godard: Son + Image, 1974–1991* (New York: Museum of Modern Art, 1992), 159–68.

Delsarte, François, *Delsarte System of Oratory: All the Literary Remains of François Delsarte*, trans. Abby L. Alger (New York: Edgar S. Werner, 1893).

Dienst, Richard, *Still Life in Real Time: Theory after Television* (Durham/London: Duke University Press, 1994).

Drakakis, John (ed.), *British Radio Drama* (Cambridge: Cambridge University Press, 1981).

Dworkin, Denis, *Cultural Marxism in Postwar Britain: History, the New Left and the Origins of Cultural Studies* (Durham/London: Duke University Press, 1997).

Dyer, Richard, ' "There's nothing I can do! Nothing!": femininity, seriality and whiteness in *The Jewel in the Crown*', *Screen*, 37:3 (Autumn 1996), 225–39.

Edgar, David, 'On drama documentary', in F. Pike (ed.), *Ah! Mischief* (London: Faber & Faber, 1982).

Eisenstein, Sergei, *The Film Sense*, trans. Jay Leyda (London: Faber & Faber, 1968).

Eliot, T. S., 'Tradition and the individual talent' (1920), in Eliot, *The Sacred Wood: Essays in Poetry and Criticism* (London: Methuen, 1960), 47–59.

Ellis, John, *Visible Fictions: Cinema, Television, Video* (2nd edn.; London: Routledge, 1992).

—— 'The discourse of art cinema', *Screen*, 19:3 (1978), 9–50.

Elsaesser, Thomas (ed.), *Writing for the Medium: Television in Transition* (Amsterdam: Amsterdam University Press, 1993).

Fiske, John, *Television Culture* (London/New York: Methuen, 1987).

Foucault, Michel, 'What is an author?' [1969], extracted in John Caughie (ed.), *Theories of Authorship* (London: Routledge & Kegan Paul/British Film Institute, 1981), 282–91.

Friedman, Lester (ed.), *British Cinema and Thatcherism: Fires Were Started* (London: UCL Press, 1993).

Frith , Simon, 'Hearing secret harmonies', in Colin MacCabe (ed.), *High Theory, Low Culture: Analysing Popular Television and Film* (Manchester: Manchester University Press, 1986), 53–70.

Fuller, Graham (ed.), *Loach on Loach* (London: Faber & Faber, 1998).

Gardner, Carl and Wyver, John, 'The single play', *Screen*, 24:4/5 (1983), 114–29.

GASCOIGNE, BAMBER et al., *The Making of 'The Jewel in the Crown'* (London: Granada Publishing, 1983).

GIELGUD, VAL, 'Policy and problems of broadcast drama', *BBC Quarterly*, 2:1 (1947), 18–23.

—— 'Drama in television and sound', *BBC Quarterly*, 5:4 (1950/1), 200–5.

GILBERT, W. STEPHEN, *Fight and Kick and Bite: The Life and Work of Dennis Potter* (London: Hodder & Stoughton, 1995).

GRADE, MICHAEL, 'Getting the right approach: Channel Four and the British film industry', in John Hill and Martin McLoone (eds.), *Big Picture, Small Screen: The Relations between Film and Television* (Luton: John Libbey Media/Luton University Press, 1996), 177–82.

GRAY, ANN, *Video Playtime: The Gendering of a Leisure Technology* (London: Routledge, 1992).

GREENBERG, CLEMENT, *Art and Culture: Critical Essays* (Boston: Beacon Press, 1981).

GREENE, HUGH CARLETON, 'Television transcription: the economic possibilities', *BBC Quarterly*, 7:4 (1952/3), 216–21.

GRIERSON, JOHN, *Grierson on Documentary*, edited by Forsyth Hardy (London: Faber & Faber, 1966).

—— 'Grierson on television', *Contrast*, 2:4 (1963), 220–4.

GRIFFITHS, TREVOR, 'Countering consent: an interview with John Wyver', in F. Pike (ed.), *Ah! Mischief* (London: Faber & Faber, 1982).

GROTOWSKI, JERZY, *Towards a Poor Theatre* (London: Methuen, 1969).

GUNNING, TOM, 'The cinema of attractions: early film, its spectators and the avant garde', *Wide Angle*, 8:3/4 (1986); reprinted in Thomas Elsaesser (ed.), *Early Cinema: Space, Frame, Narrative* (London: BFI Publishing, 1990), 56–62.

HABERMAS, JÜRGEN, 'Modernity—an incomplete project', trans. Seyla Ben-Habib, in Hal Foster (ed.), *Postmodern Culture* (London/Sydney: Pluto Press, 1985), 3–15.

HACKER, JONATHAN and PRICE, DAVID, *Take Ten: Contemporary British Filmmakers* (Oxford: Oxford University Press, 1991).

HALL, STUART, 'Encoding/decoding', in Stuart Hall et al. (eds.), *Culture, Media, Language: Working Papers in Cultural Studies, 1972–79* (London: Hutchinson/Centre for Contemporary Cultural Studies, 1990), 128–38.

—— and WHANNEL, PADDY, *The Popular Arts* (London: Hutchinson Educational, 1964).

HARE, DAVID, *Licking Hitler* (London: Faber Paperback, 1978).

—— *Dreams of Leaving* (London: Faber Paperback, 1980).

—— 'Ah! mischief: the role of public broadcasting', in F. Pike (ed.), *Ah! Mischief* (London: Faber & Faber, 1982).

HEATH, STEPHEN and SKIRROW, GILLIAN, 'Television: a world in action', *Screen*, 18:2 (1977), 7–60.

HERBERT, HUGH, '*Tutti Frutti*', in G. W. Brandt (ed.), *British Television Drama in the 1980s* (Cambridge: Cambridge University Press, 1993), 178–95.

HEWISON, ROBERT, *In Anger: Culture in the Cold War, 1945–60* (London: Weidenfeld & Nicolson, 1981).

—— *Culture and Consensus: England, Art and Politics since 1940* (London: Methuen, 1995).

HIGSON, ANDREW, *Waving the Flag: Constructing a National Cinema in Britain* (Oxford: Oxford University Press, 1995).

—— (ed.), *Dissolving Views: Key Writings on British Cinema* (London: Cassell, 1996).

HILL, DEREK, 'Intellectual attitudes: writers and television—1', *Contrast*, 2:2 (Winter 1962), 117–23.

HILL, JOHN, *Sex, Class and Realism: British Cinema, 1956–1963* (London: BFI Publishing, 1986).

—— 'British television and film: the making of a relationship', in John Hill and Martin McLoone (eds.), *Big Picture, Small Screen: The Relations between Film and Television* (Luton: John Libbey Media/Luton University Press, 1996), 151–76.

—— and McLOONE, MARTIN (eds.), *Big Picture, Small Screen: The Relations between Film and Television*, Academia Research Monograph 16 (Luton: John Libbey Media/Luton University Press, 1996).

HOBSON, HAROLD, 'What we want in television plays', *BBC Quarterly*, 5:2 (1950), 77–80.

HOGGART, RICHARD, *The Uses of Literacy* (London: Chatto & Windus, 1957).

HOUSTON, BEVERLE, 'Viewing television: the metapsychology of endless consumption', *Quarterly Review of Film Studies*, 9:3 (1984), 183–95.

HUNNINGHER, JOOST, '*The Singing Detective*: Who done it?', in G. W. Brandt (ed.), *British Television Drama in the 1980s* (Cambridge: Cambridge University Press, 1993), 234–57.

HUNT, ALBERT, 'Alan Plater', in G. W. Brandt (ed.), *British Television Drama* (Cambridge: Cambridge University Press, 1981), 137–67.

HUTCHEON, LINDA, *A Theory of Parody: The Teachings of Twentieth-Century Art Forms* (London: Methuen, 1985).

—— *Irony's Edge: The Theory and Politics of Irony* (London/New York: Routledge, 1994).

HUYSSEN, ANDREAS, *Twilight Memories: Marking Time in a Culture of Amnesia* (New York/London: Routledge, 1995).

JACKSON, MICHAEL, 'Cinema versus television', *Sight & Sound* (Summer 1980), 178–81.

JACOBS, JASON, *British Television Drama: The Intimate Screen* (Oxford: Oxford University Press, 2000).

JAKOBSON, ROMAN, 'On realism in art', in Ladislav Matejka and Krystyna Pomorska (eds.), *Reading in Russian Poetics: Formalist and Structuralist Views* (Ann Arbor: Michigan Slavic Publications, 1978), 82–7.

JAMESON, FREDRIC, 'Reading without interpretation: postmodernism and the video-text', in N. Fabb *et al.*, *The Linguistics of Writing: Arguments between Language and Literature* (Manchester: Manchester University Press, 1987), 199–223.

—— *Postmodernism, or, The Cultural Logic of Late Capitalism* (London: Verso, 1990).

—— *Late Marxism: Adorno, or, The Persistence of the Dialectic* (London: Verso, 1990).

KAPLAN, ALICE and ROSS, KRISTIN, Introduction to a Special Issue on 'Everyday Life', *Yale French Studies*, 73 (1987), 1–4.

KERR, PAUL, 'London Documentary Drama Group—a response to John Caughie', *Screen*, 22:1 (1981), 101–5.

KUEHL, JERRY, 'Truth claims: drama documentaries', *Sight & Sound* (Autumn 1981), 272–4.

LAMBERT, STEPHEN, *Channel Four: Television with a Difference* (London: BFI Publishing, 1982).

LANGLEY, NOEL, 'The nature of the television play', *BBC Quarterly*, 8:3 (1953), 149–52.

LAPLANCHE, J. and PONTALIS, J.-B., *The Language of Psycho-Analysis*, trans. Donald Nicholson-Smith (London: The Hogarth Press and The Institute of Psycho-Analysis, 1973).

LAVENDER, ANDREW, '*Edge of Darkness*', in G. W. Brandt (ed.), *British Television Drama in the 1980s* (Cambridge: Cambridge University Press, 1993), 103–18.

LEAVIS, F. R. and THOMPSON, DENYS, *Culture and Environment: The Training of Critical Awareness* (London: Chatto & Windus, 1930).

LEAVIS, Q. D., *Fiction and the Reading Public* (London: Chatto & Windus, 1932).

LEFEBVRE, HENRI, *Critique of Everyday Life*, vol. 1 (1947), trans. John Moore (London: Verso, 1991).

LEJEUNE, ANTHONY (ed.), *The C. A. Lejeune Film Reader* (Manchester: Carcanet Press, 1995).

LEJEUNE, C. A., 'Films and plays in television', *BBC Quarterly*, 4:4 (1949–50), 224–9.

LOVELL, ALAN, 'Television playwright: David Mercer', *Contrast*, 2:4 (Summer 1963), 251–8.

LUKÁCS, GEORG, *Studies in European Realism: A Sociological Survey of the Writings of Balzac, Stendhal, Zola, Tolstoy, Gorki and others*, trans. Edith Bone (London: Merlin Press, 1978).

—— *The Historical Novel*, trans. Hannah and Stanley Mitchell (London: Merlin Press, 1989).

—— 'To narrate or to describe?' (*Erzählen oder beschreiben*, 1936). Translated as 'Idea and form in literature', in Lukács, *Marxism and Human Liberation* (New York: Delta, 1973).

LUNN, EUGENE, *Marxism and Modernism: An Historical Study of Lukács, Brecht, Benjamin and Adorno* (London: Verso, 1985).

LYOTARD, JEAN-FRANÇOIS, *The Postmodern Condition* (Manchester: Manchester University Press, 1986).

MCARTHUR, COLIN, *Television and History*, BFI Television Monograph 8 (London: British Film Institute, 1978).

—— '*Days of Hope*', *Screen*, 16:4 (1975/6), 139–44; also in Bennett *et al.* (eds.), *Popular Television and Film: A Reader* (London: Open University/BFI, 1981), 305–9.

MACCABE, COLIN, 'Realism and the cinema: notes on some Brechtian theses', *Screen*, 15:2 (1974), 7–27.

—— 'Days of Hope: a response to Colin McArthur', Screen, 17:1 (1976), 98–101; also in Bennett et al. (eds.), Popular Television and Film: A Reader (London: Open University/BFI, 1981), 310–13.

—— 'Memory, phantasy, identity: Days of Hope and the politics of the past', Edinburgh '77 Magazine (Edinburgh: Edinburgh International Film Festival, 1977); also in Bennett et al. (eds.), Popular Television and Film (London: Open University/BFI, 1981), 314–18.

—— (ed.), High Theory/Low Culture: Analysing Popular Television and Film (Manchester: Manchester University Press, 1986).

—— and STEWART, OLIVIA (eds.), The BBC and Public Service Broadcasting (Manchester: Manchester University Press, 1986).

McGIVERN, CECIL (Head of Television Programmes), 'The Big Problem', BBC Quarterly, 5:3 (1950), 142–9.

—— 'Let's get it moving again', Contrast, 1:3 (Spring 1962), 160–8.

McGRATH, JOHN, 'TV drama: the case against naturalism', Sight & Sound (Spring 1977), 100–5.

McINTYRE, IAN, The Expense of Glory: A Life of John Reith (London: Harper Collins, 1994).

McKNIGHT, GEORGE (ed.), Agent of Challenge and Defiance: The Films of Ken Loach (Trowbridge: Flicks Books, 1997).

MacMURRAUGH-KAVANAGH, M. K., ' "Drama" into "news": strategies of intervention in "The Wednesday Play" ', Screen, 38:3 (1997), 247–59.

MADDEN, CECIL, 'Television: problems and possibilities', BBC Quarterly, 2:4 (1948), 225–8.

MADDEN, PAUL, 'Jim Allen', in G. W. Brandt (ed.), British Television Drama (Cambridge: Cambridge University Press, 1981), 36–55.

MADDISON, JOHN, 'What is a television film?', Contrast, 3:1 (Autumn 1963), 6–9, 71–5.

MANVELL, ROGER, 'Drama on television and the film', BBC Quarterly, 7:1 (1952), 25–30.

MARTIN, TROY KENNEDY, 'Nats go home: first statement of a new drama for television', Encore, 48 (March/April 1964), 21–33.

—— 'Up the Junction and after', Contrast (Winter/Spring 1965/6), 137–9.

MARX, KARL and ENGELS, FREDERICK, 'Manifesto of the Communist Party', in The Communist Manifesto: A Modern Edition [with introduction by Eric Hobsbawn] (London: Verso, 1998).

MELLENCAMP, PATRICIA (ed.), Logics of Television: Essays in Cultural Criticism (Bloomington/Indianapolis: Indiana University Press, 1990).

MERCER, DAVID, Collected TV Plays, vols. 1 & 2 (London: Methuen, 1990).

MILLINGTON, BOB and NELSON, ROBIN, 'Boys from the Blackstuff': The Making of a TV Drama (London: Comedia, 1986).

MODLESKI, TANIA, 'The terror of pleasure: the contemporary horror film and postmodern theory', in Modleski (ed.), Studies in Entertainment: Critical Approaches to Mass Culture (Bloomington: Indiana University Press, 1986), 155–66.

MORLEY, DAVID, Family Television (London: Comedia, 1986).

—— 'Where the global meets the local: notes from the sitting room', Screen, 32:1 (1991), 1–15.

MORRISON, BLAKE, *The Movement: English Poetry and Fiction of the 1950s* (London: Methuen, 1986).

MORSE, MARGARET, 'The ontology of everyday distraction: the freeway, the mall and television', in Patricia Mellencamp (ed.), *Logics of Television: Essays in Cultural Criticism* (Bloomington/London: Indiana University Press/BFI Publishing, 1990), 193–221.

MULLAN, PETER, 'Tearing the roof off: Liese Spencer talks to Peter Mullan about *Orphans*', *Sight and Sound*, 9:4 (1999), 13–14.

MULVEY, LAURA, 'Visual pleasure and narrative cinema', *Screen*, 16:3 (1975), 6–18.

MURDOCK, GRAHAM, 'Authorship and organisation', *Screen Education*, 35 (Summer 1980), 19–34.

MUSTAFA, KHALID EL MUBARAK, 'David Mercer', in G. W. Brandt (ed.), *British Television Drama* (Cambridge: Cambridge University Press, 1981), 82–109.

NOWELL-SMITH, GEOFFREY, 'On history and the cinema', *Screen*, 31:2 (1990), 160–71.

OSBORNE, JOHN, *Look Back in Anger* (London: Faber & Faber, 1957).

PAGET, DEREK, *True Stories: Documentary Drama on Radio, Screen and Stage* (Manchester: Manchester University Press, 1990).

PARKINSON, DAVID (ed.), *The Graham Greene Film Reader: Mornings in the Dark* (Manchester: Carcanet Press, 1993).

PATERSON, RICHARD, 'Restyling masculinity: the impact of *Boys from the Blackstuff*', in J. Curran *et al.* (eds.), *Impacts and Influences: Essays on Media Power in the Twentieth Century* (London: Methuen, 1987), 218–30.

PEARSON, ROBERTA E., *Eloquent Gestures: The Transformation of Performance Style in the Griffith Biograph Films* (Berkeley and Los Angeles: University of California Press, 1992).

PETRIE, DUNCAN (ed.), *New Questions of British Cinema* (London: BFI Publishing, 1992).

PIDDUCK, JULIANNE, 'Travels with Sally Potter's *Orlando*: gender, narrative, movement', *Screen*, 38:2 (1997), 172–89.

—— 'Of windows and country walks: frames of space and movement in 1990s Austen adaptations', *Screen*, 39:4 (Winter 1998), 381–400.

PIKE, FRANK (ed.), *Ah! Mischief: The Writer and Television* (London: Faber & Faber, 1982).

POOLE, MICHAEL, 'The cult of the generalist: British television criticism, 1936–1983', *Screen*, 25:2 (March/April 1984), 41–61.

—— and WYVER, JOHN, *Powerplays: Trevor Griffiths in Television* (London: BFI Publishing, 1984).

POTTER, DENNIS, 'Realism and non-naturalism', 'Programme of the Edinburgh International Television Festival', 1977.

—— and FULLER, GRAHAM, *Potter on Potter* (London: Faber & Faber, 1993).

PURSER, PHILIP, 'Landscape of TV drama', *Contrast*, 1:1 (Autumn 1961), 11–20.

—— 'Head of Drama', *Contrast*, 2:1 (Autumn 1962), 33–6.

—— 'ITV drama: review of the quarter', *Contrast*, 3:3 (Spring 1964), 172–6.

—— 'Critic exposes himself', *Contrast*, 4:5/6 (Winter/Spring 1965/6) 143–4.

—— 'Dennis Potter', in G. W. Brandt (ed.), *British Television Drama* (Cambridge: Cambridge University Press, 1981), 168–93.

PYM, JOHN, *Film on Four: A Survey, 1982–1991* (London: BFI Publishing, 1992).

REITH, J. C. W., *Into the Wind* (London: Hodder & Stoughton, 1949).

Report of the Committee on Broadcasting, 1960 [Pilkington Committee] (London: HMSO, 1962), Cmnd. 1753.

Report of the Committee on the Future of Broadcasting [Annan Committee] (London: HMSO, 1977), Cmnd. 6753.

Report of the Committee on Financing the BBC [Peacock Committee] (London: HMSO, 1986), Cmnd. 9824.

RIDGMAN, JEREMY (ed.), *Boxed Sets: Television Representations of Theatre* (London: Arts Council/Libby, 1998).

ROBINSON, DAVID, 'Shooting on tape', *Contrast*, 3:1 (Autumn 1963), 30–3.

RUSSELL, DAVID, 'TV drama: a world in action', *Sight & Sound* (Summer 1990), 174–9.

SAVILLE, PHILIP, 'Director and writer: writers and television—3', *Contrast*, 2:2 (Winter 1962), 134–6.

SAYNOR, JAMES, 'Writers' television', *Sight & Sound* (November 1982), 28–31.

SCANNELL, PADDY and CARDIFF, DAVID, *A Social History of British Broadcasting, vol. 1: 1922–1939* (Oxford: Basil Blackwell, 1991).

SCHOR, NAOMI, *Reading in Detail: Aesthetics and the Feminine* (London/New York: Routledge, 1989).

SCHUMANN, HOWARD, 'Video-Mad: An American writer in British television', in F. Pike (ed.), *Ah! Mischief* (London: Faber & Faber, 1982).

SELDES, GILBERT, *Writing for Television* (New York: Doubleday, 1952).

SELF, DAVID, *Television Drama: An Introduction* (London: Macmillan, 1984).

SENDALL, BERNARD, *Independent Television in Britain*, vol. 1: *Origin and Foundation, 1946–1962* (London: Macmillan, 1982), vol. 2: *Expansion and Change, 1958–1968* (London: Macmillan, 1983).

SHUBIK, IRENE, *Play for Today: The Evolution of Television Drama* (London: Davis-Poynter, 1975).

SILVERSTONE, ROGER, *Television and Everyday Life* (London: Routledge, 1994).

SILVEY, ROBERT (Head of BBC Audience Research), 'An enquiry into "viewing"', *BBC Quarterly*, 4:4 (1949–50), 230–5.

SLOTERDIJK, PETER, *Critique of Cynical Reason* (Minneapolis: University of Minnesota Press, 1987).

SMITH, ANTHONY, *The Shadow and the Cave: A Study of the Relationship between the Broadcaster, his Audience, and the State* (London: Allen & Unwin, 1977).

—— *Books to Bytes: Knowledge and Information in the Postmodern Age* (London: BFI Publishing, 1993).

SPIGEL, LYNN, *Make Room for TV: Television and the Family Ideal in Postwar America* (Chicago/London: University of Chicago Press, 1992).

STEAD, PETER, *Dennis Potter* (Bridgend: Seren Books, 1993).

STEADMAN, CAROLINE, *Landscape for a Good Woman* (London: Virago, 1986).

STRASHNOV, G. (Asst. Director, European Broadcasting Union), 'Copyright obstacles to the international exchange of television programmes', *BBC Quarterly*, 6:2 (1951), 88–95.

SUTTON, SHAUN, *The Largest Theatre in the World* (London: BBC Publications, 1982).

SWIFT, JOHN, *Adventures in Vision: The First Twenty-Five Years of Television* (London: John Lehmann, 1950).

SWINSON, ARTHUR, *Writing for Television* (London: Adam and Charles Black, 1955).

TAYLOR, DON, *Days of Vision—Working with David Mercer: Television Drama Then and Now* (London: Methuen, 1990).

—— 'Style in drama (1): the Gorboduc stage', *Contrast* 3:3 (Spring 1964), 150–208.

TAYLOR, JOHN RUSSELL, *Anatomy of a Television Play: An Inquiry into the Production of Two ABC Armchair Theatre Plays* (London: Weidenfeld & Nicolson, 1962).

—— 'Drama 66', *Contrast* (Winter/Spring 1965/6), 132–4.

TAYLOR, RONALD (ed.), *Aesthetics and Politics* (London: NLB, 1977).

THOMAS, HOWARD (ed.), *The Armchair Theatre* (London: Weidenfeld & Nicolson, 1959).

THOMPSON, DENYS (ed.), *Discrimination and Popular Culture* (Harmondsworth: Penguin, 1964).

TILSLEY, VINCENT, 'The Doomsday planners', *Contrast*, 4:1 (Winter, 1964–5), 7–11.

TRIBE, KEITH, 'History and the production of memories', *Screen*, 18:4 (1977/8), 9–22.

TRUFFAUT, FRANÇOIS, 'Une certaine tendance du cinéma français', *Cahiers du cinéma*, 31 (January 1954), 15–28.

TULLOCH, JOHN, *Television Drama: Agency, Audience and Myth* (London/New York: Routledge, 1990).

WHITEMORE, HUGH, 'Learning the lingo', *Contrast*, 3:3 (Spring 1964), 154–7.

—— 'Word into image: reflections on television drama', in F. Pike (ed.), *Ah! Mischief* (London: Faber & Faber, 1982).

WIGGIN, MAURICE, 'The future of television: as a critic sees it', *BBC Quarterly*, 7:1 (1953), 28–34.

WILDE, ALAN, *Horizons of Assent: Modernism, Postmodernism and the Ironic Imagination* (Baltimore: Johns Hopkins University Press, 1981).

WILLEMEN, PAUL, 'Letter to John', *Screen*, 21:1 (1980), 53–66.

WILLETT, JOHN (ed.), *Brecht on Theatre* (London: Eyre Methuen, 1977).

WILLIAMS, RAYMOND, *The Long Revolution* (Harmondsworth: Penguin, 1965).

—— *Television: Technology and Cultural Form* (London: Fontana/Collins, 1974).

—— 'A lecture on realism', *Screen*, 18:1 (1977), 61–74.

—— 'Base and superstructure in Marxist cultural theory', in *Problems in Materialism and Culture* (London: Verso, 1980), 31–49.

—— *The Politics of Modernism: Against the New Conformists* (London: Verso, 1989).

—— *Raymond Williams on Television: Selected Writings*, edited by Alan O'Connor (London/New York: Routledge, 1989).

WILLIS, TED, 'Look back in wonder', *Encore* (March/April 1958).

WILSON, COLIN, *The Outsider* (London: Victor Gollancz, 1956).

WITT, MICHAEL, ' "*Qu'était-ce que le cinéma, Jean-Luc Godard?*", An analysis of the cinema(s) at work in and around Godard's *Histoire(s) du cinéma*', in the 'Godard dossier', *Screen*, 40:3 (Autumn 1999), 304–47.

WORDSWORTH, WILLIAM, 'Poetry and poetic diction', in E. Jones (ed.), *English Critical Essays: Nineteenth Century* (London: Oxford University Press, 1947), 1–32.

ZOLA, ÉMILE, *The Experimental Novel & Other Essays*, trans. Belle M. Sherman (New York: Haskell House, 1964).

Index